STRENGTH IN NUMBERS?

STRENGTH IN NUMBERS?

THE POLITICAL MOBILIZATION OF
RACIAL AND ETHNIC MINORITIES

JAN E. LEIGHLEY

PRINCETON UNIVERSITY PRESS
PRINCETON AND OXFORD

Copyright © 2001 by Princeton University Press
Published by Princeton University Press, 41 William Street,
Princeton, New Jersey 08540
In the United Kingdom: Princeton University Press,
3 Market Place, Woodstock, Oxfordshire OX20 1SY
All Rights Reserved

Library of Congress Cataloging-in-Publication Data

Leighley, Jan E., 1960–
Strength in numbers? : the political mobilization of racial and ethnic minorities /
Jan E. Leighley.
p.   cm.
Includes bibliographical references and index.
ISBN 0-691-08670-2—ISBN 0-691-08671-0 (pbk.)
1. Minorities—United States—Political activity.   2. Political participation—United
States.   I. Title.
E184.A1 L43 2001
323'.042'08900973—dc21   2001016379

British Library Cataloging-in-Publication Data is available

This book has been composed in Caledonia

Printed on acid-free paper. ∞

www.pup.princeton.edu

Printed in the United States of America

10   9   8   7   6   5   4   3   2   1

10   9   8   7   6   5   4   3   2   1
(Pbk.)

To my parents
Roger and Betty Leighley

CONTENTS

FIGURES AND TABLES

FIGURES

TABLES

PREFACE

ALTHOUGH presidential nominating conventions have always been
spectacles of one sort or another, the 2000 Republican and Democratic National Conventions were replete with symbols of racial
and ethnic diversity. With a strong national economy and a fairly popular
president, it is perhaps not surprising that the parties shifted their symbolic focus from economics and national defense to the faces of African-
Americans, Latinos and Asian-Americans—among others—on national
television. The post-convention debate, of course, was to what extent the
abstract symbols and claims of inclusion, integration, and incorporation
made by both parties would be translated into concrete federal policies.
This debate is surely one that will continue for years to come. But that we
are engaged in it at this moment is indeed hopeful.

This book, too, focuses on the nature of inclusion, integration, and incorporation—but with respect to mass political behavior. I hope to engage a
broad spectrum of scholars to look more carefully at how political institutions structure political behavior—and how an increasingly diverse electorate is likely to respond to these efforts. Although this is but one very
narrow slice of the issues raised by the political conventions this year, it is
nonetheless an important one. Thus, I hope that scholars of political participation, voter turnout, African-American politics, Latino politics, and political parties find this work valuable as an extension of their own.

The intellectual debts that I have accumulated during my career are
many. But I would like to make special note of three mentors who have
influenced me beyond the scope of this book: John Sprague, Bob Salisbury, and Jewel Prestage. John's graduate seminars at Washington University were always memorable—in several dimensions—but what has influenced me the most is his passion for the work that he does and the life
that he leads. When I was first beginning this project, Bob gave me some
simple advice: if you are going to write a book, make it a really good one.
Jewel, whom I met only a few short years ago, has, in her own very elegant
way, tutored me in the politics of race and gender. For this passion, this
wisdom, this grace, I am indebted.

I would like to acknowledge the support and assistance of numerous
colleagues and institutions over the past few years. Sidney Verba, Kay
Schlozman, and Henry Brady were kind enough to provide me with data
from their Citizen Participation Study, which serves as the basis of this
project. This, as well as their comments at numerous panels at the Midwest and APSA meetings, have meant a great deal to me.

Funding for additional data collection and writing time came from the

Department of Political Science, the Bush School of Government and Public Service, the Center for Presidential Studies, the Center for Public Leadership, and the Race and Ethnic Studies Institute at Texas A&M University. I would like to thank Charlie Johnson, Chuck Hermann, George Edwards, Arnie Vedlitz, and Mitch Rice for their leadership of these academic units and for their support of my work.

Colleagues at Texas A&M University, including Kim Hill, George Edwards, Jon Bond, and Ken Meier, have provided thoughtful comments on various drafts of these chapters as have Michael Alvarez, Peggy Conway, Louis DeSipio, Luis Fraga, Rodney Hero, Paula McClain, Gary Segura, Joe Stewart, and Jerry Wright, among others too numerous to list. Jonathan Nagler deserves a special thank-you for his encouragement along the way (which was sprinkled with insightful observations about book publishing) and for detailed comments on more than one draft of the manuscript.

I would also like to express my appreciation to graduate students who ably assisted in data collection and analysis; this includes: Whitney Grace, Patrick Ellcessor, Stacy Ulbig, Patricia Garcia, Alesha Doan, and Abby Lorenz.

While the professional obligations are numerous, I should note that it is my family who has had to live with this project for more years than anyone—including me—would have preferred. I thank both the Leighleys and the Johnsons, especially James and Ted, for encouragement, patience, and good humor, and remind them that they really needn't read one more word in this book!

Most important, I would like to thank my husband, Rick Johnson, for the professional and personal sacrifices he has made for my career and this book in particular. His confidence in me has never wavered. His first priority has always been to see that I had enough time to get my work done; his second to make sure that I played hard, too. Recently he asked me, "Will there ever be a time in your career when you don't work in the evenings?" There will be, sweetheart—and it will be spent with you.

STRENGTH IN NUMBERS?

Chapter One

RACE, CLASS, AND POLITICAL PARTICIPATION:

THE ARGUMENT

ONE of the striking features of political life in the United States at the beginning of the twenty-first century is that racial and ethnic minorities are becoming political majorities. California, Florida, New York, and Texas project that "whites" will be racial *minorities* in their states within decades, while other states' immigrant populations have increased substantially in selected communities. Whether potential or realized, these demographic changes have seemingly changed the dynamics of national, state, and local politics.

Political analysts and commentators offer decidedly mixed views of the political consequences of these changes. To some, it is inevitable that this diversity will be embraced by political and social institutions, as well as citizens. This positive response to diversity will thus result in greater integration and, ultimately, a society in which "color" is irrelevant. Others are far less positive, anticipating that racial/ethnic diversity will threaten Anglos as well as minorities and lead to heightened political conflict.[1]

These predictions, however, are typically based on anecdotal accounts of dramatic or unusual cases of racial/ethnic integration or conflict. For example, the Rodney King "incident" in Los Angeles—when protests and rioting erupted after police officers accused of brutality against King (an African-American) were acquitted of criminal charges—is often used as the specter of an uncontrollable and divisive racial politics of the twenty-first century.

On the other hand, some politicians use the language of racial and ethnic integration as a symbol of hope and progress, often demonstrating their commitment to this ideal by choosing minority individuals for appointed positions or as informal political advisors. Both Republican and Demo-

---

[1] Throughout the text I use the terms "Anglo," "white," and "Anglo-whites" interchangeably to refer to non-Hispanic Caucasians; "Black" and "African-American" to refer to non-whites who identify as either; and "Latino" and "Hispanic" interchangeably for individuals of Hispanic or Latino origin. Where possible, I use whichever labels were used in previous research, or by elite subjects. While I use the term "minority" to refer generally to racial and ethnic minorities, the evidence I offer focuses almost entirely on African-Americans and Latinos as ethnic minorities. Finally, I occasionally simplify the phrase "racial and ethnic minority" to "racial minority," though I nonetheless am referring to both groups.

cratic presidents alike have made it a priority to select a cabinet (as well as other political appointees) that is to some extent racially and ethnically diverse, while political candidates from Jesse Jackson to George W. Bush have sought the advice and endorsement of individuals from a variety of racial and ethnic backgrounds. If individuals of different races and ethnicity can govern together, then different racial and ethnic groups can learn to live together.

But will they? Aside from the strategic use of race by political candidates and officials, how will citizens respond to increasing racial and ethnic diversity in their neighborhoods, their jobs, their communities? And will the reactions of citizens of minority (i.e., racial/ethnic) status to diversity be the same as those of Anglos? These questions are important for they reflect on individuals' fundamental political responses to their social environments.

Consider, for example, the potentially distinctive reactions of two individuals—one Anglo-white, the other African-American—to change in the racial composition of their neighborhood. The first, upon seeing an increased number of Blacks in the previously "white" neighborhood, might view such changes as a positive sign of social progress and embrace the new neighbors by engaging with them socially and politically. Alternatively, this change in social composition might be interpreted as an omen of bad things to come—declining property values, increasing crime, etc.—and thus a threat to house and home. The political response might well be to either mobilize against such a threat or demobilize by remaining silent or exiting the community.

The second citizen in this vignette might likewise embrace such change as a positive sign of social progress, one that would provide this individual with the potential for enriched social interaction and political involvement. It is less likely to imagine a Black individual residing in an increasingly Black neighborhood perceiving this change as a threat, but it is not logically impossible.

The problem is that we simply do not know how individuals—Anglo-whites, Blacks, or Latinos—respond politically to the racial composition of their neighborhoods and communities. Following Hirschman (1970), three options are conceivable: exit, voice, or loyalty. Certainly evidence of white flight in residential neighborhoods confirms that whites have often reacted to increasing neighborhood diversity by exiting. But, for various reasons, exiting is not an option or a choice for many—and important questions regarding how individuals react to racial and ethnic diversity remain. Do political elites, as well as citizens, mobilize or demobilize? And under what conditions do they do so?

INTELLECTUAL CONTEXT

Scholarly analyses of the consequences of racial diversity for individuals' political behavior are rare. Hero's (1998) recent work on state politics—by far the most encompassing treatment of the concept of racial/ethnic diversity—focuses only marginally on political behavior. And, despite the centrality of individual political participation to democratic politics, few studies of mass political behavior explicitly consider the more narrow question of how individuals' social contexts structure their political participation. Thus, how citizens react to diversity is unknown. Do individuals engage or disengage, and under what conditions do they do so?

The dominant paradigm in the study of political participation over the past thirty years has emphasized socioeconomic status as the primary determinant of individuals' engagement in politics and repeatedly demonstrated that those with greater status are more likely to participate than those with lesser status. *Why* such a relationship exists has been addressed at length by Verba, Schlozman, and Brady (1995), who identify three resources (i.e., skills, time, money) associated with socioeconomic status. According to Verba, Schlozman, and Brady, individuals without such resources are less able to bear the costs of political activity. Hence the importance of socioeconomic status in explaining who participates.

Theories of racial and ethnic participation, in contrast, tend to emphasize contextual characteristics such as candidate and group mobilization. Motivating this emphasis is the underlying premise that individuals of lesser social status rely on the political mobilization of organized groups more heavily than do individuals of greater social status (see, e.g., Verba, Nie, and Kim 1978).[2] Given the lower level of individual resources that minorities typically control, engagement in politics is tied to group characteristics that subsidize the cost of participation through the provision of information or psychological benefits. Although this argument resounds throughout a voluminous case-study literature on minority politics, systematic empirical studies of minority political participation—particularly those that consider more than one ethnic group—rarely incorporate measures of political mobilization.[3] Furthermore, findings regarding the validity of the

[2] More specifically: "Lower-status groups, in contrast, need a group-based process of political mobilization if they are to catch up to the upper-status groups in terms of political activity. They need a self-conscious ideology as motivation and need organization as a resource. The processes that bring them to political activity are more explicit and easily recognized. They are more likely to involve explicit conflict with other groups. Our argument is consistent with Michels's contention that organization—and we might add ideology—is the weapon of the weak" (Verba, Nie, and Kim 1978: 14–15).

[3] Throughout the book, I use the terms "recruitment" and "mobilization" interchangeably

socioeconomic status model for minority individuals are somewhat inconsistent when tested using empirical data.

And therein lies the rub: our theories of participation assumed to be generalizable across racial and ethnic groups are tested primarily on Anglos and typically ignore the contextual characteristics emphasized in theories of minority participation, while theories of group mobilization are rarely tested empirically in a systematic fashion across racial and ethnic groups. Thus, the relative importance of individual and group (i.e., contextual) characteristics as predictors of participation across racial and ethnic groups is unknown.

More broadly, the goal of incorporating individual and group factors into our theories of political participation challenges two fundamental and related assumptions in the study of political participation: first, that participation in democratic political activities is individualistic (i.e., motivated within the individual participant) and second, that political behavior more generally is independent of the social context within which the individual resides. The socioeconomic status model is a perfect example of the first assumption; social and political processes beyond the individual are not considered essential to explanations of political behavior. Explanations of minority participation that emphasize the critical importance of political mobilization (i.e., being asked to participate) to individuals' participation decisions challenge this first assumption by posing individuals' decisions to participate as being structured by political elites rather than individuals' resources.[4]

The second assumption, though similar to the first, reflects more on the methods used to study political participation than it does on the theories offered to explain it. Specifically, the widespread use of survey research and its reliance on large-scale, national probability samples in the study of political participation have sustained decades of research, for which the only appropriate and available data are on characteristics of the individual—randomly chosen from an unspecified political environment—rather than the individual's political context.[5] Hence, in part due to the lack of

---

to refer to direct requests of individuals to participate in a particular way (to vote, to campaign, to attend a local meeting, etc.). In contrast, "participation" refers to engaging in political behavior with the intention of influencing government or policy outcomes. This usage is distinct from various studies that use the term "mobilization" to refer to voter turnout or racial/ethnic group voting patterns. I also use the word "mobilization" when referring to *elite* mobilization activities such as party targeting, campaign spending, and grassroots outreach by group leaders.

[4] Note that this use of the term mobilization differs from that often seen in urban politics, minority politics, and comparative politics studies. Individuals who are mobilized (i.e., asked or encouraged) to participate in politics may or may not choose to participate; whatever their choice, the fact that they have been mobilized is beyond their immediate control.

[5] An elegant exception to this generalization is Huckfeldt and Sprague (1995).

data on individuals' political environments and to the wealth of data on individuals' demographic characteristics, our explanations of political participation focus on individual characteristics, independent of the social and political context. The argument forwarded in the following chapters thus takes issue with the assumption that individuals' political environments are essentially irrelevant to their political engagement.

THEORETICAL FRAMEWORK

The underlying theoretical model on which this empirical analysis rests is drawn from rational-choice models of voter turnout and collective action, described in greater detail in chapter 2. These models posit individuals' decisions to participate as a comparison of the costs of contributing (i.e., voting or engaging in collective action) to the benefits gained by contributing (i.e., preferred policies being pursued by successful candidates, or as a result of some other group effort such as protest). The "paradox of participation" is that, contrary to the model's prediction (zero turnout, in most cases), voting or engaging in collective action is fairly common.

Various solutions to this paradox essentially require that "extra-individual" considerations such as group identity or benefits, social interaction, and elite mobilization be considered in the calculus. These are the very types of contextual factors identified in the minority politics literature as critical to the understanding of minority participation. Some of these factors—in particular those relating to social interaction and mobilization— are occasionally identified in contextual studies of (Anglo) political participation as well.

I conceptualize the contextual influences discussed in these literatures as consisting of three types, with each type either reducing the costs or increasing the benefits of participation. *Elite mobilization* refers to the explicit or implicit solicitation of individuals' engagement in political activity by elites, who provide an information subsidy (i.e., regarding where to vote, or how to become registered, or when the meeting is scheduled) to individuals. *Relational goods*, as developed by Uhlaner (1989b), refer to a set of incentives enjoyed by individuals as members of groups. These incentives—available only to group members—range from group identity to social interaction and recruitment, but the essential mechanism is again that of information provision: the group provides information that reduces the costs of participation.

The third type of contextual influence is the *racial/ethnic context*, which refers to the racial/ethnic composition of the individual's immediate social context. This contextual influence may indirectly reduce the costs of participating by affecting the likelihood of elite mobilization and the provision of relational goods, but more important, it increases the benefits of participating more directly. For minority individuals, the potential benefits of participating are greater as the racial/ethnic group increases in size because the group consequently enjoys a higher probability of being successful in its political efforts.[6] For Anglos, an increase in minority group size acts as an informational cue of group threat—which again should increase the potential policy benefits of engaging in political activity.

This threefold conceptualization of contextual influences is drawn from numerous studies of race, politics, and political behavior in the United States and justified further in chapters 2 and 3. Based on this conceptualization, I advance the following thesis:

> *Contextual influences that reduce the costs of participation have a greater effect on minority participation than on Anglo participation, while contextual influences that increase the perceived benefits of participation have a greater effect on Anglo participation than on minority participation. Moreover, the nature of this relationship differs for Blacks and Latinos.*

More specifically, I offer three distinct models of how contextual influences structure Anglo, Black, and Latino participation, distinguished primarily by whether the racial context influences elite mobilization and relational goods, and whether racial context directly influences participation, of each specific group. These distinctions rely in part on previous empirical findings on political participation, as well as extensions of various theoretical frameworks used more broadly in the study of political behavior.

I model Anglo participation as a function of relational goods, elite mobilization, and racial context, with the latter having no independent effect on either elite mobilization or relational goods (see figure 1.1). The basic argument here is that Anglos are more likely to participate when there are greater relational goods incentives, when there are higher levels of elite mobilization, and when Anglos reside in more racially diverse contexts.[7]

---

[6] To be more accurate, it is not "being large" that matters for the group, but being pivotal. By definition, however, due to the relatively small proportion of minorities in most electoral districts, I assume that the larger the group size, the more likely it is to be pivotal.

[7] An alternative interpretation regarding the behavior of Anglos in minority contexts is that Anglos who do not want to reside in a minority context self-select by moving elsewhere. What we then observe is the result of this self-selection process rather than a "real" relationship between context and participatory behavior. As with most research on contextual effects, I assume that whites' decisions to move (or not move) are guided by considerations other than their desired level of political participation or social interaction. Therefore, the evidence offered in the chapters that follow should reflect on how the racial context influences whites' behaviors.

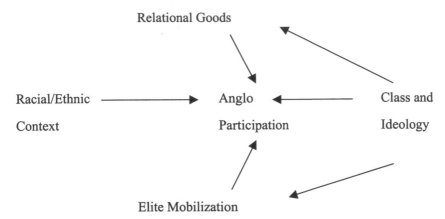

Figure 1.1. Model of Anglo Participation: Race, Class, and Mobilization

In contrast, for both Latino (figure 1.2) and African-American (figure 1.3) participation, I argue that the racial context—the size of individuals' racial groups—structures the provision of both relational goods and elite mobilization. This set of hypothesized relationships reflects the importance of strong group-oriented (social or political) institutions where minority citizens live in concentrated areas and therefore enjoy greater opportunities for social interaction and organization.

Socioeconomic status, relational goods, and elite mobilization are hypothesized to increase participation for both African-Americans and Latinos. The notable difference between the African-American and Latino models relates to the effect of the racial context on individuals' participation decisions. Specifically, I argue that the racial context will directly af-

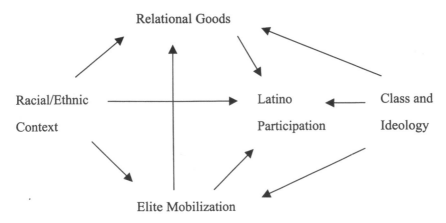

Figure 1.2. Model of Latino Participation: Race, Class, and Mobilization

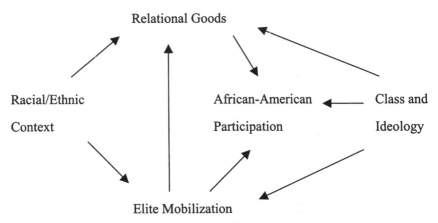

Figure 1.3. Model of African-American Participation: Race, Class, and Mobilization

fect Latino but not African-American participation, for three reasons. First, African-Americans have few opportunities to be true political majorities (i.e., pivotal), as their potential size in any political or electoral coalition is undoubtedly lower than that of Latinos. Although there are notable exceptions, of course, African-Americans are most likely to be minorities in most states and cities (and most likely majorities in electoral districts drawn specifically for that reason). In contrast, Latinos have become dominant electoral forces in a much wider array of cities and states and have far greater potential in the coming decades. Thus, group size has far greater potential to be of political consequence, and I believe that individuals' decisions to participate will reflect this calculus.

Second, the greater assimilation of Latinos into non-Latino neighborhoods (largely by virtue of their relatively higher levels of economic success, as compared to African-Americans) also suggests that Latinos are additionally advantaged with incentives to participate as their presence increases: viewing a more diverse neighborhood or electorate signals that such economic success might be translated into greater political success.

Third, the distinctiveness of contextual influences on Blacks and Latinos reflects on the political histories of these groups in the United States, which have been marked by repeated attempts to gain full citizenship and participation. This political history has, for Blacks, been accompanied by the development of a highly complex set of political institutions that seek to foster their members' political involvement, while for Latinos such mobilizing structures are fewer in number and scope (McClain and Stewart 1999: 44–51).

The literature on minority politics suggests that African-Americans have the strongest infrastructure to facilitate participation, due to the historical role of the Black church and civil rights organizations in mobilizing their members. Furthermore, the dramatic increase in the number of African-American candidates in the post–Civil War era along with the significant residential segregation of the African-American community suggest that the level of elite mobilization is relatively high compared to that of other ethnic groups.

With the exception of Cuban-Americans, Latinos generally have a much weaker infrastructure to facilitate participation.[8] The Mexican-American community has fewer groups organized to mobilize political participation. Until recently, fewer (though increasing) Mexican-American candidates ran for or were elected to office; unlike the majority of African-American candidates, successful Mexican-American candidates have used various political strategies and displayed more diverse ideological stances, both resulting in different types of political coalitions seemingly less tied directly to Latino interests. Additional barriers to broad-based mobilization of Latinos result from nationality and language differences, a less concentrated population, and the relatively lower proportion of citizens within the Mexican-American community (Hero 1992: 194–201).[9]

Cuban-American politics, on the other hand, is marked by "a remarkable level of cohesiveness" sustained by a significant increase in native-born Cuban-Americans over the last two decades (Diaz 1996). The relatively high socioeconomic status enjoyed by Cuban-Americans as well as high levels of English usage in second-generation Cuban-Americans suggest that the Cuban-American population is becoming both "more mainstream and more Latino (in terms of identification with other Hispanics)" (Hill and Moreno 1996: 178). These advantages in mobilization infrastructure are likely reflected in high levels of electoral organization and participation in Cuban-American communities (Diaz 1996: 162–63).[10]

Absent this high level of organization, and despite its diversity, the size of the Latino population acts as an indirect measure of the potential policy benefits of participating in a way that does not necessarily hold for African-

[8] There are other exceptions such as local, highly organized, and mobilized Latino or Chicano groups, many of which are in California, while others are scattered across local communities in the United States.

[9] The Asian-American community similarly struggles with nationality and language differences among an even smaller population and has no mass-based groups devoted to political mobilization. Unfortunately, the data used in this book do not include sufficiently large samples of Asian-Americans to incorporate in the analysis.

[10] This distinction between Mexican-American and Cuban-American clearly suggests that the "Latino" label is an oversimplification that masks a wide variety of interests, beliefs, and behaviors. However, it is impossible to consider these native-origin differences in the analyses in later chapters due to the low number of cases even from countries such as Cuba and Mexico.

Americans, who are able to rely on more formal organizations and social institutions for the collective representation of their political interests.

CHAPTER OUTLINE AND DATA SOURCES

As noted above, this theoretical framework is justified in greater detail in chapters 2 and 3, along with some initial confirmatory evidence. I then test various implications of these models more fully. Chapters 4 and 5 examine several propositions associated with elite mobilization, while chapter 6 tests various hypotheses regarding individuals' (self-reported) recruitment to political activities by other individuals. Chapters 7 and 8 then consider the relative importance of racial context, relational goods, and elite mobilization, controlling for socioeconomic status, across these three racial/ethnic groups.

The empirical analyses rely on a variety of data sets. The first is the biennial American National Election Study (NES), consisting of nationally representative samples taken in every presidential election year from 1956 to 1996 (Sapiro et al. 1998). The NES time series provides the opportunity to assess changes in the mobilization (i.e., party contacting) of African-Americans, as well as its impact on participation levels, over time.

The second data source is a survey of party county chairs conducted in 1996. These survey data were collected from Republican and Democratic Parties' county chairs in Texas, primarily through telephone interviews conducted between November 16 and December 7, 1996. Questions on the survey focused on a number of topics, including characteristics of the county chair; organizational characteristics (e.g., money spent, staff, office); the priority and nature of get-out-the-vote efforts in the county; the presence of other party or nonparty organizations devoted to get-out-the-vote efforts in the county; the ideology of various groups in the county; and early versus election-day campaign strategies, among others (see appendix A for the questionnaire).

The party chair data are valuable, for I know of no other existing data in which political elites are asked to report on which groups they mobilized, or targeted, in an election campaign. Although my argument that elites are strategic in their decisions to mobilize voters is not necessarily new, the ability to test that argument using elite reports, rather than voter self-reports, is important. With its relatively large African-American and Latino populations (discussed in greater detail in chapters 4 and 5), the state of Texas is a reasonable venue for preliminary data collection on elite mobilization of racial and ethnic minorities. The findings using this data must be interpreted cautiously, however, as a case study of Texas elites rather than evidence suitable for generalizing to all party elites in the 1996 presidential election.

The third data set used in the analyses that follow is Verba, Schlozman, and Brady's (1995) Citizen Participation Study (CPS), a national public opinion survey that I have supplemented with data on minority group size and political empowerment.[11] This survey provides individual-level data on individuals' resources, political attitudes, and civic skills, as well as self-reports on recruitment and participation. Conducted in 1989–90, the CPS includes oversamples of political activists, Blacks, and Latinos (see Verba, Schlozman, and Brady [1995] and Verba et al. [1993] for a more detailed description of the sampling and weighting details).

In addition, in chapters 4 and 8 I use or refer to the Texas Minority Survey, a statewide public opinion survey of Texans that oversampled African-Americans, Mexican-Americans, and Asian-Americans.[12] The survey was conducted using randomly selected telephone households in Texas between October 29, 1993, and February 23, 1994. An extended analysis of these data is provided in Leighley and Vedlitz (1999). Also reported in chapter 8 are analyses published in Hill and Leighley (1999) using data on the racial composition of state electorates, state mobilizing institutions, voter registration requirements, and voter turnout in the 1950s, 1980s, and 1990s. The state-level data set confirms the analyses of the survey data reported in chapter 7 and generalizes these findings by using a different level of contextual analysis (i.e., states as electoral units).

CONTRIBUTIONS

The empirical evidence that follows confirms the critical importance of integrating contextual influences in studying individuals' decisions to participate. Moreover, it demonstrates that these contextual influences vary across racial/ethnic groups. Taken as a whole, this work highlights the critical importance of developing and validating general models of political

[11] I owe each of these scholars numerous intellectual debts, as well as gratitude for their gracious assistance in sharing the data they originally collected. This book would have been impossible to write without them.

[12] Research funding for this project was provided primarily by the Office of the Associate Provost for Research and Graduate Studies, Texas A&M University; through the Interdisciplinary Research Initiatives Program, along with the Center for Biotechnology Policy and Ethics; through the Institute of Biosciences and Technology; the Racial and Ethnic Studies Institute (RESI); the Public Policy Research Institute (PPRI); and the Department of Political Science, all academic units of Texas A&M University. Principal investigators are: James Dyer, PPRI; Jan Leighley, Department of Political Science; George Rogers, Hazard Reduction and Recovery Center, Texas A&M University; and Gail Thomas, RESI.

behavior that incorporate distinctive, group-related features of race and ethnicity.

The models introduced above are generally supported in the chapters that follow, though not in the exact manner that I anticipated. In particular, I find some interesting variations across racial/ethnic groups in how the racial context, elite mobilization, and relational goods affect different types of participation.

Nonetheless, these analyses address several notable gaps in our empirical evidence regarding elite mobilization and mass political participation. First, the evidence suggests that standard models developed in the study of "mass" political behavior in the United States are not as powerful in explaining minority behavior as they are in explaining Anglo behavior. Second, the evidence also points to the critical importance of minority group size in structuring mobilization for minorities and, in contrast, structuring the participation decisions of Anglos. This finding thus broadens the utility of the group-conflict model used previously in studies of vote choice rather than political participation. Third, the analyses provide unique evidence regarding the importance of race/ethnicity to political elites' mobilization strategies. Fourth, the analyses integrate and extend the political empowerment model developed in the study of Black politics to Latino politics.

More broadly, the chapters that follow suggest that at the most fundamental level, citizens' responses to racial/ethnic diversity are indeed complex. Anglos respond to diversity differently than do African-Americans or Latinos. These variations in response patterns primarily reflect the incentives associated with majority/minority status—as structured by political institutions—rather than class differences across these groups. These chapters also demonstrate the underlying principle that racial/ethnic homogeneity enhances citizens' engagement in the political system. Thus, democratic politics will likely thrive in a more diverse society only if elites seek to mobilize not "just" racial and ethnic minorities (as currently defined), but instead minorities as determined by the social context, *independent of race and ethnicity*.

Chapter Two

MASS AND MINORITY PARTICIPATION:

THEORETICAL FRAMEWORKS

U NDERSTANDING how and why individuals participate in politics is critical for understanding how citizens are likely to respond to politics in an increasingly diverse society. Citizen participation is often considered a key element of democracy, with high levels of participation viewed as a sign of vitality. Although this theory is by no means universal, many scholars have argued that participation in democratic decision making acts as a "safety valve," allowing dissatisfied citizens avenues to pursue their goals and possibly achieve better outcomes from the political system. Moreover, there is some empirical evidence that individuals who participate in politics learn more and develop more positive political attitudes (see Leighley 1995 for a review of the consequences of participation) and that elected officials reward those who participate (Hill and Leighley 1992).

But most studies of political participation in the United States rely on national samples consisting primarily of Anglos and assume that the theories supported by this evidence are essentially generalizable to racial and ethnic minorities. In contrast, studies of minority participation are motivated by different theoretical frameworks and typically focus on a single group, ignoring the question of the extent to which these alternative theories might generalize to other groups.

Together, these research findings lead to an incomplete understanding of participation in a diverse society: do the same factors that influence Anglo participation influence Latino or African-American participation? And do the factors that influence African-American participation influence Anglo participation? Without knowing the answers to these questions, we cannot assess how citizens—whether Anglo, Latino, or African-American—will respond politically in an increasingly diverse society.

In this chapter I discuss in greater detail the theoretical framework introduced in chapter 1. I then provide an overview of traditional studies of mass political participation, followed by a discussion of group-oriented studies of African-American and Latino political participation. I conclude the chapter with a discussion of how the analyses in chapters 3 through 8 extend and integrate these literatures, both theoretically and empirically.

THEORETICAL MOTIVATION

The theoretical framework introduced in chapter 1 relies heavily on formal models of voter turnout as well as collective action.[1] Classic formal decision-theory models of voter turnout—which now serve as the basis of "the calculus of voting"—were first offered by Downs (1957) and Riker and Ordeshook (1968).[2]

With respect to voter turnout, the calculus is as follows: an individual compares the costs, C, to the benefits, B, of turnout (or engaging in other forms of collective action such as protest). The costs of turnout include factors such as the physical time and effort it takes to vote, as well as informational costs, while the benefits of voting are the policy benefits one receives when one's preferred candidate is elected. However, the individual will receive B only if his preferred candidate is elected, and so the value of B must be weighted by the probability of the individual's vote being decisive. Since in most cases any given individual's probability of determining the outcome of an election almost always approaches zero, the costs of voting will always outweigh the benefits ($C > B \times p$, the probability of determining the outcome) and individuals will therefore abstain.

That the model's prediction stands in stark contrast to the reality that individuals do, indeed, actually turn out to vote has troubled formal theorists for decades. A number of solutions to this paradox have been proposed. Downs (1957) added a "D" term, representing the individuals' value, in the long run, of maintaining democracy. As Fiorina (1976: 392) notes, however, maintaining democracy, whether in the short run or long run, is a collective good. It is thus a weak contender for a solution to the paradox. Later scholars interpreted Downs's D term as representing the expressive or consumptive values of voting (Hinich 1981; Riker and Ordeshook 1968, 1973; also see Fiorina's [1976] "hybrid" model, which includes both instrumental and expressive values).[3] Aldrich (1993) argues that reinterpreting Downs's D term to include both consumptive (expres-

[1] Although the "calculus of voting" focuses on electoral turnout, it is often extended to other types of participation (see, e.g., Aldrich 1976). Given that participation types vary in the costs and benefits they provide, it is likely that a direct extrapolation is not appropriate. At minimum, we might expect to see some predictable differences in the model results—and empirical evidence—when considering alternative types of participation. For that reason, many of the analyses in chapters 6 through 8 examine differences in model results across types of participation.

[2] For a review of these models and research that followed, see Aldrich 1976, 1993; on game theoretic models, see Aldrich 1993; Grafstein 1991; Palfrey and Rosenthal 1985.

[3] Alternatively, Ferejohn and Fiorina (1974) propose the "minimax regret" decision rule; rather than being determined by the probability of affecting the election outcome, individuals' decisions to vote are guided by their preference to minimize the probability that their least preferred option (candidate) occurs (wins).

sive) and long-term beliefs and values is particularly appropriate because voting is a relatively low-cost, low (potential) benefit activity (also see Hinich and Munger 1997, chapter 5).

Uhlaner (1989b) provides an alternative solution to this paradox by incorporating "relational goods"—incentives that depend on the interaction, or sociability, of individuals—into the standard formal model. While most decision-making models assume that individuals will maximize individually possessible goods, Uhlaner argues that such a restriction is neither necessary nor helpful and that models incorporating "sociability" are more realistic approximations of the mixed motives, or incentives, that structure individual behavior. The uniqueness of relational goods is that they can "only be 'possessed' by mutual agreement that they exist after appropriate joint actions have been taken by a person and non-arbitrary others. . . . Moreover, the others must either be specific individuals or drawn from some specific set" (254).

More specifically, relational goods include social approval, identity, a desire to experience one's history, friendship and its benefits, the desire to be recognized or accepted by others, the desire to maintain an identity, other aspects of sociability, and some instances of fulfillment of a duty or moral norm.

Uhlaner uses game theory and decision theory to model the consequences of incorporating sociability into standard rational-choice approaches to the paradox of participation. She demonstrates the various conditions under which the combination of costs and benefits (both relational and nonrelational) result in individuals' deciding to participate. The results point to the importance of coordination or negotiation between players (two individuals deciding whether to vote, where the benefits are a function of what the other decides to do). This leads her to emphasize the critical role of leadership in mobilizing participation: "The ways leaders can facilitate negotiations include facilitating side-payments . . . enhancing communication, providing means for players to make binding commitments, and providing a forum for bargaining. Thus, mobilization could occur through the organization of negotiations" (263).

Moreover, extending the two-person game to a larger group, Uhlaner finds that group leadership is particularly important, in that leaders can modify individuals' sense of group identification, individuals' assessments of the costs and benefits of others' participating, and the relative importance that others place on relational goods—each of which is critical to the decision of whether to participate. As a result, group leaders can be successful in mobilizing participation by stressing that "everyone" in the group is participating.

Uhlaner (1989b: 279) derives several specific hypotheses based on her relational goods model of participation. First, groups with more unanimous support for a candidate have higher levels of turnout. Second, groups that are concentrated geographically and that have higher levels of interpersonal interaction within the group have higher levels of turnout. Third, group members are more effective in mobilizing group turnout than are nongroup members. Fourth, the stronger the individual's identity with the group, the more likely that mobilization appeals will be successful.

The striking feature of these implications of Uhlaner's model for our purposes here is that they point toward the importance of the social and political context in structuring individuals' and, in particular, minorities' incentives for participation. Thus, the models introduced in chapter 1 are broadly consistent with this approach to the paradox of participation. The variations in these models across racial/ethnic groups, however, are justified by previous research on minority politics.

MINORITIES, MOBILIZATION, AND PARTICIPATION

Although Uhlaner provides no empirical data related to these hypotheses, her model's implications are broadly consistent with much of the research on Black and Latino political participation. Chong (1991: 48–72), for example, emphasizes the importance of reputation as an incentive for participating in collective actions associated with the civil rights movement. Leaders emphasized the importance of everyone contributing, and this appeal was enforced by the relatively dense social networks in the Black church: members who shirked were clearly identifiable (Chong 1991: 31–37, 100–102).

Moreover, the importance of group identity in stimulating participation is noted by Dawson (1994), who argues that Black institutions reinforce Blacks' group identity and behavior, and do so in part by emphasizing the precedence of racial group identity over class identity for Blacks. The mobilization networks associated with the civil rights movement as well as the more recent voter mobilization campaigns by Black candidates such as Harold Washington in Chicago and Jesse Jackson emphasize the importance of race over class (McAdam 1982; Morris 1984; Pinderhughes 1987; Tate 1993, 1994). Hence, individuals' decisions to participate reflect both individual and group considerations.

Historical and case-study research on Black political participation is consistent with Uhlaner's expectations as well, in that it emphasizes the efforts of African-American candidates to mobilize participation in particular races, the most recent notable example being Jesse Jackson (see, e.g., Cavanagh 1985; Barker and Walters 1989). The potential impact of candidates on Black participation is also underscored by candidates' self-described campaign strategies. At a Joint Center for Political Studies roundtable, for example, Odessa Shannon, the first Black elected in Montgomery County, Maryland, reports visiting every Black church in Montgomery County, as well as most poolrooms and the *real* old dance halls, "[a]ll of this before it was really a big campaign, to let the Black folks know a Black was running, because they wouldn't have known it otherwise" (Cavanagh 1987: 19). She then emphasized how difficult it was to decide whether or not to put her picture on posters—a perceived advantage in mobilizing Blacks (and their votes), but a decided disadvantage within the white community.

In perhaps the most systematic analysis of Black electoral behavior to date, Tate (1993) argues more generally that higher Black turnout in 1984 and 1988 resulted from the increasing number of Black candidates, including Jesse Jackson (as well as the number of voter registration drives and the policies of the Reagan administration) (see also Williams 1987). Higher turnout of Blacks in races with Black candidates, Tate suggests, may result from increased targeting of Black voters by Black candidates, but she has no direct evidence that this is the case (1993: 81). Neither does she have any systematic evidence that the number of Black candidates is directly related to Black turnout. But Tate concludes that "individual candidates . . . can most strongly affect Black rates of participation" within the context of "their ties to the Black community, the strength of their political organizations, and the competitive nature of the race" (117).[4]

Similar conclusions are drawn in the study of Latino participation, which is notable for the sometimes dramatic variation in participation patterns across states and local communities. De la Garza, Menchaca, and DeSipio (1994: 17), for example, report that petition signing in the Latino community during the 1990 midterm elections ranged from 8.8 percent in Los Angeles to 23.2 percent in New York, while Latino attendance at rallies ranged from 3.5 percent in Los Angeles to 10.5 percent in Chicago (see also Garcia and Arce 1988). *Why* such variations exist has not been addressed, although Garcia and Arce posit several possible explanations: "In these locations, situational factors such as local personalities and ethnically defined political races, local issues compelling to Chicanos, historical patterns, and sophisticated organizational activities increase awareness and participation" (1988: 129).

Hardy-Fanta's (1993) study of participation within the Latino community in Boston emphasizes the role of nonelectoral groups in stimulating, or structuring, political participation. Consistent with Uhlaner (1989a,

---

[4] Browning, Marshall, and Tabb (1984: 78) report that "previous research had shown that turnout peaked at times of major challenges to conservative coalitions and then fell, even though minority candidates continued to win elections." This suggests that candidate mobilization does not have long-term effects or that other elements associated with campaigns might be necessary to produce enhanced turnout that endures over a series of elections.

1989b), Hardy-Fanta argues that group activities socialize individuals, establishing social ties and developing interpersonal connections. When these social ties are developed, individuals are more likely to participate—particularly when the issues are important to the Latino community (e.g., government housing or social welfare programs)—*when political leaders encourage such involvement.*

While Hardy-Fanta (1993) uses Mujeres Unidas—a local Latina women's protest organization—as an example of this mobilization process, other scholars point to different types of groups. De la Garza, Menchaca, and DeSipio (1994: 26), for example, cite the important role of community organizations in stimulating turnout: in the two study sites without community organizations, turnout was around 25 percent; in two sites where community organization activities were stronger, turnout was around 40 percent (see also Sierra [1992: 59] on the efforts of community organizations in Albuquerque to register and educate "Hispanos").

Despite this rich case-study literature on the importance of candidate and group mobilization for Latino political participation, systematic individual-level evidence regarding the importance of mobilization is rare or even nonexistent. Numerous studies using data from the Latino National Political Study, for example, focus exclusively on whether demographic and attitudinal characteristics are associated with Latino participation. Arvizu and Garcia (1996) find that education, income, and occupational status, as well as life-cycle factors such as age, home ownership, and years in the United States, are associated with voter turnout. Likewise, Hero and Campbell (1996) report that education and income are associated with alternative types of participation as well, and in most cases they account for differences in the level of participation between Latinos and Anglos. The absence of *any* mention of group or candidate mobilization in these survey-based studies of Latino participation is striking, particularly in contrast to Tate's (1993) emphasis on the role of candidate mobilization in explaining participation.

Thus, systematic, survey-based studies of minority participation focus almost exclusively on individual-level attributes and ignore mobilization, despite the emphasis on group and candidate mobilization in the historical and case-study literatures. A more accurate understanding of minority *participation* thus requires a more systematic analysis of the process of political *mobilization*—which should in turn reflect on our models of mass political behavior.

ON MAINSTREAM STUDIES OF RACE, CLASS, AND PARTICIPATION

One of the most consistent findings in the study of mass behavior over the past forty years is that high-status individuals are more likely to participate in political activity than low-status individuals (see, e.g., Campbell et al. 1960; Verba and Nie 1972; Wolfinger and Rosenstone 1980; Leighley and Nagler 1992). The dominant interpretation of this research is that high-status individuals have more resources (i.e., time, money, and skills) available to facilitate engaging in political activity. Most recently, Verba, Schlozman, and Brady (1995) elaborate on the many ways these resources structure individuals' political participation.

Two alternative explanations for how socioeconomic status translates into political activity receive far less attention. Verba and Nie (1972) emphasize the importance of civic attitudes in explaining political participation: high-status individuals are more likely to participate because they have more positive civic orientations that either reduce the costs of participation or increase the benefits—the net effect being a higher probability of participating. Reflecting the critical importance of Verba and Nie's study, later participation studies routinely include various attitudinal indicators as predictors of participation.

A second alternative to the resource interpretation of the relationship between socioeconomic status and participation focuses on political mobilization. This interpretation argues that socioeconomic status is a primary determinant of political mobilization and that high-status individuals are more likely to participate in part because they are more likely to be asked, or recruited, to participate. More broadly, Rosenstone and Hansen (1993) argue that mass participation levels reflect the mobilizing activities of political elites and suggest that much of the decline in voter turnout since the 1960s reflects changes in mobilization patterns.

Aside from Rosenstone and Hansen (1993), however, there has been relatively little work done on the political mobilization of mass participation. The most extensively studied questions have been how party systems, or attributes, affect turnout (see, e.g., Hill and Leighley 1993) and the patterns and effects of party contacting on individual-level participation (see, e.g., Oliver 1996; Wielhouwer and Lockerbie 1994). This literature consistently finds positive effects of party attributes or activities on voter turnout. But we know very little about the strategies parties follow in seeking to mobilize turnout. Nor do we know whether the effectiveness of such activities is contingent on any particular individual or contextual characteristics.

The failure to systematically test the importance of mobilization as well as group characteristics in structuring minority participation is likewise evident in studies of minority participation that compare the predictors of Anglo participation to those of Blacks, Latinos, and, occasionally, Asian-Americans. The standard modeling strategy in these studies is to include a variety of demographic and attitudinal indicators, as well as dummy variables indicating whether the individual is a member of each ethnic group, in a multivariate model. Statistically significant coefficients for the race/

ethnicity dummy variables indicate that members of that particular group participate more or less (depending on the sign of the coefficient) than Anglos (typically excluded from the equation and used as the reference group). By estimating a series of models with different combinations of independent variables, these analyses provide some insight as to why certain ethnic groups participate less than Anglos.

Several factors—socioeconomic status, group identity, language, and culture—are typically offered as explanations for differences in participation levels across minority groups. Socioeconomic status often accounts for these differences, though it is far from consistent as a predictor of participation within groups. Uhlaner, Cain, and Kiewiet (1989) find that differences in participation levels between Blacks and Anglos can be accounted for by socioeconomic status, while differences between Latinos and Anglos can be accounted for by differences in socioeconomic status and group consciousness.[5] Similarly, Verba, Schlozman, and Brady (1995) report that once the resource differences associated with socioeconomic status are accounted for, Latinos and Blacks are no less likely to participate than are Anglos.

The greatest focus on mobilization in these comparative studies is provided by Verba, Schlozman, and Brady (1995: 151), who document how race structures who is asked to participate: Anglos are far more likely to report being asked to participate than either African-Americans or Latinos (56 percent compared to 40 percent and 25 percent, respectively). Further, African-Americans are most likely to report being asked by other African-Americans, while Latinos are most likely to report being asked by Anglos. Although Verba, Schlozman, and Brady do not explicitly test whether these requests for political activity are associated with greater participation, they do consider whether institutional mobilization—requests to participate directed toward the respondent in church, on the job, or in a voluntary association—is associated with individuals' participation. They find that, controlling for socioeconomic status, time, and resources, individuals who are mobilized are more likely to engage in political activity.[6]

Interpretations of the empirical findings in the "mainstream" literature on race and participation introduced above typically reflect two assumptions regarding the generalizability of political behavior that might be questioned. First, conclusions regarding the basic relationships among socioeconomic status, political attitudes, and political participation, based

[5] Differences between Asian-Americans and Anglos are not explained in Uhlaner, Cain and Kiewiet's study: controlling for socioeconomic status, immigration factors, and group consciousness, Asians are less likely to participate than are Anglos and Latinos. For one possible explanation, see Cho (1999).

[6] No details are provided as to whether these patterns of recruitment have similar effects on participation across ethnic groups or in contrast to Anglos.

primarily on samples of whites, are assumed to hold for all individuals in the sample *regardless of minority status*.[7] That is, estimating the relationship between socioeconomic status and political attitudes using a primarily Anglo-white sample assumes that the estimated relationships hold equally across minority groups. But is it appropriate to assume that education and income, for example, enhance the participation of ethnic minorities in the same way they enhance the participation of (majority) whites?

Second, conclusions regarding the political behavior of African-Americans are often assumed to generalize to other minority groups. Because data on the political behavior of Hispanics and Asian-Americans, for example, are relatively rare compared to that on African-Americans, empirical evidence regarding African-American political behavior is either explicitly or implicitly extrapolated to provide "insight" into the political behavior of other minority groups such as Hispanics and Asian-Americans. In the few cases where differences among minority groups are demonstrated empirically, the results are treated as random occurrences rather than as theoretically significant findings (see, e.g., Uhlaner, Cain, and Kiewiet 1989). Absent of any theoretical perspective from which we can analyze these differences, it is likely that scholars of mainstream political behavior will continue to assume that various ethnic groups, with their unique political histories and goals, reflect the same linkages among socioeconomic status, political attitudes, and political participation.

Without some empirical evidence with regard to these two assumptions, one might reasonably argue that the study of mass political behavior has been the study of *white* political behavior. That, in essence, is the argument eloquently advanced by Hanes Walton, Jr., in *Invisible Politics* (1985). Walton argues that behavioralists' emphasis on individualistic explanations of participation ignores the "overwhelming systemic influences and forces" that have structured Black political behavior for decades, if not centuries. Walton also argues that scholars should not assume that Blacks' and other ethnic groups' political behavior are linked to individualistic or systemic factors in the same way:

> [B]lack political behavior . . . is inspired and shaped *by some features and currents that do not form the basis of all American political behavior because it is rooted in the black experience in America.* And this experience is radically different from the experience of other immigrant groups. In fact, to fully understand black political behavior one must know the context from which it sprang and the factors that influenced and nurtured that context (italics in original). (8)

---

[7] This assumption applies to those studies cited above that rely on national surveys with a small set of minority (usually Black) respondents, where the discussion of race is restricted to the question of comparative participation levels and the interpretation of the dummy variable for race.

Further, he takes issue with the simplistic comparison of Blacks and whites in terms of demographics and without accounting for the political context:

> Behaviorally oriented researchers, in setting up experimental and control groups mandated by the scientific method, invariably developed black and white samples that were equal on demographic variables. Each sample has similar educational, economic, age, regional, housing, and social status levels. This pairing of demographic realities leads one to assume that the two groups are equal, politically and socially. Then, when comparisons between the two groups are drawn and vast gaps inevitably emerge, explanations are sought only in terms of individual variables, which are inherent in the very nature of the behavioral approach. But the disparities might be due to the differences in the two groups themselves. On this point, the literature is silent. Similar demographics do not make groups equal—politically or socially. (12)

The richness of Walton's argument is matched by the diversity of empirical evidence on which he draws to support his case—evidence rarely referred to in studies of mass political behavior. He cites various studies of Black politics published at the same time as Verba and Nie's (1972) classic study of political participation, each of which emphasizes the importance of legal and political factors—not socioeconomic status, political attitudes, or group consciousness—in determining Blacks' levels of participation. In part due to the fact that much of this evidence relies on subnational data, these findings have never been incorporated into mainstream studies of political participation.

ANALYTICAL STRATEGY AND OVERVIEW OF THEORETICAL CONTRIBUTIONS

I have drawn from previous research on mass political behavior and minority participation to identify several factors described in both literatures as central to understanding both who is mobilized and who chooses to participate. These five factors—class, ideology, relational goods, group size, and political empowerment—form the basis of the empirical analyses. Because recruitment and mobilization are key elements in Uhlaner's relational goods argument, the empirical analyses test how these five factors structure both mobilization and participation, from the perspective of elites as well as citizens, and whether these relationships differ for Anglos, African-Americans, and Latinos.

The centrality of socioeconomic status to theories of participation and mobilization was discussed in chapter 1. Although far less attention has been paid to the role of ideology as a stimulus of participation, various empirical studies suggest that both elite mobilization strategies and the mass public responses are so structured. Partisanship (or ideology) is likewise associated with both participation and mobilization. To the extent that parties target swing voters, we might also expect to see Independents more likely to be mobilized as well. These two expectations thus suggest that partisans and Independents will be more likely to be mobilized and to participate than will individuals who fail to identify with the electoral system in this way.[8]

Further, Beck and Jennings (1979) demonstrate that who participates reflects the opportunities available to do so and that these opportunities are structured by ideology. They conclude that liberals were significantly more likely to participate in the 1970s because there was a higher level of organization and mobilization among liberals than among conservatives. Consistent with this finding, Nie et al. (1988) report that Black participation has declined since the 1970s because the decline of the civil rights movement resulted in fewer opportunities for Blacks to participate.

The Beck and Jennings finding is broadly consistent with the common belief that political elites target individuals who are likely to be supporters. Participation, or voter turnout, is not an "end" for political elites, but rather a means—a means to being elected, or winning a policy decision through initiatives or referenda, for example. Hence, elites will seek to target supporters, rather than opponents, and mobilization patterns will reflect their perceptions of the ideological or policy affinity of potentially targetable groups.

The evidence on this point, however, is mixed. For Blacks and Latinos, this has resulted in fewer efforts directed toward them by the Republican Party, for example, because these groups are perceived to be ideologically liberal. Yet Black leaders often complain that the Democratic Party fails to mobilize, or target, Blacks because they have been so loyal to the Democratic Party that party leaders believe there is little risk in ignoring this core support group.

Anecdotal evidence abounds as to the importance of both group size and political empowerment in structuring both participation and mobilization. The importance of group size to minority participation is suggested by Dawson's (1994) argument that group interests motivate Black political behavior. Accordingly, this claim requires that one aspect of the calculus of voting be modified in the case of Blacks (and other minorities): instead of the individual's rationality of participating in an election contest reflecting the probability of casting the winning vote, minority decisions to participate will reflect the potential of the minority group to determine the out-

[8] Note that this expectation undoubtedly reflects a psychological attachment to the system as well as the likelihood of being targeted by parties.

come of the election or attain another instrumental end. This probability, I argue, is a function of group size, but as I noted in chapter 1, I believe that the direct effect of group size is more important for Latino participation than it is for African-American participation.

Group-conflict theory, and empirical studies associated with it, likewise confirm the importance of group size in structuring political behavior. According to this theory, historical as well as present conflicts between whites and Blacks result in conflict between these groups for limited resources (including political power). The greater the threat perceived by whites, the more they will engage in behaviors that seek to limit or control Blacks. Giles and various coauthors have documented how a variety of electoral behaviors—including candidate choice, party identification, and group identity—are influenced by threat, which is operationalized as the size of the Black population in the local community (see, e.g., Giles and Buckner 1996; Giles and Evans 1985, 1986; Giles and Hertz 1994).

But this empirical evidence focuses on Anglo (not minority) attitudes such as partisanship or candidate preference rather than participation and relies almost exclusively on aggregate-level data. Responding to this, Leighley and Vedlitz (1999) offer individual-level evidence that, indeed, threat depresses rather than mobilizes the participation of Anglos and that minority individuals are not influenced by group threat. But this evidence is based on a statewide public opinion survey in Texas, and thus the generalizability of this conclusion is limited.

Elite mobilization also reflects the importance of the size of the minority group and its impact on the ultimate electoral contest or policy decision. Specifically, where minorities make up a large, or significant, portion of the electorate, they will more likely be targeted. This results in higher mobilization levels when minorities are segregated and lower mobilization levels when minorities are integrated (or dispersed) as a smaller proportion throughout a population.[9]

Finally, as Bobo and Gilliam (1990) have demonstrated, minorities will be more likely to participate when they are empowered. That is, when minorities are successfully elected to office, Blacks' psychological involvements in politics increase, and therefore they participate more. However, it is also possible that political empowerment is associated with greater levels of mobilization within minority communities. Hence, where Blacks and Latinos hold public office, we should expect to see higher levels of mass

[9] As noted above, to be more pivotal is clearly more important than being large, but the relatively small size of minority populations in most districts makes this point moot. I have, however, done many of the analyses in chapters 4–8 with alternative measures of pivotalness, but these measures produce few differences in results. For reasons of parsimony, I have chosen to use the group-size measures.

participation by Blacks and Latinos in both electoral and nonelectoral activities.

Related to this, elites will be more likely to target minorities when minorities *are* the political elites. This expectation follows from Dawson's (1994) claim that Black institutions and candidates tend to emphasize group interests: this emphasis has to be directed toward minorities themselves or it falls on deaf ears. It is also likely that minorities are more likely to be elected to office in local communities where the level of social interaction and organization—and perhaps politicization—within the minority community is high, as these networks may be critical for successful election campaigns of minorities. Thus, we should expect to find minorities targeted more by political elites, as well as other minorities, when minorities hold public office.

Thus, the analyses that follow extend previous empirical studies on the determinants of mobilization and participation with respect to African-Americans and Latinos. However, one (not uncommon) limitation of this research is that not all individual and contextual influences can be incorporated into the empirical tests of the models. This reflects a practical reality—especially when relying on existing data sources—as well as my preference for both theoretical and statistical parsimony.

Moreover, one of the most severe limitations of existing data is the virtual impossibility of linking specific forms of elite electoral mobilization to the available survey data on individual characteristics and self-reported participation. In short, most of the existing data sets provide insufficient geographic locator codes to match individuals to specific electoral contests (and, therefore, elite mobilization efforts such as campaign spending or get-out-the-vote efforts). Nor are self-reported voter turnout measures regarding particular elections especially reliable, even when they are available.

The analyses of the Citizen Participation Study (CPS) thus operationalize "elite recruitment" as "minority empowerment," which Bobo and Gilliam (1990) originally measured as the presence of elected Black (i.e., minority) mayors in the survey respondent's metropolitan area. Further, when using the CPS data, I operationalize participation in three ways: frequency of voting in local elections, frequency of voting in presidential elections, and the number of political activities (both electoral and nonelectoral) the individual reports doing.

To summarize, formal models of individuals' decisions to participate provide a rationale for including more directly various aspects of individuals' social and political contexts into empirical tests of participation models. These contextual features tend to be emphasized in studies of minority politics. Thus, the empirical analyses that follow seek to explicate how these contextual features are critical to understanding both elite mobilization and citizen participation decisions.

Chapter Three

MOBILIZATION AND PARTICIPATION:
PRELIMINARY EVIDENCE

THE models in chapter 1 suggest that both political recruitment and political participation are (in various ways for different groups) structured by class, racial context, relational goods, and elite mobilization. This chapter focuses on several preliminary issues relating to these models. To what extent are racial/ethnic differences in mobilization and participation simply or solely a function of class? To the extent that class accounts for racial/ethnic differences in participation levels, the argument that contextual influences matter for racial/ethnic participation is severely weakened. And, to what extent are racial/ethnic differences in mobilization and participation associated with two particular contextual features, group size and minority empowerment? These preliminary analyses allow us to focus on the contrasting importance of class and race as individual predictors of political mobilization and participation, as is typically done in mainstream studies. The more detailed relationships concerning racial context, relational goods, and elite mobilization are thus left to later chapters.

I begin with a discussion of the literature on class, race, and participation, supplemented with U.S. census data on voter turnout in the 1996 presidential election. I then introduce Verba, Schlozman, and Brady's CPS and examine the relationships among class, race, and alternative forms of participation. The concluding sections then review the minority politics literature's approach to the nature of contextual influences on participation and how class and race structure recruitment to alternative forms of participation as well.

SOCIOECONOMIC STATUS, RACE, AND PARTICIPATION

No reasonable discussion of the factors that influence political participation could afford to ignore the importance of socioeconomic status (SES). In fact, most discussions begin *and end* with "the standard socioeconomic status model." The most common interpretation of the SES model was initially developed by Verba and Nie (1972; see also Almond and Verba 1963; Milbrath 1965), who emphasize the importance of individuals' civic orientations as the linkage between SES and participation. Because high-status individuals are located in social environments that encourage and enforce positive attitudinal and participatory norms, they are more likely to participate in politics than are low-status individuals.

The most recent embellishment on the SES model is offered by Verba, Schlozman, and Brady (1995), who focus on individuals' acquisition of resources, with particular attention given to gender and race (see also Verba et al. 1991, 1993a, 1993b). Verba, Schlozman, and Brady (1995) conceptualize individuals' decisions to participate as reflecting the resources accumulated through the individual's life cycle (see also Strate et al. 1989).[1] One's job type, organizational memberships, church attendance, and family structure determine the skills that one brings to the political sphere. And Verba, Schlozman, and Brady's (1995) exhaustive analyses offer persuasive evidence that various skills associated with socioeconomic status help explain why high-status individuals are more likely to participate.

Evidence in support of the SES model is abundant. Individuals with high levels of education are more likely to participate in politics than individuals with low levels of education; the evidence is almost as persuasive for the relationship between income and participation, though the effect of income on participation is typically less powerful than that for education, and these findings are generally consistent across different types of participation (Acock and Scott 1980; Barnes and Kaase 1979; Conway 1991; Dalton 1988; Kenny 1992; Leighley 1990; Nie et al. 1988; Salisbury 1980; Verba, Nie, and Kim 1978; Verba, Schlozman, and Brady 1995; Verba et al. 1993a).[2]

Nowhere is the association between socioeconomic status and political participation more evident than in the case of voter turnout, as shown in figure 3.1. In the 1996 presidential election, for example, approximately 54 percent of the nation's voting-age population and 58 percent of the nation's citizen voting-age population reported voting. But barely 39 percent of citizens with less than a high school education reported voting, compared to 83 percent of citizens with advanced degrees. Similarly, less than 40 percent of citizens in the lowest income categories reported voting, compared to over 75 percent of those citizens in the highest income group.

[1] Although Verba et al. do not explicitly incorporate civic orientations in their political resource model, one might interpret the new study's focus on resources as explicating the processes whereby high-status individuals accumulate both skills and attitudes that predispose them toward political activity.

[2] Studies focusing on one particular form of participation are far too numerous to list, but for recent representative analyses on voter turnout, see Conway 1981; Leighley and Nagler 1992; Tate 1991, 1993; Teixeira 1987, 1992; Wolfinger and Rosenstone 1980. On group activism, see Cook 1984; Curtis, Grabb, and Baer 1992; Knoke 1990a, 1990b; Rothenberg 1992. On campaign contributions, see Brown, Hedges, and Powell 1980; Kenny and Parent 1991. On citizen-initiated contacting, see Hero 1986; Hirlinger 1992; Sharp 1982, 1984; Thomas 1982; Vedlitz, Durand, and Dyer 1980; Zuckerman and West 1985. On political protest and violence, see Barnes and Kaase 1979; Chong 1991; Gibson 1989; Mason 1984; Nice 1988.

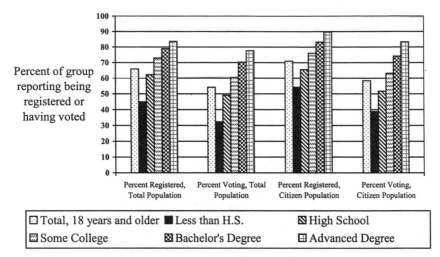

Figure 3.1. Self-Reported Registration and Voting in the November 1996 Presidential Election
Source: U.S. Bureau of the Census, Current Population Survey. "Voting and Registration in the Election of November 1996." *Current Population Reports: Population Characteristics*, P20–504.

The CPS data confirm this well-established pattern with respect to voter turnout as well as other forms of political participation. Figure 3.2 presents the proportion of respondents at four different education levels who report engaging in nine different types of participation: doing campaign work, making campaign contributions, contacting federal appointed officials, contacting federal elected officials, contacting local appointed officials, contacting local elected officials, voting in local elections, voting in presidential elections, and being registered to vote. With one exception (voting in local elections), the higher one's level of education, the greater the probability of participating, with the biggest increase in participation typically evidenced between high school graduates and individuals with some college education.

The primary question that has been addressed by scholars studying mass political behavior is whether African-Americans participate more or less than whites, with some attention given to whether Latinos participate more or less than whites.[3] Bivariate analyses of participation levels typically

---

[3] The other race-related question that has received a modest amount of attention from scholars in the mass political behavior literature is whether reported race-related differences in voter turnout are a function of differences in misreporting rates of Blacks and whites (Silver, Anderson, and Abramson 1986; but see Leighley and Nagler 1992). Shaw, de la Garza, and Lee (2000) report that Latinos substantially overreport on voter turnout, but it is not clear to what extent this overreporting is greater than that documented previously for Anglos.

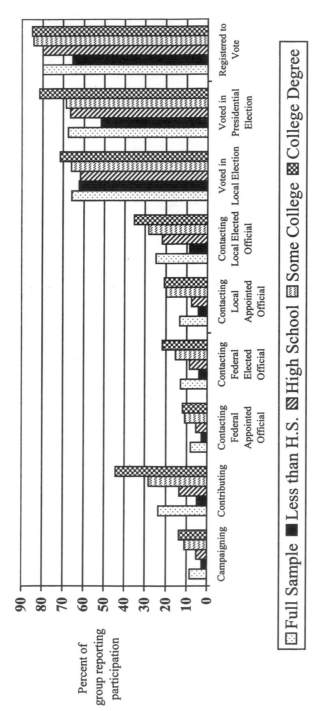

Figure 3.2. Self-Reported Participation, Controlling for Education
Source: Citizen Participation Study (CPS). Data are weighted.

suggest that minorities are less likely to participate, though the magnitude of the difference depends on the type of participation considered. This, too, is the pattern evidenced in the CPS.

Figure 3.3 presents the proportion of respondents who reported engaging in the nine types of participation, controlling for race/ethnicity; data are presented separately for Latinos and Latino citizens, so that the effects of noncitizenship are not confounded with those of race/ethnicity. Anglos are most likely to report participating in each type of activity, except for campaign work, where African-Americans report participating at about the same level (18 percent). Latinos are far less likely than Anglos and African-Americans to report participating, regardless of the type of activity, and restricting our attention to Latino citizens narrows this gap only slightly. Perhaps not surprisingly (and consistent with previous research), voting is the type of participation in which the smallest race/ethnicity-related differences in participation levels are documented.

The usual question raised by patterns such as these is whether the lower participation rates of African-Americans and Latinos "simply" reflects distributional differences relating to class across groups—that is, that the overall rate of minority participation is less than that for Anglos because minorities tend to be poorer. The analytical strategy typically used to address this question is to include race along with education, income, age, and gender in a multivariate regression model predicting whether, or how much, the individual participates in politics. Race is typically measured as a dummy variable, with values of one indicating that the individual is a member of a particular minority group and values of zero indicating that the individual is not a member of a minority group. A statistically significant estimate of the race coefficient is interpreted to mean that, controlling for socioeconomic status, individual members of the particular minority group participate more or less (depending on the sign of the coefficient) than those who are not.

Using this approach, evidence regarding race-related differences in participation rates varies. Controlling for socioeconomic status, minorities are sometimes more and sometimes less likely than whites to participate, depending on the exact type of participation and time period investigated (Berry, Portney, and Thomson 1990; Bobo and Gilliam 1990; Ellison and Gay 1989; Nie et al. 1988; Uhlaner, Cain, and Kiewiet 1989; Verba and Nie 1972; Verba et al. 1993a, 1993b). Race-related differences in voter turnout are probably small in magnitude.[4] When controlling for education and

---

[4] This statement is based on studies focusing primarily on differences in turnout between Blacks and whites in presidential elections. Turnout differences between Blacks and whites in lower-stimulus races are likely to be greater, though the difference is reduced in racially-divided races, which often coincides with Black candidates' running for office (Engstrom and Caridas 1991).

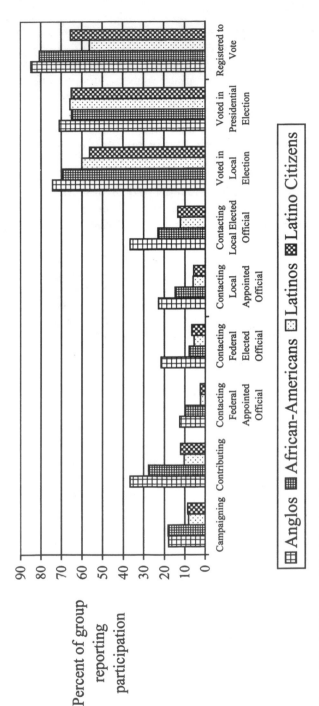

Figure 3.3. Self-Reported Participation, Controlling for Race/Ethnicity
Source: Citizen Participation Study (CPS). Data are unweighted.

income, Blacks are about as likely to vote as are whites; yet when controlling for demographics and civic orientations, Blacks are slightly more likely
to vote (Teixeira 1992).[5]

Although more complex multivariate analyses are presented in later
chapters, for now I would like to present some initial evidence from the
CPS on the question of whether the lower participation rates of minorities
are entirely accounted for by class differences. Table 3.1 presents the proportion of each racial/ethnic group that reported working in a campaign,
contributing money to a campaign, contacting a local elected official, and
voting in a local election. In general, the association between socioeconomic status and participation is supported, as the proportion of activists within each racial/ethnic group increases as one reads across the column entries. However, there remain substantial differences across groups
that are not accounted for by class.

For example, African-Americans tend to be more active in campaign
work (and occasionally in voting in local elections and contributing money)
than Anglos, while Latinos are less active in each activity at each level of
socioeconomic status. These "exceptions" to the "socioeconomic status
rule" suggest that other factors are at play in determining whether
racial/ethnic minority individuals engage in politics at the same rate as
do Anglos.

CONTEXTUAL CHARACTERISTICS AND MINORITY PARTICIPATION

Previous research on minority political participation tends to emphasize
that mobilization factors are more important than socioeconomic status in
predicting participation and tends to incorporate a broader set of factors as
critical to understanding who participates than does more traditional research. These factors include registration requirements, group mobilization, candidate mobilization, party mobilization, political empowerment,
and size/geographic concentration.[6] The discussion below reviews the main
arguments and evidence on each of these factors for both African-Americans and Latinos.

[5] Many of the standard treatments of race-related differences in voter turnout, however,
typically ignore the role of group consciousness as a predictor of participation, despite studies
of Black politics that demonstrate its importance. See Bobo and Gilliam 1990; Miller et al.
1981; Shingles 1981; Tate 1993; Uhlaner 1991; Uhlaner, Cain, and Kiewiet 1989.

[6] Both literatures portray registration requirements, group mobilization, and elite mobilization as especially important, while the significance of the other factors differs across the two
groups. This reflects either the "absence" of a factor for one group (e.g., little party mobilization of Latinos compared to Blacks) or a difference in the magnitude of the effect (e.g., group
consciousness having less impact on Latinos due to nationality differences).

TABLE 3.1
Participation by Education, Controlling for Race/Ethnicity

	Less than High School (%)	High School (%)	Some College (%)	College Degree (%)
Engaging in campaign work				
Anglos	2.2	11.3	21.8	25.8
African-Americans	8.7	11.4	19.2	37.4
Latinos	5.9	5.6	14.1	10.3
Latino Citizens	7.7	4.7	16.0	5.6
Contributing				
Anglos	5.6	19.5	37.9	59.0
African-Americans	8.7	18.1	32.5	54.5
Latinos	5.9	4.5	18.3	24.1
Latino Citizens	6.2	4.7	24.0	27.8
Contacting local elected official				
Anglos	8.4	31.2	39.2	47.8
African-Americans	8.7	10.9	33.3	43.4
Latinos	3.0	13.6	19.7	20.7
Latino Citizens	4.8	14.3	18.0	27.8
Voting in local election				
Anglos	61.4	68.8	72.7	81.2
African-Americans	69.0	55.6	73.8	80.5
Latinos	62.5	55.3	55.3	77.8
Latino Citizens	56.3	51.4	53.3	76.9
Registering to vote				
Anglos	62.9	82.5	88.3	90.8
African-Americans	70.7	76.5	85.0	91.9
Latinos	46.1	59.6	63.4	65.5
Latino Citizens	60.0	62.5	70.0	83.3

Source: CPS. Data are unweighted.
Note: Table entries indicate the proportion of each racial/ethnic group at each level of education that reports having engaged in each political activity.

Registration Requirements

Barker and Jones (1994: 70) describe securing the right to vote as dominating "the black political agenda from Emancipation through the 1960s," with the passage of the Voting Rights Act of 1965 being the final step toward satisfying the goal of the (potential) full participation of African-

Americans in U.S. politics.[7] And there is strong and consistent evidence that eliminating the barriers imposed by registrars in local communities drastically increased registration among African-Americans:

> On the first supervised registration day under the new statute (Voting Rights Act of 1965), Negro voter lists in nine counties with a history of rampant discrimination in Alabama, Louisiana, and Mississippi increased by 65 percent. . . . Extending their work to four other counties, the federal voting examiners had registered almost 20,000 Negroes within ten days. (quote from Henry J. Abraham in Walton 1985: 76)

Decades later, the large gaps between African-American and white' registration and voting rates have closed considerably, primarily due to the elimination of legal barriers, including the easing of registration requirements. Barker and Jones (1994), for example, cite census bureau data estimating the registration rate of the total population in 1966 as 70.3 percent, compared to only 60.3 percent for African-Americans. By 1988, the registration rates differed by only three percentage points: the registration rate of the total population was 67 percent and 64 percent of Blacks were registered. Furthermore, these gains in registration have been associated with gains in voter turnout. Barker and Jones (1994: 71) report that between 1966 and 1988, the Black voting population increased from 7 percent to 10 percent.

The same legal factors noted in historical analyses of Black voter turnout—for example, literacy tests, poll taxes, annual registration systems—are noted by Garcia and Arce as depressing electoral participation by Chicanos (1988: 131). As has been done in the African-American community, institutional structures have developed to assist individuals in overcoming these barriers to participation. Garcia and Arce (1988: 128) note that groups such as the Southwest Voter Registration Education Project (SWVREP) and the Mexican-American Legal Defense and Educational Fund, along with local efforts, have increased Chicano participation levels (but also see de la Garza and DeSipio's discussion in de la Garza, Menchaca, and DeSipio 1994: 27, 35).

Little disagreement exists, however, regarding another legal requirement of the voter registration process: citizenship. Of particular importance within the Latino communities in Texas and California, the requirement that voters be citizens eliminates a significant proportion of the Latino community from voting, though it may not necessarily depress participation in other activities that do not require citizenship (see, among others,

---

[7] On the disenfranchisement of Blacks in Southern politics, see Matthews and Prothro 1966: 13–20; on more recent trends in the participation of Blacks in the South, see Wright 1987.

de la Garza and DeSipio 1992, 1996; Hero 1992: 60; MacManus and Cassel 1982).

Group Mobilization

The importance of civic groups such as the League of United Latin American Citizens (LULAC), SWVREP, farm workers unions, and various local neighborhood groups is documented in scholarship on the Chicano movement of the 1960s and community organizing (Barrera 1985; Hero 1992; Mormino and Pozzetta 1987). The purpose of most of this research is either to provide accurate historical details of the political struggles of Latinos (or Chicanos) or to discuss successful community organizing techniques.

Historians have to an even greater degree documented the activities of African-Americans during the civil rights movement. One of the distinguishing features of the civil rights movement of the late 1950s and 1960s was the variety of political activities African-Americans engaged in to effect political change: registering to vote, voting in local elections, economic boycotts, protests, and letter-writing campaigns (see, e.g., Cameron 1974; Carson 1981; Chong 1991; Clark 1970; McAdam 1988; Morris 1981). In all likelihood, this heightened level of participation among African-Americans resulted from a number of factors, including the improved socioeconomic status of Blacks in the post–World War II era, the development of a Black professional or middle class, and a sense of political opportunity within the Democratic Party (McAdam 1982).

Greater participation also likely resulted from the high level of social organization within the Black community. Matthews and Prothro (1966), for example, argue that Blacks in the South, with limited personal resources and segregated from white political institutions, needed to form their own organizations to gain power. They demonstrate that Blacks in counties with strong Black organizations were more likely to be registered and more likely to vote. However, organizations do not have to be *political* to facilitate participation: Matthews and Prothro report that the church provided Blacks additional opportunities to participate (1966: 232–34; see also Barker and Walters 1989; Dawson 1994: 58–61; Gurin, Hatchett, and Jackson 1989: 73–75; McAdam 1982, 1988; Morris 1981, 1984; Tate 1993: 77–79).

Much of the systematic empirical evidence regarding the important role of political organizations (including churches) in mobilizing Black or Latino political participation, however, is typically indirect.[8] Most studies incorporate individuals' self-reports of church attendance or group member-

---

[8] The same problem holds for whites (Leighley 1996).

ship as indicators of organizational mobilization. Tate (1991, 1993), for example, finds that (self-reported) church membership and group membership are associated with turnout while controlling for demographics and political attitudes (see also Gurin, Hatchett, and Jackson 1989). Similarly, Dawson, Brown, and Allen (1990) find that religious guidance is significantly related to voter participation, as well as political involvement (other than turnout). And in perhaps the only systematic study of organizational mobilization of Latino participation, Diaz (1996) finds that, with the exception of Cubans, Latinos' self-reported memberships in voluntary associations are associated with higher levels of voter registration and turnout.

The most direct, systematic evidence on group (or, more specifically, church) mobilization of minority participation is offered by Verba, Schlozman, and Brady (1995), who stress how nonpolitical, or civic, groups mobilize participation both by developing skills that are transferable to political activity as well as by directly mobilizing individuals. They focus most extensively on the former and provide rich evidence in support of their civic voluntarism model: gaining communication and organizational skills in church, on the job, and in voluntary associations increases the likelihood that an individual engages in political activity. Moreover, they note that African-Americans are particularly likely to have the opportunity to gain these skills due to the congregationally oriented nature of Black churches, in contrast to the fewer opportunities provided Latinos through the Catholic Church.

Figure 3.4 presents CPS data on institutional mobilization patterns by race/ethnicity. Individuals were asked whether they were either asked to vote for a specific candidate or requested to take some other political action in church or a voluntary organization, and in addition whether they were asked to contribute money to an election campaign at work. Based on individuals' responses to these questions, additive scales ranging from 0 to 2 for church and voluntary organization mobilization, and ranging from 0 to 3 for job mobilization, were created. Adding these three scales together resulted in another scale that I refer to as "institutional mobilization."

The notable feature of these mobilization patterns across racial/ethnic groups is how starkly it contrasts with the patterns of participation displayed above in table 3.1. Simply put, there are far fewer discrepancies across racial/ethnic groups in mobilization patterns. Regardless of the locus of the mobilization efforts, African-Americans, Latinos, and Latino citizens generally report being asked to participate at about the same rate as Anglos. This seems to confirm the emphasis placed in studies of minority participation on the importance of political mobilization for racial/ethnic minorities.

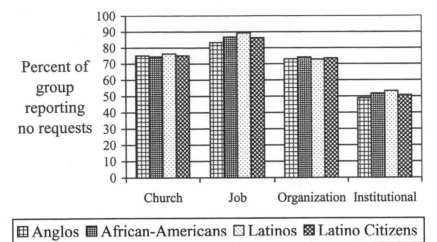

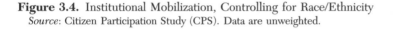

Figure 3.4. Institutional Mobilization, Controlling for Race/Ethnicity
Source: Citizen Participation Study (CPS). Data are unweighted.

Candidate Mobilization

With the increasing number of African-American candidates and elected officials over the past three decades, it is perhaps not surprising that scholars have emphasized the importance of African-American candidates and officials in mobilizing the participation of the Black community. This is particularly true in case studies of Jesse Jackson's 1984 presidential bid as well as in studies of mayoral races in major U.S. cities.[9]

Similarly, de la Garza and DeSipio emphasize the importance of the local context in determining the extent to which political campaigns mobilize Latinos (de la Garza, Menchaca, and DeSipio 1994: 27). In fact, the importance of candidates' engaging in traditional campaign activities directed toward the Latino community is underscored by their discussion of the depressing effects of modern campaign technology, which selectively targets people who already vote. Most observations regarding the importance of candidate mobilization focus on whether candidates in a particular election contacted members of the Latino community. DeSipio and Rocha (1992: 11, 16), for example, describe the efforts of the Dukakis campaign

[9] On Blacks' reaction/mobilization by the Jackson campaign, see also Cavanagh 1985; Walters (in Barker and Walters) 1989.

to mobilize Latinos, reporting that initial promises to have get-out-the-vote drives never materialized (also see Sierra 1992: 59).[10]

The *effectiveness* of such efforts is another question. Falcon (1988: 183) reports that

> in New York City, [Jesse] Jackson's campaign and appeal for a Rainbow Coalition served to dramatically motivate blacks to have the highest turnout rate in recent memory in a primary held in the city, with 52 percent of registered black Democrats turning out to vote compared to only 38–39 percent of whites and Latinos on April 3, 1984. Absent the Jackson candidacy in the general election that year, black turnout once again fell to previous low levels, but it apparently had little or no effect on Latino voters either way.

Finally, there are numerous examples of particular issues in local elections stimulating significantly higher turnout within the Latino community. The assumption in these studies is that a notable issue appearing on the ballot motivates (minority) political entrepreneurs to organize in the local community to work for or against the issue, and that this organization subsidizes the cost of participation (and possibly enhances the benefits gained by contributing to a collective enterprise). Saiz, for example, claims that the presence of an "English-only" initiative on the ballot increased registration and turnout greatly among Latinos in Colorado in 1988 (1992: 72).

We can assess the extent to which minorities are mobilized to become active in local politics using the CPS data, although the particular issue motivating such involvement is not identified. As shown in figure 3.5, for example, Anglos are most likely to report being mobilized to contact a government official or to "take an active role in a local political or public issue" (40.1 percent and 28.7 percent, respectively) compared to African-Americans, Latinos, and Latino citizens (19 percent and 21.1 percent, 9.3 percent and 9.6 percent, and 11.7 percent and 11.7 percent, respectively). Unlike the responses to the questions on institutional mobilization, these patterns are more reflective of the lower levels of participation exhibited by Latinos and Latino citizens. This suggests that the level of noninstitutional mobilization (i.e., mobilization occurring outside the church, job, or voluntary association) directed toward minorities might account for lower levels of participation.

Party Mobilization

In contrast to the common references to candidate mobilization in the African-American and Latino participation literatures, little is said about

[10] An alternative claim regarding the importance of candidate mobilization is that the presence of Latino candidates on the ballot—independent of any mobilization efforts the candidate undertakes—is associated with higher voter turnout (Flores and Brischetto 1992: 96).

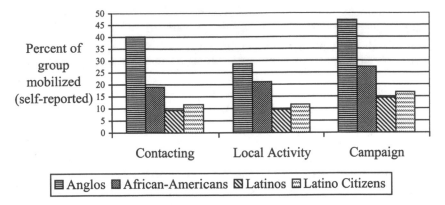

Figure 3.5. Mobilization to Particular Activities, Controlling for Race/Ethnicity

partisan mobilization—and the little that *is* said emphasizes how rarely partisan mobilization occurs among either minority group. For Blacks, the argument is that because the group typically makes up a very small percentage of any given (city, state, or national) electorate, and because in contemporary politics it has been overwhelmingly loyal to the Democratic Party, neither of the major parties has an incentive to mobilize Black voters. But systematic evidence on the level and effectiveness of party mobilization of Blacks is almost nonexistent.

One exception to this is Carton's (1984) analysis of the effects of party organizational activity and community leader activity in Detroit, Michigan. Carton's intensive study of a two-week referendum campaign focused specifically on the effectiveness of various canvassing efforts to increase turnout and win voter support. Based on precinct-level data, he concludes that face-to-face contacts are more likely to mobilize turnout than are literature distributions; that party organizational activity is effective in both low- and high-status Black precincts; and that party organizational activity is more effective in mobilizing turnout than is community leader mobilization.

The lack of partisan mobilization of Latinos is documented somewhat more systematically in the literature on Latino participation. The strongest statement on the importance of partisan mobilization is offered by de la Garza and DeSipio, who claim that Latinos vote as much as Anglos when socioeconomic status is controlled for; the reason Latinos do not vote is because electoral institutions do nothing to mobilize these resource-poor individuals (de la Garza, Menchaca, and DeSipio 1994: 34). Hence, instead of interpreting the relationship between socioeconomic status and participation as a reflection of individuals' resources, de la Garza and DeSipio interpret it as an indicator of the likelihood of being mobilized by political parties.

Most scholars reach similar conclusions as to the political party's proclivity to engage in such activities.[11] DeSipio and Rocha argue that the loyalty of Latinos to the Democratic Party limits the incentives for the parties to mobilize them (1992: 7, 9). Hero claims that both parties were completely indifferent to the Latino vote in 1988 in Arizona, with the Democrats being able to identify few efforts targeting Latinos and Republicans unable to identify any (de la Garza and DeSipio 1992: 79). Garcia reports that Salces and Colby find Spanish-Americans in Chicago participate less due to an unresponsive Democratic Party (1988: 121). And Hardy-Fanta reports that the limited participation of Latinos in Boston reflects the lack of partisan mobilization and subsequent unresponsiveness of the party system (1993: 173).

In contrast to the case-study evidence on the level of party mobilization, the *effects* of the party system on Latino participation have been documented more broadly by Calvo and Rosenstone (1989), who test for party and group mobilization effects using census data. They demonstrate that Hispanics living in areas with strong parties are more likely to vote and that Hispanics living in areas with highly organized groups are more likely to vote. Mexican-Americans in Texas and Cubans in Florida, for example, have higher turnout levels than Hispanics living in areas with weakly organized groups. They conclude

> that differential political mobilization explains why individual political resources have a smaller effect on Hispanic than on non-Hispanic turnout and why individual political resources have a negligible impact on Cuban-American rates of participation. Strong political parties underwrite the cost of voting among Hispanics; they do not subsidize non-Hispanic turnout. . . . When groups mobilize people to participate in politics, they boost the perceived benefits and subsidize the costs of participation for those who do not otherwise have the resources to take part. (22)

As shown in figure 3.5, however, the level of campaign mobilization that racial/ethnic minorities are exposed to is substantially lower than that reported by Anglos: only 27.4 percent of African-Americans, 14.4 percent of Latinos, and 16.8 percent of Latino citizens report being asked to become involved in campaign work or contribute money, compared to 47.1 percent of Anglos. Thus, consistent with the mobilization patterns for local activity and contacting officials, racial/ethnic minorities are simply exposed to fewer requests to participate. Political party and candidate organizations

---

[11] On a more positive note, de la Garza and DeSipio describe the two-party system in Texas as becoming more competitive recently, with one faction of the Democratic Party now actively soliciting the support of Mexican-Americans (1994: 8). And Sierra (1992: 47, 49) notes the important role of strongly organized parties in New Mexico, where Latino participation is high.

either explicitly or implicitly adopt mobilization strategies that discriminate across racial and ethnic groups, a point I investigate in greater detail in chapters 4 and 5.

Political Empowerment

Browning, Marshall, and Tabb's (1984) pioneering work on the requisites of minority policy success in local governments highlights the critical importance of minority officeholders becoming members of governing coalitions. More recently, Bobo and Gilliam (1990) considered the implications of Black officeholding for Black political behavior. Using data from the 1987 General Social Survey, Bobo and Gilliam find that Blacks living in high-empowerment areas (where a Black serves as mayor) tend to know more and feel more positive about government and politics. This results in Blacks in high-empowerment areas participating more than whites of the same socioeconomic status living in the same areas (1990: 383). Thus, greater Black participation is attributed almost entirely to the greater levels of political knowledge of Blacks in empowered areas.

That the presence of Black candidates and elected officials enhances Black participation might be explained by two different mechanisms. Minority turnout might be higher because the presence of a minority candidate on the ballot, or the presence of an elected Black official, changes individuals' calculations of the (potential) benefits or costs of voting. This is the linkage mechanism emphasized by Bobo and Gilliam: empowerment enhances participation because it enhances Blacks' attitudes toward and knowledge of politics.

Alternatively, minority turnout might be higher when minority candidates are on the ballot because minority candidates direct more resources toward mobilizing minority groups. This is clearly the common explanation alluded to in the case studies discussed above, while it is basically ignored by Bobo and Gilliam (1990). Without more systematic evidence on minority candidacies, mobilization, and participation, however, it is impossible to distinguish between these two alternative linkage mechanisms. Moreover, no systematic evidence on the effects of political empowerment on Latino mobilization and participation has been documented.

Table 3.2 presents some preliminary evidence on the relative importance of political empowerment for racial/ethnic mobilization and participation. These data were collected by supplementing the CPS data with data on political empowerment. More specifically, CPS respondents were coded as living in "empowered" areas if the county in which the CPS respondent resides had an elected Black or Latino mayor at the time of the survey. The percentage of respondents who reported being mobilized to a particular activity (i.e., had been asked to work in a campaign, contact

TABLE 3.2
Mobilization and Participation, by Race and Ethnicity, Controlling for Political
Empowerment

	Black Empowerment		Latino Empowerment	
	Low	High	Low	High
Summary mobilization				
Anglos	63.6%	63%	63.3%	65.8%
	(1,262)	(381)	(1,487)	(114)
African-Americans	37.8%	46.7%	41.1%	42.4%
	(275)	(195)	(428)	(33)
Latinos	24.6%	18.5%	25.4%	20.9%
	(224)	(65)	(173)	(110)
Institutional mobilization				
Anglos	52.5%	46.2%	51.9%	43%
	(1,262)	(381)	(1,487)	(114)
African-Americans	49.1%	47.7%	49.1%	45.5%
	(275)	(195)	(428)	(33)
Latinos	47.8%	44.6%	46.2%	50%
	(224)	(65)	(173)	(110)
Overall participation				
Anglos	80%	80.1%	79.8%	83.3%
	(1,262)	(381)	(1,487)	(114)
African-Americans	63.3%	77.4%	69.9%	57.6%
	(275)	(195)	(428)	(33)
Latinos	51.8%	43.1%	47.4%	52.7%
	(224)	(65)	(173)	(110)

Source: CPS. Data are unweighted.

Note: Table entries represent the proportion of each racial/ethnic group that reports being mobilized or having participated; numbers in parentheses below percentages represent the number of individuals in each racial/ethnic group within that empowerment context (low or high), upon which the percentage is based. The mobilization and participation measures are dummy variables, where individuals who were not mobilized, or who did not participate, are coded 0, and individuals who were mobilized or did participate were coded as 1.

a local official, or become active on a local problem, which I refer to as activity mobilization) or in particular contexts (at work, in church, or through a voluntary association, which I refer to as institutional mobilization) is reported separately for those living in low- and high-empowerment areas, controlling for the respondent's race/ethnicity, in the first part of the table. Similar reports for participating in any one of the participation items listed in figure 3.2, except the registration status variable, are presented in the second part of the table.

The evidence presented in table 3.2 suggests that mobilization patterns are not structured by political empowerment, with perhaps two exceptions. First, and consistent with Bobo and Gilliam's (1990) findings, African-Americans living in areas of political empowerment are significantly more likely to report being mobilized than are African-Americans not living in areas of political empowerment.[12] Second, Anglos are significantly less likely to report being mobilized on the job, at church, or in political associations in areas of Black or Latino empowerment. Finally, for Latinos, neither type of mobilization is associated with political empowerment.

Bobo and Gilliam's findings are again supported when considering whether empowerment structures individuals' participation levels: African-Americans are significantly more likely to report participating when residing in areas of political empowerment. Once again, however, this same pattern does not hold for Latinos and Latino political empowerment.

Size/Geographic Concentration

The size and geographic concentration of minority communities typically act to limit minority political power in electoral politics. Most scholars point to the small proportion of the electorate that the Hispanic community represents as depressing participation levels (see, e.g., DeSipio and Rocha 1992; de la Garza and DeSipio 1992; Garcia 1988: 121; MacManus and Cassel 1982; Tostado 1985: 240). Alternatively, Moreno and Warren claim that the power of Cubans in Florida is derived from their concentration in Dade County (Portes and Mozo 1988).

For African-Americans, the study of politics in the South, particularly with respect to securing the right to vote, is one of numbers as well as strategy: Blacks could organize and seek power most effectively where their numbers were relatively large, and whites fought this through a variety of legal and illegal methods (e.g., gerrymandering, annexation, and physical intimidation; see Barker and Jones 1994).

The premise underlying many references to the disadvantages of a minority group's accruing to its size is that individuals—at both mass and elite levels—are strategic. Individuals have less of an incentive to vote when the likelihood of their vote's affecting the outcome is essentially zero (Downs 1957; Riker and Ordeshook 1968). On the other hand, elites are strategic as well and are less likely to seek to expend scarce resources in inefficient ways. According to this logic, candidates should be less willing to spend resources mobilizing groups that are not critical to winning. And it is likely that group size is one factor determining the perceived importance of minority groups.

---

[12] A χ^2 test of statistical significance was computed for each of these relationships and was significant at $p < .05$ (one-tailed) for the first two.

Aggregate-level studies of voter turnout in local and presidential elections suggest that the size of the African-American population is positively associated with turnout (see, e.g., Affigne 1994; Affigne and Tate 1993). In a recent study, Schlichting, Tuckel, and Maisel (1998) conclude that racial segregation increases turnout, perhaps due to segregation's positive effect on racial group identity or, alternatively, because there are fewer cross-pressures in racially homogeneous districts. However, Fort (1995) finds that the size of the Black population (as well as the proportion of the population of Spanish origin) is positively associated with voter registration but *negatively* associated with voter turnout in county-wide voting on referenda issues in Washington and California from 1976 to 1980. These conflicting findings might well be attributed to differences in research design—the types of elections considered, geographical focus (Baltimore and Bridgeport versus Washington and California), the use of aggregate data, etc. Whatever the explanation, it seems that such discrepancies should be considered in light of broader (geographically speaking), individual-level evidence on mobilization and turnout. Doing so allows us to test whether the relationship between minority population size and participation reflects elite behavior, rather than individual assessments of the rationality of registering or voting.

Initial evidence on this point—and the first that I know of that links individual-level reports of mobilization and participation to the contextual characteristics of racial group size—is presented in table 3.3. These data were generated by supplementing the individual-level CPS data with census data indicating the proportion of the individual's "neighborhood" (more specifically, zip code region) made up of Anglos, African-Americans, and Hispanics. Table 3.3 shows the correlations between these various measures of population size and three measures of mobilization and participation: summary mobilization (a scale ranging from 0 to 8); institutional mobilization (a scale ranging from 0 to 3); and overall participation (a scale ranging from 0 to 8).

Overall, there is little support for the notion that group size structures patterns of political mobilization or participation. In no case is Black or Hispanic group size significantly correlated with either mobilization or participation for Blacks or Latinos. Instead, Anglos are more likely to be mobilized within civic institutions where the size of the Anglo population is larger and more likely to participate where the size of the Black population is larger. The only other significant correlation in the entire table is a positive correlation between Anglo population size and Latino mobilization: the greater the Anglo proportion of the neighborhood, the more likely Latinos are to report being mobilized. This correlation disappears, however, when the analysis is restricted to Latino citizens. Thus, at the outset we have little evidence that suggests that group size matters—but we will pursue this question with greater precision in later chapters.

TABLE 3.3
Correlations between Group Size, Mobilization, and Participation

	Summary Mobilization	Institutional Mobilization	Overall Participation
Anglos (n = 1,558)			
Anglo group size	.00	.06°	−.02
Black group size	.03	−.04	.07°°
Hispanic group size	−.03	−.04	−.02
African-Americans (n = 449)			
Anglo group size	.03	.06	−.01
Black group size	−.001	−.06	.03
Hispanic group size	−.04	−.02	−.05
Latinos (n = 273)			
Anglo group size	.12°	.01	−.03
Black group size	−.05	−.09	−.04
Hispanic group size	−.09	.03	.07

Source: CPS. Data are unweighted.

Note: Table entries are Pearson correlation coefficients and indicate the correlation between each group (population) size and level of summary mobilization, institutional mobilization, or overall participation for individuals within each racial/ethnic group.

°$p < .05$, two-tailed test of significance. °°$p < .01$, two-tailed test of significance.

A NOTE ON DIVERSITY AND CULTURE

While the factors discussed above underscore the similarities in factors associated with participation of Blacks and Latinos, it should be emphasized that a distinctive feature of Latino politics is the diversity of the Latino community. Language, country of origin, and immigration differences are but a few of the factors that contribute to a cultural diversity—and possibly a heterogeneity—of political values, interests, and incentives. Hence, leaders within the Latino community cannot appeal to a shared history in the way that African-American leaders can, and the political institutions within the Latino community reflect this.

Related to this diversity, language is cited as a factor that depresses participation rates of Latinos. MacManus and Cassel (1988: 203–4), for example, find that Spanish language preference is associated with lower levels of political interest (see also Calvo and Rosenstone 1989: 22, 27). Verba, Schlozman, and Brady (1995), however, find no association with speaking English at home and participation of any type. It is likely that the richness of their model—with details regarding a variety of civic skills, attitudes, and mobilization—overwhelms the relationship between language skills and participation that others, with more simple models, have suggested.

However, note that language *preference* likely indicates something distinct from language *skill*, with the former being interpreted as an attachment to the minority culture. In its weakest form, this interpretation suggests that non-English-speaking individuals are not integrated into U.S. society and therefore are removed from its politics; to the extent that this is observed in newly immigrated individuals, we might expect this barrier to be minimized, or even eliminated, over time (and thus the importance of "life-cycle" effects noted by Arvizu and Garcia [1996] and others).

In its strongest form, however, language preference as an indicator of cultural attachment becomes a "cultural" explanation for why Latinos, or other minorities, participate less. The "cultural" argument is based on the negative stereotype that Latinos are passive, lazy, etc.; therefore, lower participation levels simply reflect their indifference to political and social life (also see Hardy-Fanta 1993: 32). Hero offers evidence against this argument: Puerto Ricans in Puerto Rico vote at 80–90 percent. Thus, their lower participation in the United States must result from "the importance of context" and "perhaps other factors, such as sense of 'attachment' and language, in understanding Latino political participation" (1992: 60). But *not* political culture.

Garcia and Arce (1988: 130) also note that this argument regarding the effects of attachment to "things Mexican" (a negative influence on participation) contrasts with supposed positive effects of (ethnic) group consciousness, as discussed above. It seems that cultural attachment is most often offered as an explanation of why Latinos are *less* likely to participate. One could argue, however, that Latinos who are most culturally attached to their homeland or immigrant culture are also those who are least likely to be mobilized. Hence, without systematic evidence regarding the role of mobilization, the validity of the "cultural attachment" argument is open to question.

This is a particularly important point when one considers the typical evidence regarding language preference or cultural attachment offered in these studies. Most often cultural attachment is offered as an alternative explanation for lower levels of participation when the factors hypothesized to influence participation do not account for lower rates of participation. Hence, systematic evidence of the importance of this factor is not necessarily offered but is included as a list of possible (but untested) explanations.

In more quantitative research, the same phenomenon occurs when all factors that the researcher could possibly imagine might influence participation fail to account for lower participation levels of Latinos or Asian-Americans. In these econometric models, this occurs when estimating a multivariate model and a dummy variable indicating the ethnicity of the respondent remains significant while controlling for many other variables.

This significant coefficient is often interpreted as an indicator of cultural differences across population groups. But it should be noted that such a dummy variable will pick up the effects of *any* variable that depresses participation when excluded from the model. Which variable it is—cultural attachment or political mobilization, for example—we do not know.

CONCLUSION

This chapter has provided some preliminary evidence regarding the relationships among race, mobilization, and participation. Clearly socioeconomic status has a significant effect on individuals' levels of participation, regardless of race or ethnicity. Yet class differences across these groups do not account for all of the variation in activity levels across groups. Consistent with the models presented in chapter 1, both participation and mobilization are structured by individuals' socioeconomic status as well as their race and ethnicity.

Beyond these individual-level characteristics, however, this initial overview suggests that contextual factors indeed matter. Political empowerment is also associated with individuals' mobilization to and engagement in political activity, especially for Latinos and African-Americans. Seemingly less important, however, is group size, which appears to be least consequential for African-Americans.

The chapters that follow expand on these initial findings in three respects. First, they consider the relative importance of class, race, and ethnicity as predictors of participation and mobilization. Second, the analyses consider how both individual-level as well as contextual factors structure mobilization and participation patterns. Third, they consider mobilization from an elite, as well as citizen, perspective.

To address the lack of systematic evidence on the nature of elite mobilization, in chapters 4 and 5 I present the results of a study of party chairs during the 1996 presidential election, investigating both the explicit and implicit ways in which their mobilization and targeting strategies advantage or disadvantage racial and ethnic minorities. Then in chapters 6, 7, and 8, I return to using individual-level survey data from the CPS to examine how race and class structure the nature of both political mobilization and participation of racial and ethnic minorities in the United States.

Chapter Four

ELECTORAL MOBILIZATION: ELITE
CONCEPTUALIZATION AND TECHNIQUE

P ROBABLY the most well-established research on elite mobilization
focuses on electoral politics. Systematic empirical studies of party
mobilization most commonly rely on individuals' reports of having
been contacted by a party taken from the American National Election
Studies biennial surveys (see, e.g., Rosenstone and Hansen 1993; Wielhouwer 1999). Rosenstone and Hansen (1993: 164–66) argue that parties
mobilize strategically, targeting individuals who are likely to participate as
well as individuals who are likely to be supporters. Consistent with this,
they find that strong partisans are about 5 percent more likely to be contacted by parties in presidential election years than are Independents.

Alternatively, various studies emphasize the importance of the nature of
the party system more broadly in mobilizing participation, reporting that
party competitiveness, elite ideology, and campaign spending increase
turnout (see, e.g., Hill and Leighley 1993; Jackson 1993, 1996; Patterson
and Caldeira 1983). But both of these approaches essentially focus on the
result of party-elite activity. If, in fact, elites are strategic and their decisions accumulate to create contexts in which individuals make decisions
about whether to participate or not, then it seems that we should study
elite behavior—or reports thereof—more directly than rely on mass reports of elite behavior.

This chapter and the next do exactly that, using data from in-depth,
focused interviews of political elites as well as a survey of party chairs in
Texas in 1996 and 1997. These interviews and survey data are used to
describe how party elites conceptualize voter mobilization efforts, to assess
the nature of mobilization activities undertaken by chairs, and to determine what factors are associated with party chairs' targeting racial and
ethnic minorities.

Examining the nature of elite mobilization efforts provides a unique and
important vantage point from which to view minority participation. The
models introduced in chapter 1 suggest that the racial context influences
elite mobilization. In this chapter and the next I consider more specifically
two ways in which the presence of minority groups might be associated
with distinct patterns of mobilization. First, I consider whether minority
individuals are exposed to unique mobilization contexts due to either

elites' choices of certain mobilization techniques or minorities' residing in areas of particular mobilizing strength (or weakness). Second, I consider whether minorities are exposed to higher levels of mobilization when they reside in areas of large minority group size. The first distinction in mobilization levels is passive, even accidental, with respect to race and ethnicity, while the latter indicates a more conscious, strategic effort to mobilize individuals on the basis of race or ethnicity.

I begin the chapter with a brief overview of minority and party politics in Texas, with references to the historical setting as well as contemporary electoral context. Although this material is admittedly brief, it nonetheless provides an important perspective from which to view the reports of Texas party elites on how they conceptualize their mobilization efforts, both in general and with respect to racial and ethnic minority groups. This qualitative investigation into the nature of elite mobilization is valuable because very little work has been done on theoretical models of elite mobilization. Moreover, these reports of political elites in Texas help motivate the models of mobilization tested more systematically in the last part of the chapter.

TEXAS COUNTY PARTY CHAIRS AS ELITES

Studying elite mobilization in a systematic fashion necessarily requires restricting one's attention to a particular set of elites acting strategically to achieve a particular set of goals. Given the centrality of electoral politics in the study of political participation, as well as minority politics, focusing on electoral mobilization and the role of party elites seemed as reasonable a focus as any. The subsequent choice to focus on party elites in Texas was motivated both by practical convenience as well as demographic realities. The population of the state of Texas is racially and ethnically diverse, with 1990 census data indicating that the state's population comprised approximately 75 percent Anglos, 12 percent Blacks, 2 percent Asian/Pacific Islanders, and less than 1 percent Native Americans/Eskimos. At the same time the state's Hispanic-origin population, primarily made up of Mexican-Americans, was estimated to be 26 percent of the population—and growing at a high rate relative to other racial/ethnic groups. Recent census bureau projections for the year 2000 suggest that at the turn of the century Hispanics will likely make up 34 percent of the population.[1]

[1] These population estimates were calculated by the author using census data from www.census.gov/population/projections/state/stpjrace.txt (May 20, 2000); for more details, see PPL #47, "Population Projections for States, by Age, Sex, Race, and Hispanic Origin: 1995 to 2025." The percentages add up to more than 100 percent because race and ethnicity were measured separately in the 1990 census (i.e., Hispanics and non-Hispanics could report their race as white, Black, Asian Pacific Islander, or American Indian, Eskimo, or Aleut).

Consistent with these data, Hero's work (1998) ranks Texas high on minority diversity (a score of .673, with a mean [for all states] of .33 and standard deviation of .17), following only California and New Mexico, and quite low on white ethnic diversity (a score of .109, with a mean [for all states] of .17 and standard deviation of .09, making it the eighth lowest state). This contrast of a relatively homogeneous Anglo population and high levels of numerous minority communities suggests that the state provides a suitable context for studying how race and ethnicity structure party activities. Also, Hill and Leighley's (1999) analysis indicates that this level of racial/ethnic diversity has been relatively stable in Texas since the 1950s.

The projected growth in the Hispanic population in the state had, by the mid-1990s, come to be identified as the kingmaker in electoral politics in the twenty-first century. Most projections suggest that by 2030, Anglos will be a racial/ethnic minority group in the state, with Hispanics as the new majority. In terms of electoral politics, party elites are responding to this eventuality in predictable ways.

Democratic officials in Texas claim that they will continue to benefit from the strong loyalties of Latinos to Democratic candidates, while Republican officials claim that Latinos' strong "family values" and socially conservative views are ripe for the picking. Absent the highly charged, racialized nature of Republican rhetoric witnessed in California under Governor Pete Wilson and with the relatively strong showing of George W. Bush in counties with high proportions of Latinos in the 1998 gubernatorial election, some shift in partisan loyalties might indeed be possible. Both Republicans and Democrats are aware of this: statewide candidates from both parties now regularly advertise and campaign in Spanish, signaling the importance of the Latino vote.[2]

As in most states, this partisan battle for statewide offices will be conducted primarily by candidates' campaign organizations, with party officials providing various support services to the candidates as needed. Bibby (1999: 205) argues that while state party organizations can no longer control nominations in this era of candidate-centered campaigns, they nonetheless play significant roles in candidates' efforts to win office. Moreover, county-level party offices—though not romanticized in the same manner as urban political machines of earlier years—have become increasingly important to these efforts, "their principal function [being] . . . grassroots outreach: recruiting volunteers and getting voters to the polls" (Bibby 1999: 206).

My decision to survey county party chairs follows from their presumed importance in developing and implementing a localized effort to mobilize

[2] See, e.g., "Parties Roll Out Strategies to Court Hispanic Vote," *Bryan-College Station Eagle*, September 20, 1998.

voters and the probability that these "local" officials would be most likely to be aware of and respond to important constituencies in their communities. Of course, the mobilization efforts of these party chairs are certainly not the only form of elite mobilization—other party organizations, citizen groups, and the national presidential campaigns certainly engaged in activities oriented toward various constituencies to get-out-the-vote through media advertising and direct mail, among other things.

Subervi-Velez and Connaughton (1999) report, for example, that the 1996 presidential election was the first in which the national Democratic reelection campaign effectively implemented a media strategy oriented toward Latinos and Latino news organizations. At the same time, Subervi-Velez and Connaughton report that substantially less was spent on media in Texas ($72,120) compared to other states in which the campaign had identified Latinos to be an important swing vote: for example, Florida at $390,665; Arizona at $175,207; and New York at $112,172.[3] (on the efforts of the national presidential campaigns to target Hispanics through advertising in the 1988 campaign, see Subervi-Velez 1992; also see Martinez' [1996] description of the national campaign efforts targeted toward Latinos during the 1992 campaign.

Montoya (1999) identifies organizational mobilization efforts in Texas as occurring at three levels. First, a "Just Vote! '96 Tour" organized by the national Democratic campaign included Texas in its series of events emphasizing the importance of Latinos voting in the presidential election; along with Latino political leaders and celebrities, the tour included neighborhood canvassing, press events, and rallies in various Democratic and Latino neighborhoods. Second, the Southwest Voter Registration Education Project (SWVREP) continued its efforts to increase Latino voter registration in the state, organizing registration drives in several large cities. This effort was coordinated with and enhanced by the Morales (for senator) campaign efforts to increase Latino voter registration and turnout. Third, a party-related group, the Tejano Democrats, organized get-out-the-vote drives in various cities across the state in the last two weeks of the campaign. As Montoya (1999) notes, the effectiveness of these efforts is difficult to measure. But initial evidence was not particularly encouraging, as Montoya reports that "in an October 1996 survey by the Tomas Rivera Policy Institute, 80 percent of Latinos said that they had not been contacted by candidates, public officials, or any other groups and invited to register to vote in the general election" (151).

The latter point suggests that, at minimum, the activities of the county

---

[3] On the efforts of the national presidential campaigns to target Hispanics through advertising in the 1988 campaign, see Subervi-Velez 1992; also see Martinez's (1996) description of the national campaign efforts targeted toward Latinos during the 1992 campaign.

party chairs I focus on are not likely to be overwhelmed by a massive amount of activity by either the national campaign or local, Latino organizational efforts. However, the analyses offered below should be interpreted carefully in two respects. First, these data should not be interpreted as reflecting the overall level of mobilization in the particular county—only those efforts engaged in by county chairs. Second, it is possible that the party chairs' responses reflected socially desirable responses or, alternatively, rationalizations of non–socially desirable behavior. For example, a chair who did not target a group might then describe the group as being ideologically distant from the chair's party—as a rationalization for her decision not to target the group. Or it might be that Democratic chairs feel obligated to at least say that they target African-Americans; likewise, it might be that while Democratic chairs say that they target poor people, Republicans are hesitant to report that they target rich people. The analyses and interpretations of the party chair data are done in such a way as to minimize these two concerns to the extent that it is possible to do so.

Finally, although these political elites operate in the world of Texas politics, I had strong expectations—based on conventional wisdom as well as research findings on party contacting—regarding how they would conceptualize get-out-the-vote efforts and approach mobilizing racial/ethnic minorities. As Huckfeldt and Sprague (1995) put it, "Everybody lives in a South Bend," or, in this case, "Everybody lives in a Texas." That is, Huckfeldt and Sprague argue that their single-city study of political communication during an election campaign can nonetheless provide generalizable findings, for everyone lives in a community, or state, with a particular political and social configuration. Although it is indisputable that minority politics can be "community specific," because minority groups are often defined and limited by particular political majorities, both past and present, I would argue that it is possible to theorize and empirically test generalizations regarding minority/majority political behaviors in distinct communities. By explicitly incorporating the way in which the contexts in which minorities reside vary, it is also likely that we can more clearly identify the relative importance of individual and contextual characteristics— even if the nature of these relationships is somewhat muted due to omitting some context-specific characteristics from the model analyses.

THE ELECTORAL CONTEXT

A few additional comments on the electoral context are in order. First, Davidson (1990) describes Texas as characterized by muted class conflict, where the "have's" (i.e., oil, cotton, cattle, and manufacturing fortunes) have systematically bested the "have-nots." The class conflict has been

ELECTORAL MOBILIZATION 55

muted, for the most part, as one-party dominance of the Democrats in the post–New Deal system has "concealed issues from the disadvantaged: issues of tax fairness, educational opportunities, job safety, and public utility regulation" (242). To its credit, the Democratic Party in the 1970s, dominated by moderates and liberals, was effective in stifling a conservative reaction against extending basic voting rights to minorities and has since become the home to working-class and racial and ethnic interests.

By the 1990s, however, the Democratic Party saw its monopoly on statewide offices literally evaporate, with all Republicans elected to statewide office in 1994 and many local elections uncontested by the Democratic Party. After the 1996 elections, the Democrats lost control of the Texas Senate (17 versus 14 seats), but maintained control of the House (14 versus 17 seats, and 82 versus 68 seats, respectively; Thielemann 1998).

At the same time that decades of organizational investments started paying off for the Republicans in their efforts to gain election to public office, the party became vulnerable to intra-party conflict with increased activism of the Christian Right. The 1996 state convention, for example, witnessed Senator Kay Bailey Hutchinson being threatened with losing her delegate seat at the national Republican convention due to her unwillingness to support a right-to-life plank in the state party platform (Lenchner 1998).

It is this seeming change—and potential change—in party fortunes that has captured the attention of observers of Texas politics and shifted greater attention to issues of racial and ethnic politics in the state. On the one hand, the changing population projections suggest that the growth of the Republican Party—traditionally viewed as hostile to the interests of racial and ethnic minorities—will soon reach a natural limit. Davidson, for example, argues that various tensions within the Republican Party have been

eased by the racial solidarity of their lily-white party; and it was the race issue, perhaps more than any other, that undercut the potential solidarity of the Democrats. For, despite gradually changing attitudes, Texas was still a state in which blacks and whites faced each other with suspicion, fear and animosity. The situation was complicated by the presence of Mexican Americans, themselves long the victims of Anglo discrimination and hostility. Blacks continued to live in largely segregated enclaves, although survey evidence indicated that they would greatly prefer to live in racially mixed areas. Hispanics were more dispersed, but many still clustered in urban barrios. Both groups contained huge numbers of the poor. (1990: 257)

On the other hand, if a new generation of political leaders in the Republican Party can appeal to minority voters, then the Republican Party could come to dominate Texas politics in the twenty-first century as the Democratic Party did in the twentieth century. One of the early successes of the Republican Party was the appointment (and subsequent election) of Tony

Garza as secretary of state in 1994. With Garza running successfully for a spot on the Railroad Commission—a powerful regulatory board in the state—many claimed that Garza was the face of the new Republican Party, open to and representative of the interests of Latinos.

Similarly, many argue that how party fortunes—as well as racial and minority interests—might play out is related to the increasingly large number of minority officeholders in Texas. According to Davidson (1990: 249), the number of Black and Latino elected officials in the 1980s was dramatically higher than that of the 1970s (29 versus 228 for Blacks, and 298 versus 1,427 for Latinos). By the 1990s, over 2,000 Latinos had been elected to public office in the state (Bullock 1999).

In addition to the historical affiliation of racial and minority groups with the parties and the increased number of minority elected officials, the changing fortunes of the Republican and Democratic Parties in Texas are likely to reflect the political views of minorities and the extent to which these groups' views differ from Anglos, as well as their level of political involvement. Public opinion data from the last two decades suggest that the significant shift in party identification toward the Republican Party in the state electorate as a whole has not been accompanied by a similar shift in ideology. By 1994, the electorate was about equally split among Democrats, Republicans, and Independents. But ideologically, conservatives barely dominated moderates (approximately 43 percent versus 40 percent), with liberals making up just under 20 percent of the statewide population (Dyer, Leighley, and Vedlitz 1998).

The shift in party identification between 1984 and 1994 resulted largely from shifts in Anglo and Hispanic, but not Black, party identification. In 1994, 6 percent fewer Anglos and 6 percent fewer Hispanics identified with the Democratic Party than in 1984, with this shift in party identification seemingly more of a dealignment than a realignment: Independents among both groups increased by 4 percent, while Republicans increased by 2 percent among Anglos and by 1 percent among Hispanics (Dyer, Leighley, and Vedlitz 1998). Hence, these data suggest that Republican leaders might well be able to accelerate this microscopic shift in Hispanics' identification from the Democratic to the Republican Party.

A statewide survey of public opinion conducted in 1993 provides some additional detail as to how party elites might view the possible payoffs of targeting or mobilizing various ethnic groups in the state. As shown in table 4.1, Anglos statewide are far more likely to identify with the Republican Party than are African-Americans, whose party loyalties lie overwhelmingly with the Democratic Party. Mexican-Americans likewise tend to identify with the Democratic Party, though not nearly as strongly as African-Americans, while Asian-Americans tend to spread across the party continuum, tending to have relatively weaker party attachments.

TABLE 4.1
Selected Characteristics of Texans, by Race/Ethnicity

	Anglos (%)	African-Americans (%)	Mexican-Americans (%)	Asian-Americans (%)
Party identification				
Strong Republicans	18.7	5.0	8.9	12.1
Republicans	20.2	5.0	16.2	16.0
Weak Republicans	16.0	6.4	8.6	18.3
Weak Democrats	20.0	19.6	20.1	26.2
Democrats	9.9	24.9	14.9	14.8
Strong Democrats	15.3	39.1	31.3	12.6
	(476)	(281)	(383)	(420)
Political interest				
Not at all	5.3	11.0	15.1	14.3
Somewhat	16.5	20.8	22.7	29.4
Most of the time	45.8	41.8	36.9	40.5
All of the time	32.4	26.3	25.3	15.7
	(537)	(509)	(537)	(523)
Voted in 1992	80.4	65.0	52.2	36.6
	(565)	(511)	(545)	(524)
Vote choice in 1992				
Clinton	28.0	86.7	61.2	34.7
Bush	45.9	8.0	24.4	50.6
Perot	25.4	3.1	12.4	14.2
Other	0.7	2.1	1.9	0.6
	(410)	(286)	(258)	(176)
Nonvoters' candidate preference				
Clinton	24.2	77.6	45.3	31.3
Bush	35.2	4.8	30.4	41.7
Perot	31.9	7.5	13.6	23.3
Other	8.8	10.2	10.7	3.8
	(91)	(147)	(214)	(288)

Source: Texas Minority Survey, 1993.

Note: Table entries represent the proportion of each racial/ethnic group in each response category; the number of cases on which these percentages are based is included in parentheses for each group on each item. For purposes of groupings, we relied on individuals' willingness to identify themselves as "Anglo, African-American, Mexican-American or Asian-American, or something else." Each group is a representative sample of the minority group in the state of Texas.

As we would expect, voters' self-reports on presidential candidate choice in 1992 reflected these partisan orientations, with the majority (or plurality) of Anglos and Asian-Americans voting for Bush (45.9 percent and 50.6 percent, respectively) and majorities of African-Americans and Mexican-Americans voting for Clinton (86.7 percent and 61.2 percent, respectively).

Of particular relevance are the patterns of turnout and nonvoters' preferences across the four groups. Each racial/ethnic minority group reports voting at significantly lower rates than do Anglos. Some of this variation might reflect variations in misreporting across groups (Shaw, de la Garza, and Lee 2000; Silver, Anderson, and Abramson 1986) and, more important, socioeconomic status differences (see Leighley and Vedlitz 1999 for evidence on this point: controlling for socioeconomic status, only Asian-Americans continue to participate at lower levels than the other three groups). Regardless, these turnout rates certainly suggest that there is some potential for mobilizing these groups into the political system. Although nonvoters' retrospective reports on candidate preference must be interpreted cautiously, it is particularly interesting to note that nonvoting Mexican-Americans tended to prefer Bush at a higher rate than did Mexican-American voters (though Clinton was still reported as the most preferred candidate among nonvoters).

Martinez (1996: 119–20) reports similar results from 1992, claiming that turnout of Texas Latinos increased (from 46 percent in 1988 to 52 percent in 1992 of registered voters; statewide, voter turnout increased from 66 percent to 73 percent), while support for the Democratic ticket declined to approximately 70 percent (from 85 percent support for Dukakis in 1988). While Clinton received his highest support from those counties with the largest proportion of Latinos (Starr, Webb, Maverick, Jim Hogg, and Zavala), turnout in these counties was at least ten percentage points lower than in those counties with the largest number of Latinos (Harris, Bexar, El Paso, Hidalgo, and Dallas), where support for the Democratic ticket was substantially lower.

ELITE REPORTS ON VOTER MOBILIZATION

Little systematic research on the strategies party leaders adopt to mobilize voter turnout even exists. Goldenberg and Traugott (1984), for example, report that congressional campaign managers target supporters and Independents, although many believed that they needed to "target" all voters, or at least some nonsupporters, in their districts to win. Whether local *party* leaders adopt these same strategies or not—and the extent to which race structures these strategies—is unknown.

During the summer of 1996, I conducted several in-depth interviews with party leaders, political consultants, and elected minority officials in several major cities in Texas. The purpose of the interviews was to document party and candidate strategies in trying to mobilize turnout. Interviews began with several broad questions about what parties or candidates do to stimulate turnout, and then eventually moved to questions concerning targeting minority groups.[4]

As expected, the party leaders and elected officials I interviewed generally agree on the importance of targeting registered voters, while Democratic leaders are more likely than Republican leaders to cite the importance of voter registration drives. One of the Republican state party's campaign management publications, for example, suggests to candidates that: "Ideally, you will only stop at the homes of registered voters. . . . In a large district you may only want to stop at the homes of registered voters who have a history of voting in important elections. There is no point in talking with unregistered citizens, or registered voters who rarely vote" (Masset, "Precinct Walking," 5). Likewise, a minority city council member in Houston reports that her district has relatively high voter turnout— approximately 35 percent for local elections—and thus mobilizes voters by targeted mailings to previous voters and neighborhoods with high turnout.

An experienced consultant to statewide Democratic candidates, in contrast, describes voter registration efforts as an important first step in getting-out-the-vote, where sending out voter registration applications is effective in reducing the costs of voting: "Convenience has a lot to do with voting." The Republican state political director, however, reports few efforts devoted to voter registration: "They've [the Democrats] made it so easy—every time you renew your driver's license. Unless [registering drives] are targeted, you are more likely to mobilize opponents."

All of the party leaders and elected officials agree that targeting swing voters is the key to a successful campaign. The Democratic strategist reports that where districts/precincts are more than 65 percent Democratic, a successful campaign will focus on get-out-the-vote efforts, whereas in districts with less Democratic support, selective targeting must be done based on individuals' primary voting records. If the district is around 45 percent or more Democratic, then there is a possibility of victory, while in

---

[4] Interviews with elites must always be evaluated to the extent to which the individuals are "objectively" reporting on their behavior or instead providing either self-serving or socially expected answers. Although it is impossible to provide any evidence on this point, I would note that, qualitatively, I was struck by the seeming "honesty" of the self-reports of the elites I interviewed. They appeared to be motivated by electoral considerations and stated this directly, talking in a proud yet professional manner about how elections are won. The extent to which these elites viewed their jobs in a strategic rather than a "collective," public-oriented enterprise was clear.

districts that are between 35 and 45 percent Democratic, the campaign might be able to "find the angels lost in hell." Under 35 percent, according to this strategist, there is nothing to do, other than avoid "stirring up the other side."

Republican leaders likewise stress the importance of candidates' targeting swing voters, whom they assume to be most likely to be undecided and therefore persuadable. The rationale here, in terms of campaign strategy, is that this is the most efficient use of campaign resources:

> Ticket splitters, also called swing voters, split their ticket (ballot) among candidates for different parties. These are the people most likely to be genuinely undecided. Think about this. You aren't going to win new votes from strong Republicans. (But don't ignore them completely!) You aren't going to win votes from good Democrats. They'll vote straight Democrat no matter how much they may like you. The only new votes you can win are those of ticket splitters. All campaigns aim at these voters. They are the only people who are really deciding who to support—you or your opponent. (Masset, "Campaign Planning," 22)

In addition,

> There will be precincts where 40% of all voters are undecided and others where less than 10% will be undecided. You will obviously work hard in the areas where 40% of the voters are up for grabs and waste little effort where less than 10% of the votes can be won by you. (Masset, "Introduction to Campaign Management," 16)

The importance of targeting the swing vote for minority politics is noted in comments by two minority elected officials, one a former state legislator and the other a member of city council. "Republicans don't target Blacks because they're liberal," according to the state legislator, "and Democrats don't target Blacks because of their size and they're not swing—they target Hispanics." The implication is that Hispanics are targeted more than Blacks because they represent a larger proportion of the electorate in many districts—and because they are more likely to be ideologically moderate.

Also affirming the importance of group size and ideology, the city council member reports emphasizing the pan-Asian "label" and the common interests of individuals from diverse national origins, as "there aren't enough (Chinese-Americans) to put someone in office alone (like Blacks can do). Asians need to be the swing vote. That's why we've made financial contributions, because we don't have enough numbers."

Consistent with that sentiment, the National Asian Pacific American Voter Registration Campaign was undertaken in 1996 to increase voter turnout among Asian-Pacific-Americans. The mobilization campaign, led by a coalition of Asian-American social, professional, and economic groups, recognizes the importance of being the "swing vote" in its campaign manual:

Current studies demonstrate that the APA community could vote either way . . . Republican or Democrat. The APA has not been recognized for its electoral potency. . . . In the 104th Congress, there are 62 Congressional Districts with APA constituencies in excess of 5% of a district's overall population. For these districts, the APA vote can make or break an election. (*Basic Facts on Voter Registration*)

Exactly who undertakes voter mobilization efforts is not easily ascertained. All of the Republican Party leaders interviewed reported that there is no one "coordinated" campaign to mobilize voters. As suggested above, candidates are encouraged to target swing voters/precincts, while the state party devotes its mobilization efforts to securing the base—ensuring that Republicans will get out and vote on election day—by their use of an extensive phone bank system. However, the state political director emphasized how state party leaders cannot control local party activities of the county chair.

Independent of the county chair, the Republican Party supports a committee devoted to increasing voter turnout. These "VICTORY" committees—which operate independent of the local county chair—have been in existence for years and are named for the election year in which they are operating (e.g., "VICTORY '96" refers to committees operating in various counties during the 1996 presidential campaign). According to one Republican state party executive, the VICTORY committee uses phone banks and direct mail, and relies on a high level of volunteer support to target Independents and Republicans. Once contacted by phone, if an individual is unsure about whom she will vote for, she is sent a specific mailing in an effort to persuade her to vote Republican.[5]

We thus have anecdotal evidence that ideology, group size, and prior voter turnout are important factors in elites' decisions about whom to mobilize, as well as perceptions among some minority leaders that, due to these factors, minorities may be overlooked in the mobilization process. But we have little, perhaps no, *systematic* evidence as to *what party elites choose to do* and *whom they choose to do it to*. Without some systematic approach to these questions, the consequences of party-elite strategies for racial and ethnic minorities are unknown.

PARTY MOBILIZATION ACTIVITIES

The consequences of party-elite activities for minorities might be explained in one of two ways. First, elites might consciously choose to mobil-

[5] Despite numerous efforts to identify the name, structure, and function of a similar committee organized by Democrats, no information was provided to me by state officials, Democratic consultants, elected officials, or local activists.

ize a minority group because that group's electoral turnout is valued by the party. Democrats, for example, might choose to mobilize Blacks because party leaders know that they will reap most of the votes of Blacks who ultimately decide to vote. Second, elites might "unconsciously" mobilize a minority group because members of that group tend to reside in areas that are very likely (or unlikely) to bear party leaders much in the way of benefits—either because turnout in that precinct is historically low or because, based on characteristics other than race (i.e., education or income), the precincts where minorities reside might appear to be composed of party opponents rather than supporters.

Alternatively, party leaders in areas of large minority populations may—for whatever reasons—adopt different mobilization techniques or strategies, whether or not they choose to target minorities. The analyses in this chapter focus on whether minorities—due to the social or political context in which they reside—are exposed to different types or levels of mobilization by party elites. The alternative explanation—that party leaders consciously choose to target (or not target) these activities toward minorities—is addressed in chapter 5.

To address the question of whether minorities are exposed to different types of mobilization activities than are Anglos, I use the responses of Democratic and Republican county party chairs in Texas to a survey conducted just after the conclusion of the 1996 presidential election (see appendix A for a description of the survey and precise question wording). As part of the surveys, the county chairs were asked whether their organization did the following in 1996:

- Purchase advertisements or distribute literature
- Sponsor fundraising events or provide funds to candidates
- Provide voter information or volunteers to candidates
- Provide registration materials to individuals
- Provide voters transportation to the polls on election day
- Provide voters transportation to the polls during early voting

As seen in table 4.2, the two most commonly reported activities were purchasing ads or campaign literature (86.5 percent) and providing information to candidates (86 percent). The next most common programmatic activity reported was providing registration materials to individuals (80 percent), while assisting in fundraising for candidates was reported by nearly half of the chairs (49.7 percent). The two least commonly reported activities reported were providing transportation to individuals to the polls on election day (48.5 percent) and providing transportation to individuals for early voting (42.3 percent).

Based on the anecdotal evidence above, as well as conventional wisdom, I expected that the two major parties would differ significantly in their use

TABLE 4.2
Mobilization Techniques Used by Party Chairs in 1996 Presidential Election

	All Chairs (%)	Republicans (%)	Democrats (%)	Chi^2 (p)
Purchasing ads	86.5	85.7	87.4	0.58
Fundraising	49.7	53.5	45.6	0.10
Providing information/ volunteers to candidates	86.0	88.7	82.8	0.07
Providing registration materials	80.0	73.9	86.6	0.00
Providing transportation, election day	48.5	35.7	62.3	0.00
Providing transportation, early voting	42.3	30.9	54.7	0.00

Source: 1996 Survey of Texas County Party Chairs.
Note: Table entries represent the percentage of chairs in the entire sample, the percentage of Republican chairs, and the percentage of Democratic chairs who report engaging in each particular type of mobilizing activity. The Chi^2 p value indicates the probability that the difference in the percentage of Republicans and Democrats engaging in each particular type of activity is significant.

of mobilization techniques. Such differences are likely to be of consequence for the nature of minorities' mobilization contexts. The specific hypotheses tested are drawn from observations of the current party system as well as one assumption: parties know who their supporters are. Moreover, the Democratic Party has long been known for its machine-like efforts in trying to stimulate voter turnout, while the Republican Party has recently been distinguished by its high level of resources devoted to training and supporting candidates.

Both of these characterizations, of course, reflect the nature of the two parties' electoral coalitions: with Republicans being supported predominantly by upper-class individuals likely to vote in any case, it is not surprising that party efforts are devoted instead to support candidates. Alternatively, the Democratic Party derives more of its strength from working-class or poor individuals, who presumably "need" the party to underwrite the cost of participating (Verba, Nie, and Kim 1978). Hence, I expect that Democrats will be more likely than Republicans to engage in mobilizing activities oriented toward mass supporters, and that Republicans will be more likely than Democrats to engage in mobilizing activities oriented toward candidates.

Further, to the extent that it is the Democratic Party that also targets minorities more than the Republican Party, this expectation also reflects broadly on my claim that contextual features that reduce the costs of participation are more effective for minorities than for Anglos. If, in fact, elites are strategic, then they should engage in activities that are most efficient in mobilizing their supporters. This analysis, then, provides indirect evidence for the claim that reducing the costs of participation are critical to increasing minority involvement.

As shown in table 4.2, approximately the same proportion of Republican chairs report purchasing advertising as do Democratic chairs, while only a few more report engaging in fundraising activities to assist candidates. The latter difference, although in the hypothesized direction, is not statistically significant. Republican chairs are slightly more likely to report providing information to candidates than are Democratic chairs (88.7 percent versus 82.8 percent), and this difference is statistically significant at $p = 0.07$.

Perhaps more notable is the finding that Democratic chairs are significantly more likely to report providing registration materials to voters, providing voters transportation for early voting, and providing transportation on election day. The biggest difference, with 54.7 percent of Democrats claiming that they provided transportation for early voting compared to 30.9 percent of Republicans, is consistent with reports of Democrats' embracing early voting as a key strategy in the 1996 election.

Next I consider whether similar patterns hold when considering not the type of activity chosen, but the overall level of activities pursued by the party chair. While I had no expectation as to how many activities chairs would report doing, I also had conflicting expectations regarding partisan differences. On the one hand, and consistent with the argument and findings above, I thought that Democratic chairs might report doing more because they were more likely to have supporters who tend to rely on the party to reduce voting costs (i.e., providing registration materials or transportation to the polls). On the other hand, would a better-financed Republican Party attract county chairs who simply did more due to slack resources being available?

Figure 4.1 shows the distribution of mobilization activities for all chairs and for Republican and Democratic chairs separately. Although the level of activity varies substantially between the parties' chairs, there is a tendency for Democratic chairs to do more. Over 50 percent of Democratic chairs report engaging in either five or six activities, compared to only 30 percent of Republican chairs.[6] Hence, the finding above with respect to the particular types of mobilization activity is sustained in the case of the overall level of chair mobilization activity.

Next, I consider whether party chairs' use of the various mobilization activities differs according to the competitiveness of the county. If, indeed, county chairs are responsible for grassroots organizing and are acting stra-

[6] This is a statistically significant difference.

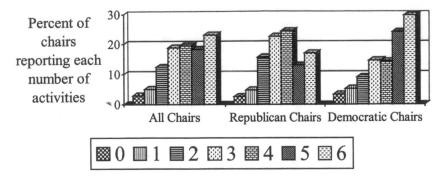

Percent of chairs reporting each number of activities

☒0 ▥1 ▤2 ▨3 ▦4 ▬5 ▧6

Figure 4.1. Number of Mobilization Activities Reported by Party Chairs

tegically, then I would expect to see chairs in competitive counties engaging in greater levels of activity overall, grassroots mobilizing activities in particular. Table 4.3 shows that there are no significant differences between chairs in competitive and noncompetitive counties in their use of different mobilization activities.[7]

To test whether African-Americans and Hispanics are exposed to different mobilization techniques, I did a similar analysis comparing party chairs' use of particular mobilizing techniques between counties with small minority (Black or Hispanic) group sizes and those with large minority group sizes. These analyses are particularly relevant to the models introduced in chapter 1, where I argued that the racial/ethnic context determines the extent to which elites mobilize minority individuals—and that elites do so by engaging in activities that are likely to reduce the costs of participating.

Table 4.4 shows that party chairs in counties with large Black populations are indeed more likely to engage in nearly each type of mobilization activity than are chairs in counties with small Black populations. This higher level of activity is especially prevalent for the types of activities that reduce the costs of participating: providing registration materials and providing transportation (both on election day and during early voting).[8] The only type of activity *not* associated with Black group size is purchasing ads—which likely suffers from a ceiling effect: such a large proportion of chairs report purchasing ads that there is simply little room for contextual effects to boost the chairs' participation in this type of activity.

In contrast, the results for similar analyses testing for contextual effects of Hispanic group size on chairs' use of mobilization techniques lead to a

---

[7] I also tested whether the total number of activities undertaken by the chairs was significantly different in competitive and noncompetitive counties, and it was not.

[8] I also found that the total number of activities undertaken by the chairs was significantly different in large Black population counties and small Black population counties.

TABLE 4.3

Mobilization Activities, by Party Competitiveness

	Noncompetitive Counties (%)	Competitive Counties (%)	Chi² (p)
Purchasing ads	86.4	86.8	.89
Fundraising	49.5	50	.92
Providing information/volunteers to candidates	85.0	87.4	.50
Providing registration materials	77.9	84.2	.11
Providing transportation, election day	48.8	48.0	.88
Providing transportation, early voting	41.6	43.7	.68

Source: 1996 Survey of Texas County Party Chairs.

Note: Table entries represent the percentage of chairs in competitive counties and the percentage of chairs in noncompetitive counties who report engaging in each particular type of mobilizing activity. Competitive counties are those counties in which the 1996 presidential vote was between 45 percent and 55 percent Democratic; noncompetitive counties include all others. The Chi² p value indicates the probability that the difference in the percentage of chairs in competitive counties and the percentage of chairs in noncompetitive counties engaging in each particular type of activity is significant.

quite different conclusion. Table 4.5 shows that party chairs in large His-panic group-size counties are no more likely to engage in any particular type of mobilizing activity—and in one type, fundraising, these party chairs are actually significantly *less* likely to do so.[9] Also important to note here are the different levels of activity reported in the large Hispanic group-size counties as compared to the large Black group-size counties (see table 4.4): when Hispanics make up the largest proportion of the population, they tend to reside in counties in which party chairs engage in fewer mobilization activities—and especially those oriented toward reducing the costs of participation (providing registration materials and transportation to voting).

To assess whether these results regarding the importance of the racial context might be spurious—instead reflecting on contextual effects of class or partisan competitiveness, or indicating the higher level of activity noted earlier on the part of Democratic chairs—I have estimated a series of multivariate models to test more stringently whether elites' choices of mobilization techniques are structured by the county's racial context.

The dependent variables are the six types of mobilizing activities re-

[9] As expected, there is no significant difference between the large Hispanic group-size counties and the small Hispanic group-size counties on the number of activities the chairs engage in.

TABLE 4.4
Mobilization Activities, by Black Group Size

	Small Black Group Size (%)	Large Black Group Size (%)	Chi² (p)
Purchasing Ads	85.6	88.2	.43
Fundraising	42.3	62.7	.00
Providing information/volunteers to candidates	83.5	90.0	.06
Providing registration materials	76.1	87.0	.01
Providing transportation, election day	44.0	56.5	.01
Providing transportation, early voting	37.8	50.3	.01

Source: 1996 Survey of Texas County Party Chairs.
Note: Table entries represent the percentage of chairs in counties with small Black population sizes and the percentage of chairs in counties with large Black population sizes who report engaging in each particular type of mobilizing activity. Large Black population size counties are those that are above the statewide average in the percentage of Blacks in the population; small Black population size counties are those that are below the statewide average of Blacks in the population. The Chi² *p* value indicates the probability that the difference in the percentage of chairs in large Black group size counties and the percentage of chairs in small Black group size counties engaging in each particular type of activity is significant.

TABLE 4.5
Mobilization Activities, by Hispanic Group Size

	Small Hispanic Group Size (%)	Large Hispanic Group Size (%)	Chi² (p)
Purchasing Ads	87.0	85.6	.69
Fundraising	54.5	40.5	.01
Providing information/volunteers to candidates	84.9	87.6	.45
Providing registration materials	79.5	81.0	.70
Providing transportation, election day	49.3	47.1	.65
Providing transportation, early voting	41.8	43.4	.74

Source: 1996 Survey of Texas County Party Chairs.
Note: Table entries represent the percentage of chairs in counties with small Hispanic population sizes and the percentage of chairs in counties with large Hispanic population sizes who report engaging in each particular type of mobilizing activity. Large Hispanic population size counties are those that are above the statewide average in the percentage of Hispanics in the population; small Hispanic population size counties are those that are below the statewide average of Hispanics in the population. The Chi² *p* value indicates the probability that the difference in the percentage of chairs in large Hispanic group size counties and the percentage of chairs in small Hispanic group size counties engaging in each particular type of activity is significant.

ported above, where 1 indicates that the chair reported engaging in the activity, and 0 otherwise. Included in the multivariate model as independent variables are the party of the chairperson; party competitiveness (which is obviously excluded from the party competitiveness model); Black group size and Hispanic group size (both measured as a percent of the county population); and the proportion of whites in the counties with a high school degree (to control for socioeconomic differences across counties). Since the dependent variables are all dummy variables, I present (MLE) probit estimates for each of the models.

Table 4.6 basically confirms the earlier findings, in that socioeconomic status is negatively associated with mobilizing activity, chairs in higher socioeconomic status counties reported doing less, and party competitiveness is not associated with engaging in any particular type of activity. The racial/ethnic context, in terms of the size of the Hispanic population, is significant in only one case: chairs in counties with smaller Hispanic populations are less likely to engage in fundraising than are chairs in counties with larger Hispanic populations. In contrast, the coefficient estimates for the size of the Black population are significant and positive for three mobilizing activities: providing registration materials, providing information to candidates, and fundraising.

Although this finding suggests that the racial context structures the activities party chairs undertake, it is nonetheless inconsistent with the argument forwarded previously: party chairs in counties with large minority populations will be more likely to engage in activities that reduce the costs of participation. Providing candidates information and doing fundraising are not typically thought of as reducing the costs of participating.

To push this finding a bit further, I reestimated each of these models but restricted the cases in the analysis to counties with a Black population percentage of more than 1 percent. When this is done, the coefficient estimate for the size of the Black population is insignificant in every equation. I thus conclude that the racial context only marginally affects the choices chairs make in what they do and these choices are structured almost entirely by the unique strategies defined by party elites.

PARTY ATTRIBUTES AND SYSTEMS AS MOBILIZATION CONTEXTS

As noted earlier, minorities can be exposed to unique mobilization contexts either because elites specifically choose to engage in different types of activities or because racial/ethnic minorities tend to reside in social contexts with particularly strong or weak political attributes. It is to this latter point I now turn. As Huckfeldt and Sprague (1995) have eloquently argued, individual political behavior by necessity occurs within a particular

TABLE 4.6
Multivariate Models of Mobilization Techniques

	Registration Materials	Transportation, Early Voting	Transportation, Election Day	Ads	Information to Candidates	Fundraising
Party (Dem = 1)	.47**	.63**	.70**	.07	-.30*	-.24*
	(.14)	(.12)	(.12)	(.15)	(.15)	(.12)
Competitiveness	.18	.06	-.04	-.02	.09	-.02
	(.16)	(.14)	(.14)	(.16)	(.17)	(.13)
Percent Black	3.07**	1.70	1.61	1.48	2.62*	2.14*
	(1.10)	(.91)	(.91)	(1.17)	(1.23)	(.88)
Percent Hispanic	.002	-.21	-.65	-.49	-.42	-.91**
	(.442)	(.38)	(.38)	(.46)	(.47)	(.37)
Education (whites)	-4.88**	-7.72**	-8.28**	-4.66*	-6.37**	-5.76*
	(1.94)	(1.68)	(1.71)	(2.06)	(2.14)	(1.65)
Constant	1.90**	1.75**	2.20**	2.53**	3.12**	1.93**
	(.67)	(.57)	(.58)	(.72)	(.75)	(.57)
N	446	444	445	445	445	445

Source: 1996 Survey of Texas County Party Chairs.
Note: Table entries are the MLE probit coefficient estimates, followed by the associated standard error in parentheses. Dependent variables are all dummy variables, where 1 indicates that the party chair reported doing the activity, and 0 indicates that the party chair reported not doing the activity. The abbreviated variable names represent, from the first to the last column: providing registration materials, providing transportation to voters for early voting, providing transportation to voters on election day; purchasing advertising; providing information to candidates; and engaging in fundraising activities. Education is the percentage of whites in the county with a high school diploma.
*$p < .05$, two-tailed test of significance. **$p < .01$, two-tailed test of significance.

social context, and to ignore that context is to misrepresent the nature of political life.

Huckfeldt and Sprague's study of South Bend, Indiana, demonstrates the subtle ways in which the nature of the community's political system— its one-party dominance, the level of social interactions, and neighborhood characteristics such as education level, income level, and partisanship— structure individuals' participation decisions, vote choices, and political opinions. Moreover, the strategic decisions and activities of political institutions—that is, political parties—respond to these social dynamics as well.

It is this intellectual tradition—which of course had V. O. Key among its earliest proponents—that motivates this investigation of the nature of the political environments in which racial and ethnic minorities are likely to reside. Huckfeldt and Sprague's study systematically excluded racial minorities, so we know little of the social dynamics structuring politics in diverse neighborhoods and communities from their "contextual" approach to the study of politics.

Traditional studies of party systems, of course, emphasize the importance of class and race as structuring electoral coalitions (e.g., Burnham, 1981, 1982, 1987; Kleppner 1979, 1982), but none of these studies addresses how the nature of the party system is associated with the racial composition of the electorate. Key (1949) and Matthews and Prothro (1966), of course, identify numerous consequences of Black population size in Southern communities, counties, or states for levels of Black voter registration, turnout, and political organization. But it is not clear how the findings of these rich, finely detailed case studies of the late 1940s and 1950s might be properly extrapolated to the political and social realities of the (post–civil rights) late twentieth century.

Drawing from historical studies emphasizing the critical importance of race to the development of political institutions and, more specifically, party systems, it might be expected that the nature of party systems in areas with high levels of ethnic diversity is significantly different from that of areas with low levels. But systematic evidence on this point is limited at best. Hero (1998) provides the most detailed consideration of the general political consequences of social (i.e., racial/ethnic) diversity for state politics, finding that diversity is associated with greater party-elite polarization, with Republican leaders in more diverse states being significantly more conservative and Democratic leaders being more liberal. Moreover, Hill and Leighley (1999) find that states with ethnically diverse populations tend to have more restrictive voter registration requirements. The analysis below is motivated by Hill and Leighley's broader assertion that ethnic diversity is likely associated with weaker mobilizing institutions in general.

To test whether minorities in Texas tend to reside in counties with weaker mobilizing contexts, I examine the association between racial/ethnic context and four different indicators of the strength of mobilizing institutions. Two of these indicators reflect on strategies of the party chair, while the others reflect on the party system more broadly. More specifically, I first use the level of *party activity*, which refers to the number of activities that the party chair reports engaging in during the presidential election. This is an additive index ranging from 0 (no activities) to 6 (all possible activities); these are the same mobilization techniques presented in the first part of the chapter.

Second, I use party competitiveness as a measure of mobilization potential, due to its association with candidate spending strategies (see, e.g., Cox and Munger 1989): electoral districts that are competitive tend to draw strong challengers, and spending by candidates is typically high (Jacobson 1996). Since most spending is done on advertising and other mobilization activities, it stands to reason that individuals residing in competitive districts should be exposed to higher levels of campaign mobilization. Party competitiveness in this model is measured as an interval-level variable, based on the party difference in the presidential vote in 1996, where higher values indicate closer electoral results in the county and thus greater competitiveness.[10]

Third, I use whether the party chair identified "increasing turnout" as the most important organizational priority for the county organization. Chairs were asked to rank in order of importance to their organization in the past election "a list of things that parties do," including:

- Increasing turnout
- Persuading voters to support the party's candidates
- Providing resources to candidates
- Registering voters

Approximately 39 percent of chairs reported that increasing turnout was their most important priority; 12.6 percent reported that registering voters was most important; 35.1 percent reported that persuading voters was most important; and 13.8 percent reported that providing resources to candidates was most important. However, figure 4.2 shows that there are substantial partisan differences in these goals: Democratic chairs are more likely (than Republican chairs) to cite increasing turnout and registering voters as their most important organizational goal, while Republican chairs are more likely (than Democratic chairs) to report persuading voters and assisting candidates as their most important organizational goal.[11]

[10] The specific measure is one minus the absolute value of the difference between the Republican and Democratic vote in the county.

[11] This is a significant difference (Chi^2 = 44.37, df = 3, p = .00). I also examined whether having turnout as the most important organizational goal differed across competitive and noncompetitive counties, and in counties with large and small minority populations. The only

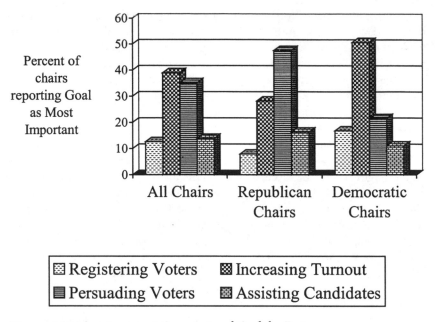

Figure 4.2. Most Important Organizational Goal, by Party
Source: 1996 Survey of Texas County Party Chairs

For the third party system measure, I use a dummy variable (where
1 = turnout as the first priority, 0 otherwise) as an alternative indicator of
the value the chair places on mobilizing voters. Given the significant partisan differences associated with this goal, I also include a dummy variable
for party in the model. Fourth, I include the party chair's self-report on
whether the county was targeted by a national or statewide campaign as
another indicator of the partisan mobilization context. I assume that counties
so targeted were likely to be exposed to more advertising and get-out-the-
vote efforts. Probit models were estimated for the two dummy variables,
Turnout as a Priority and Targeted by State and National Organization,
while OLS regression models were estimated for the number of mobilization acts and party competitiveness.

Table 4.7 shows that the racial context thesis is supported in three out of
the four cases: the larger the presence of Blacks, the more mobilizing acts
engaged in by party chairs, the more likely the county was to be targeted
by a national or state organization, and the more competitive the county.

---

statistically significant difference was that for Hispanic group size: 59.1 percent of chairs in
counties with large Hispanic populations identified increasing turnout as a primary goal, compared to only 38 percent in counties with small Hispanic populations.

TABLE 4.7
Multivariate Models of Strong Mobilization Contexts

	Mobilization Acts by Chair	Turnout First Priority	Targeted by State and National Organization	Party Competitiveness
Party (Dem = 1)	.49°°	.59°°	.15	.02
	(.15)	(.12)	(.13)	(.01)
Competitiveness	.07	−.05	.15	
	(.16)	(.14)	(.14)	
Percent Black	3.38°°	.27	3.43°°	.54°°
	(1.08)	(.91)	(.93)	(.10)
Percent Hispanic	−.78	.09	.21	.09°
	(.45)	(.38)	(.40)	(.04)
Education (whites)	−10.95°°	−1.81	−1.52	.44°°
	(1.94)	(1.62)	(1.74)	(.18)
Constant	6.96°°	−.04	−.61	.64°°
	(.67)	(.56)	(.60)	(.06)
F, p	12.17, .000			21.11, .000
Adjusted R2	.11			.15
N	442	436	439	446

Source: 1996 Survey of Texas County Party Chairs.
Note: For "Turnout First Priority" and "Targeted by State and National Organization," both dummy variables, cell entries are the MLE probit coefficient estimates, followed by the associated standard error in parentheses. For "Party Competitiveness" and "Mobilization Acts by Chair," cell entries are OLS regression coefficient estimates, followed by the associated standard error in parentheses. Education is the percentage of whites in the county with a high school diploma.
°$p < .05$, two-tailed test of significance. °°$p < .01$, two-tailed test of significance.

Support for the racial/ethnic context thesis for Hispanics is not as strong, though the size of the Hispanic population is positively associated with party competitiveness.

The latter finding should be interpreted in light of the other notable finding for party competitiveness: the higher the level of socioeconomic status in the county, the more competitive it is. This suggests that in counties with lower levels of education—as in the Rio Grande Valley, where a large proportion of the state's Hispanic residents reside—party competitiveness is lower. These Hispanic-dominated counties tend to be the least competitive in the state, suggesting that the positive coefficient on the size of the Hispanic population is driven by electoral politics elsewhere. Whatever advantage in mobilization levels is gained by large Hispanic majorities in the state is certainly not driven by the combination of class and ethnicity witnessed in the Rio Grande Valley counties.

Two additional points are important to note. First, as indicated earlier in this chapter, Democratic Party chairs are more interested in turnout and tend to report engaging in more mobilizing activities. This is certainly consistent with anecdotal (and some academic) evidence that turnout advantages the Democrats and that these leaders realize the importance of mobilizing institutions for lower-status individuals. Second, and consistent with this latter point, chairs residing in lower-status counties tend to engage in more mobilizing activities, again suggesting that elites are being efficient in their use of mobilization resources.[12]

CONCLUSION

This chapter focused on two basic questions. First, are chairs' choices of mobilizing techniques structured by the racial context of their county? Second, do minorities tend to reside where (partisan) mobilizing institutions are weak? Addressing these questions allows us to consider more subtle ways in which the *nature* of political mobilization of racial and ethnic minorities might vary, as well as the *level* of political mobilization.

The first important finding of this chapter is not likely to catch many by surprise: Democratic Party chairs are significantly more likely to engage in more mobilizing activities and more likely to engage more in mobilizing activities that tend to reduce the costs of participation. Thus, there is a substantial difference in the way in which each party approaches mobilization activities. Consistent with observations of the increasing organizational and financial capability of the Republican Party at all levels, the particularly interesting point this finding raises is whether the parties will continue to be distinctive in their mobilizing activities as they both seek to mobilize Hispanics as a newly empowered (by virtue of its size) voting bloc. Supporting candidates to run for office is certainly one way to build a party. But whether focusing party efforts on candidate support alone is sufficient to gain the loyalties of citizens—and to get them to show up at the polls—is yet to be seen.

The second important finding is that partisan mobilization strength is not necessarily associated with racial context. Hispanic group size is only associated with one aspect of the party system—party competitiveness— while Black group size is associated with the mobilization activity level of

---

[12] I also estimated the same models while restricting the cases to those counties with greater than 1 percent Black population. While the results are essentially the same for the "turnout first priority" model, there are some differences in the other models with respect to which variables are significant. Specifically, Black group size becomes significant in the "targeted by state and national" equation; Black group size becomes insignificant in the "number of mobilization acts" equation; and Hispanic group size becomes significant for party competitiveness.

party chairs, the county's being targeted by state and national organizations, and its party competitiveness. However, the latter findings wash out when the analysis is restricted to only those counties whose Black population is greater than 1 percent; this suggests that the initial findings reflected the unique (and skewed) distribution of Blacks in the states.

Just as important (in terms of context) in its association with mobilization institutions is the role of socioeconomic status. Party chairs do more in counties with lower status, while the party system is more competitive in counties with higher status. And, finally, even in terms of these mobilizing "systems," the distinctive approaches and priorities of chairs across parties is notable: Democratic chairs do more and place more emphasis on turnout than do Republican chairs.[13]

These findings might be interpreted more broadly as reflecting a certain level of responsiveness of the party system to its "constituencies" and in such a way as to be consistent with conventional perspectives on the role of parties in electoral systems. Note, for example, that socioeconomic status (measured by the percentage of whites with a high school diploma) is negatively correlated with most (party) mobilization indicators. This suggests that the party attributes likely to stimulate participation are more readily available in lower socioeconomic status populations—the very individuals who are said to "need" mass political institutions to reduce their costs of participating.

These findings, of course, must be interpreted in the context of Texas politics. It might be, for example, that the somewhat unique (and fairly recent) development of the party system—with the Democratic Party dominant for so many years, and now with the Republican Party having a strong organization dominated by the Christian Right—in some sense determines some of its particular features today. Were we to study additional states or do a nationwide sample of party chairs, these findings might not be sustained.

The question remains as to whether the racial/ethnic context is as weakly associated with the intentional decisions of party chairs to target racial and ethnic minorities in Texas. That is what I turn to in chapter 5.

---

[13] Another alternative interpretation is that respondents' answers reflect socially expected behavior, but I am less inclined to believe that given the extent to which the party leaders I interviewed were blatant about whom and what they cared about as they did their jobs. The extent to which these elites, many of whom were state-level officials, share this orientation with the county party chairs who responded to the survey is unknown. But perhaps the relative anonymity of the mail survey reduced the incentives of party chairs to provide socially expected answers.

Chapter Five

ELECTORAL TARGETING:

ELITE STRATEGIES AND CONTEXT

T HE strategies party elites use in determining what they do—and
toward which groups of potential voters these activities are directed—might have racial consequences whether or not such strategies are consciously adopted with racial or ethnic considerations in mind.
The last chapter investigated the choices of party chairs about mobilization
strategies and the political context in which minorities tend to reside as
two aspects of party mobilization that are "color-blind." In contrast, this
chapter focuses on the party leaders' conscious choices whether or not to
target minority groups. I begin with a traditional, (national) survey-based
analysis of party contacting patterns and then move to an analysis of the
Texas party chairs' targeting decisions.

PARTY CONTACTING STRATEGY

Huckfeldt and Sprague (1992, 1995) focus on the strategies parties use in
determining whom to contact, demonstrating that parties target previous
voters and party supporters. They find that 40 percent of individuals who
participated in previous primary elections report being contacted by a
party during the campaign, compared to only 25 percent of individuals
who had never participated in a primary election. Huckfeldt and Sprague
also find that parties tend to locate their fellow partisans: 32 percent of
those who only vote in Democratic primaries report being contacted by
Democrats, compared to 19 percent reporting that they were contacted by
Republicans. Similarly, 34 percent of Republican primary voters report
being contacted by Republicans, while only 15 percent report being contacted by Democrats.

Huckfeldt and Sprague also emphasize that party contacting patterns are
structured in part by the political environment. Because South Bend, their
study site, is predominantly Republican and many Democrats therefore
participate in the Republican primaries, the Democratic Party must rely
on factors other than primary voting to identify and mobilize supporters.
Huckfeldt and Sprague find that the "best" neighborhood characteristic
predicting whether an individual will be contacted by the Democratic
Party is the proportion of the *neighborhood* that is contacted (as opposed

to measures of neighborhood class or partisanship). They infer from this that the Democratic Party must identify target neighborhoods—as opposed to individuals—in an effort to find Democrats who might well participate in the Republican primaries.[1] Since this targeting is independent of the social characteristics of the individuals or neighborhoods targeted, Huckfeldt and Sprague conclude that this targeting reflects the local political structure.[2]

With the exception of Huckfeldt and Sprague, most research on party canvassing relies on the party contacting series of the American National Election Studies (NES), where individuals in each biennial survey are asked whether anyone from a political party had contacted them about the election. Rosenstone and Hansen (1993), for example, argue that mobilization by political elites is key to understanding why individuals vote and that parties are strategic in whom they mobilize, due to limited resources. Using the NES party contacting data, Rosenstone and Hansen find that strong partisans and labor union households are indeed more likely to be contacted—evidence of the claim that parties seek to mobilize supporters.

Wielhouwer (1995), also using the NES party contacting data, tests alternative hypotheses regarding whom the parties target: members of their own electoral coalition (i.e., supporters), undecided voters, or members of the opposition party's electoral coalition (in an effort to demobilize their turnout). In contrast to Rosenstone and Hansen's (1993) findings, however, Wielhouwer concludes that parties do not use their limited resources to contact supporters.[3] Democrats, for example, do not target Blacks more than whites, or the poor more than the nonpoor; and Republicans fail to target whites more than Blacks. Wielhouwer concludes that both parties target "marginal voters": those with higher levels of education and living in urban areas; individuals with a high probability of voting due to socioeconomic status; and older individuals.

Some initial evidence regarding race and mobilization is drawn from the NES presidential election-year series (1956–96). In each of these surveys, a nationally representative sample is asked whether they voted in that

[1] The most potent neighborhood characteristic associated with Republican contacting is the proportion of neighborhood respondents claiming to have voted in the 1984 Republican primary. This suggests that Republican contacting was structured more heavily by past primary participation than was Democratic contacting—a finding entirely consistent with Huckfeldt and Sprague's argument.

[2] It might also reflect differences in the organizational capabilities of the two parties (if the local Republican Party has more information available to it as to the names and locations of party supporters) or in in the types of mobilization pursued (if Republicans rely more on phone banks while Democrats rely more heavily on door-to-door contacting).

[3] The results on this point in fact provide some evidence of targeting supporters: Republicans target the elderly and the wealthy significantly more than they do the poor and young voters.

year's presidential election and whether a political party or candidate had contacted them. In addition, demographic characteristics of the respondents are gathered, along with numerous other attitudinal and behavioral reports. Although the number of Blacks in each of the surveys is extremely small (and therefore the error of the sample estimates is substantial), these data provide a starting point from which to evaluate the role of socioeconomic status and ideology in structuring political mobilization and individual political participation. Evidence on the role of group size and empowerment will be presented in later chapters, as indicators of each of these factors are not available in the NES.

Figure 5.1 presents the percentage of individuals in each presidential election-year survey reporting being contacted by the Democratic Party, the Republican Party or either party. Some of the points are interesting and intuitive—the high level of Republican Party contacting in 1964, for example, or the high level of Democratic contacting during the 1970s. Other aspects of the self-report data are somewhat troubling: if, as some scholars argue, party organizations are stronger, it is certainly not reflected in the amount of party contacting they engage in.

Figures 5.2, 5.3, and 5.4 present the proportion of respondents who had been contacted, controlling for income. Figure 5.2 is especially important to the argument that mobilization is intertwined with participation, in that it demonstrates the strong relationship between income and being mobilized by a party: individuals in the highest income group are two times or more likely to be contacted by a party than are individuals in the lowest income group. And although the absolute levels of contacting change from election to election, the greater probability that high-income individuals are contacted is consistent over time.

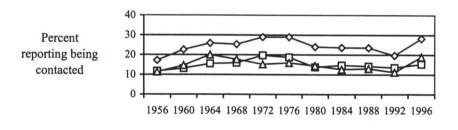

Figure 5.1. Party Contacting, 1956–96
Source: American National Election Studies Cumulative File, 1948–1997

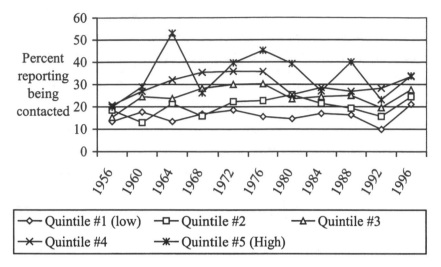

Figure 5.2. Party Contacting, by Income, 1956–96
Source: American National Election Studies Cumulative File, 1948–1997

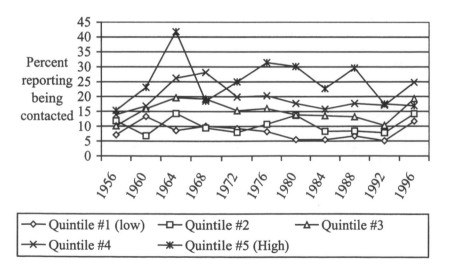

Figure 5.3. Republican Party Contacting, by Income, 1956–96
Source: American National Election Studies Cumulative File, 1948–1997

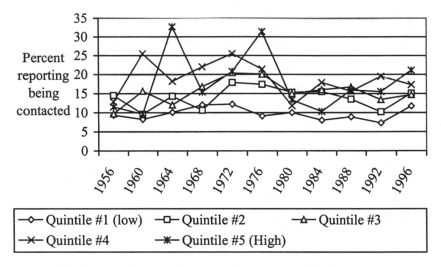

Figure 5.4. Democratic Party Contacting, by Income, 1956–96
Source: American National Election Studies Cumulative File, 1948–1997

Consistent with Wielhouwer (1995), Frymer (1995) finds that Blacks are less likely than whites to be contacted by the Democratic Party, even while controlling for income. Frymer argues—and provides qualitative interview data with Democratic Party leaders as evidence—that Democrats do not mobilize Blacks because they are exceedingly loyal supporters. Targeting loyal supporters, party leaders suggest, would be a waste of scarce resources. Instead, the party seeks to target persuadables—individuals who split their votes between Republicans and Democrats. The expected benefit from targeting these individuals, as reported to Frymer, is that these individuals are already likely to vote; the contacting effort need only persuade the individual to vote Democratic in that election, not to convince the individual both to vote *and* to vote Democratic.

Using the NES party contacting data, Frymer estimates a probit model, where the dependent variable is whether the respondent reports being contacted by a political party, and the independent variables are income and race. The negative coefficient estimated for race, while controlling for income, is offered as evidence that Blacks are systematically ignored by the parties.

There are several potential problems with his brief analysis. First, the model is rather underspecified—especially in comparison to Wielhouwer (1995), who includes nearly twenty independent variables in his model. Second, Frymer analyzes the time-series data as a cross-section—all cases from the 1956–92 series are included, with no consideration of how political and electoral changes over time might bias the estimates of the coefficients for the independent variables. Third, he fails to analyze the two parties separately—although the major parties likely target different groups.

More specifically, if we assume that parties contact their supporters, then we might expect the relationship between contacting and income to differ for the Republican and Democratic Parties, expecting that the relationship is significantly stronger for the former. That is, since high-income individuals tend to identify with the Republican Party, we would expect the Republican Party to target these individuals not just because they are likely to vote—but because they are likely to vote in the preferred manner. Democrats, on the other hand, should see some benefit from targeting low-income individuals, since they are likely to be faithful to Democratic Party candidates. Thus, Democrats have "mixed" incentives to target both high-income and low-income individuals.

This is basically what we see in figures 5.3 and 5.4. Figure 5.3 demonstrates that the Republican Party always contacts high socioeconomic status individuals more than low socioeconomic individuals. Democrats, on the other hand, seem to change their strategy of whom to contact from election to election, though generally high-income individuals are more likely to be contacted by them as well (see figure 5.4).

Figure 5.5 tells a similar story for the relationship between contacting and race. Figure 5.5 presents the percentages of Anglos (non-Blacks) and Blacks who report being contacted by the Democratic Party and by the Republican Party, and the pattern is clear: party contacting of Blacks increased dramatically in 1964, but subsequently immediately declined to a much lower level of contacting than that reported by non-Blacks.

Consistent with a "party supporters" thesis, figure 5.5 also suggests that the dramatic post-1960 increase in mobilizing Blacks was almost entirely the result of Democratic Party contacting efforts. Less than 10 percent of Blacks ever report being contacted by the Republican Party, compared to at least 13 percent of non-Blacks (at minimum) reporting that they were contacted by the Republican Party. In contrast, Blacks are occasionally more likely than non-Blacks to be contacted by the Democratic Party, and the level of Black contacting by Democrats is always more than 13 percent (and sometimes substantially so).

This last set of comparisons must be done cautiously, as we might draw some incorrect inferences regarding contacting and race if we do not control for income. To do this, I begin by estimating a model similar to that presented by Frymer (1995) to demonstrate the importance of distinguishing between Republican and Democratic contacting strategies. Table 5.1 presents the results of probit models estimating individuals' probabilities of being contacted by either party, by the Democratic Party, and by the

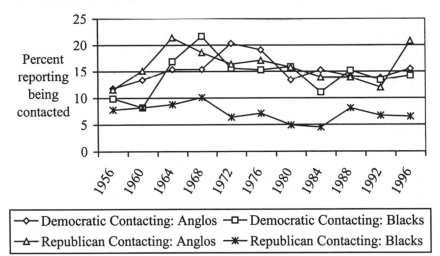

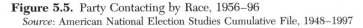

Figure 5.5. Party Contacting by Race, 1956–96
Source: American National Election Studies Cumulative File, 1948–1997

TABLE 5.1
Race and Class as Predictors of (Self-Reported) Party Contacting

	Contacted by One or Both Parties	Contacted by Democrats	Contacted by Republicans
Income	.15°°	.11°°	.17°°
	(.01)	(.01)	(.01)
Anglo	.12°°	− .03	.37°°
	(.04)	(.04)	(.05)
Constant	− 1.25°°	− 1.32°°	− 1.90°°
	(.04)	(.05)	(.06)
N	16,040	15,887	15,887
% correctly predicted	58.8	64.6	64.7
Mean contact	.24	.15	.15

Source: American National Election Studies Cumulative File, 1948–1997.
Note: Table entries are probit coefficients, with the associated standard error in parentheses. The dependent variables are dichotomous, where 1 indicates that the individual was contacted and 0 indicates that the individual was not contacted, based on self-reports, by both parties.
°$p < .05$, two-tailed test of significance. °°$p < .01$, two-tailed test of significance.

Republican Party. Following Frymer, I include only income and race as independent variables and analyze the time-series data using a cross-sectional model.

My results are similar to those of Frymer. High-income individuals and Anglos are significantly more likely to be contacted by either party than are low-income individuals and Blacks. Similar results hold for income when estimating the model for Democratic and Republican contacting separately. Yet an important difference emerges for race: while Blacks are significantly less likely than Anglos to be contacted by the Republican Party, they are contacted at similar rates to those of Anglos by the Democratic Party. This is consistent with Wielhouwer's observation that parties do not contact loyal supporters *or* opponents.

However, the parties do seem to be able to contact their supporters—as identified by individuals' self-reported party identification. Table 5.2 presents the models estimated in table 5.1 for Democratic and Republican contacting, with the addition of three independent variables: region (South versus non-South), party identification, and year. Party identification is represented in the model by two dummy variables, one for Democratic identifiers (where individuals who identify with the Democratic Party are coded as 1 and all others are coded as 0) and Republican identifiers (where individuals identifying with the Republican Party are coded as 1 and all others are coded as 0); individuals not identifying with either party, Independents, are excluded from the model specification for estimation purposes. These variables were added in the interest of more fully specifying the model (region and year) as well as to examine the "party supporters" thesis more rigorously.

The results are similar to those in table 5.1. Income is positively related to party contacting in both models, and race is associated with Republican, not Democratic, Party contacting. Note, however, that with the addition of the other independent variables, the estimated coefficient for race is substantially reduced. "Year" (where lower values represent earlier election years) is insignificant, indicating no observable increase or decrease in party contacting between 1956 and 1996. Moreover, both Democratic and Republican Party contacting are significantly less likely to be targeted toward individuals who live in the South.

Finally, Democratic and Republican identifiers are significantly more likely to be contacted by either party, though the estimated magnitude of effect is stronger in the expected direction: the Democratic Party is more likely to contact Democrats and the Republican Party is more likely to contact Republicans. Based on these self-reports, it seems that we have fairly strong evidence that parties target both likely voters (i.e., high-income individuals) as well as their (partisan) supporters. Despite the fact that the Democratic Party is far more likely to contact Blacks than is the

TABLE 5.2

Race and Class as Predictors of (Self-Reported) Party Contacting, Controlling for Region, Year, and Party Identification

	Contacted by Democrats	Contacted by Republicans
Income	.11°°	.15°°
	(.01)	(.01)
Anglo	−.02	.28°°
	(.04)	(.05)
South	−.19°°	−.08°°
	(.03)	(.03)
Democratic identifiers	.29°°	.10°
	(.04)	(.05)
Republican identifiers	.09°	.31°°
	(.05)	(.05)
Year	.001	−.001
	(.001)	(.001)
Constant	−4.92°°	.10
	(1.92)	(1.93)
N	15,579	15,579
% correctly predicted	63.3	63.4
Mean contact	.15	.15

Source: American National Election Studies Cumulative File, 1948–1997.

Note: Table entries are probit coefficients, with the associated standard error in parentheses. The dependent variables are dichotomous, where 1 indicates that the individual was contacted and 0 indicates that the individual was not contacted, based on self-reports by the Democratic or Republican Party. For purposes of estimation, a dichotomous variable where 1 indicates the individual identifies as an Independent and 0 indicates otherwise is omitted from the model.

°$p < .05$, two-tailed test of significance. °°$p < .01$, two-tailed test of significance.

Republican Party, it appears that Blacks are not necessarily "rewarded" for their loyalty.

Next, to provide a baseline for the analyses of individual behavior reported in chapters 6 through 8, I estimate a basic model of voter turnout, and these results are provided in table 5.3. The model estimates are fairly standard with respect to demographics: income is positively associated with turnout, while living in the South and being Anglo is negatively associated with turnout, controlling for year and region. Party contact, as expected, is significant and positively associated with turnout: individuals who are contacted about the election are more likely to participate in it.

Although the NES party-contacting data are a good place to start answering questions about race, mobilization, and participation, they quickly reach their limit in three ways. First, the only racial or ethnic group identified in the time series is Blacks, and even then the number of respondents

TABLE 5.3
Race, Class, Party Contact, and Voter Turnout

	Turnout
Income	.25°°
	(.01)
Anglo	.09°°
	(.04)
Year	−.002
	(.001)
South	−.30°°
	(.02)
Party contact	.58°°
	(.03)
Constant	3.21
	(1.74)
N	16,034
% correctly predicted	66.7
Mean voted	.74

Source: American National Election Studies Cumulative File, 1948–1997.

Note: Table entries are probit coefficients, with the associated standard error in parentheses. The dependent variable is dichotomous, where 1 indicates the individual reports voting in the presidential election, and 0 indicates the individual reported not voting. °p < .05, two-tailed test of significance. °°p < .01, two-tailed test of significance.

is inadequate in many years. Second, little information is provided as to the nature of the party contact—or for similar mobilization efforts by other individuals or organizations. Third, in relying on individuals' self-reports regarding whether they had been contacted by a political party, they provide indirect measures, at best, of elite mobilization strategy.

Moreover, to make inferences about elite behavior from mass survey data requires fairly strong assumptions regarding the extent to which these self-reports are accurate indicators of elite activity. It may be, for example, that strong partisans (or voters) are more likely to be contacted by parties—or instead more likely to exaggerate being asked, or more likely to remember being asked—than are weak partisans or Independents. Simply put, analyses of party contacting behavior relying on survey respondents' self-reports reflect the end product of a complex process, which is likely a function of both elite strategy as well as individual patterns of recall/survey response.[4] Hence, conclusions based on the NES party-contacting data merit review from the perspective of elite reports as well.

[4] Self-reports of party contacting are significantly correlated with independent reports of

PARTY TARGETING STRATEGIES: AN ELITE PERSPECTIVE

As described in chapter 4, interviews with party elites and candidates particularly emphasize the importance of socioeconomic status and ideology as factors determining who is mobilized in electoral campaigns. The most consistent strategy reported by elites is devoting their mobilization efforts almost exclusively to registered voters. This, in effect, results in mobilization activities being directed primarily to individuals with high levels of education and income.

Second, party elites consistently report focusing on swing voters, in that party or candidate efforts devoted to swing voters have the greatest potential to secure additional votes. Swing voters, or ticket-splitters, are those individuals who do not vote straight party tickets. Hence, individuals who claim to be ideological independents, rather than strong party supporters, are targeted, as this is where campaigns seek to gain a competitive advantage.

The third strategy identified by party leaders is targeting partisan supporters—the more you turn out your own troops, the better the chances of victory, whatever the battle. This strategy suggests a slightly different relationship between ideology and mobilization: while both parties might target Independents, Republicans would be expected to target strong Republicans and Democrats would be expected to target strong Democrats.

The analysis below tests several hypotheses consistent with these arguments; it does so, however, using elite reports of targeting and mobilization activities rather than relying on survey respondent reports as to whether individuals were contacted by a political party. More specifically:

H1: *Party leaders target supporters.* This hypothesis can be tested by comparing the social groups that party leaders report targeting and comparing the (perceived) ideological tendencies of those groups. I expect, for example, that Republicans will be more likely to target the Christian Right than will Democrats. Any groups perceived to be closer to the party's ideological position should be more likely to be targeted than groups perceived to be more distant.

H2: *Party leaders target individuals who are swing voters.* Thus, both Republicans and Democrats should report targeting Independents. In addition, both sets of leaders should be more likely to target any group they perceive to be ideologically moderate.

---

local party activity, both at the individual and aggregate level. Yet the magnitude of the correlation between the two—0.29 for Republicans and 0.39 for Democrats—suggests that substantial error is introduced by the use of individual self-reports of elite activity.

H3: *Party leaders target individuals who have a high probability of voting (or being registered to vote).* Given the widespread knowledge of the relationship between socioeconomic status and voter turnout, this hypothesis can be tested by comparing whether high-status individuals are more likely to be targeted than low-status individuals.

Testing the first three hypotheses will reflect on the broader argument that party mobilization is structured by socioeconomic status and ideology, and will have implications for understanding the extent to which minority groups are targeted. Does the lower level of mobilization perceived by African-Americans reflect the fact that African-Americans are generally poorer than whites, or does it instead reflect the distinctively liberal ideological orientation of the majority of African-Americans?

The next three hypotheses consider group size and political empowerment as alternative influences on whether African-Americans and Hispanics are targeted. Thus, I test two "race-conscious" hypotheses.

H4: *Party leaders are more likely to target minority groups when they make up a large proportion of the electorate than when they make up a small proportion of the electorate.* More specifically, I hypothesize that group size is key in determining when Blacks and Hispanics will be targeted: the larger the group size, the more likely the group will be targeted—independent of ideology and socioeconomic status.

H5: *Minority party leaders are more likely to target minority individuals than are Anglo leaders.* One of the reasons Blacks living in "empowered" areas (i.e., those having elected Black mayors) are more likely to participate, I argue, is that they are more likely to be recruited. Again independent of ideology and socioeconomic status, Blacks living in empowered areas are more likely to be recruited.

Both of these hypotheses, of course, are assumed to hold while controlling for the effects of socioeconomic status and ideology. Moreover, I anticipate that party chairs residing in competitive counties have greater incentives to use their resources efficiently and, therefore, that:

H6: *These relationships (as specified in hypotheses 1–5) will be stronger in more competitive counties.*

The final evidence presented in this chapter is a multivariate model of elite targeting, where the independent effects of socioeconomic status, ideology, group size, and political empowerment on elite targeting are tested simultaneously.

The inclusion of group size and political empowerment in this analysis is particularly valuable because these two factors have not been studied in previous research. The survey data used in the party-contacting literature simply provide no contextual information as to the characteristics of the electoral environment or the race or ethnicity of political elites engaged in mobilizing activities. Hence, previous analyses of party mobilization have necessarily been restricted to testing for the effects of individual-level attributes available in mass survey data sets.

Table 5.4 shows that party supporters were by far the most commonly targeted group, with 85.3 percent of chairs identifying supporters as a targeted group, providing strong support for hypothesis 1, that *parties will target supporters*. A distant second in targeted groups were individuals aged fifty-five and over, with 60.6 percent of chairs reporting targeting them, and Hispanics, with 60 percent of chairs reporting targeting them. Over half the chairs reported targeting women (54 percent), and individuals thirty and under (50.2 percent). Independents, the poor, and African-Americans were the next most targeted groups (44.9 percent, 43.5 percent, and 39.7 percent, respectively). The groups least likely to be targeted in the counties were the Christian Right, the rich, and Asian-Americans (21.6 percent, 20.9 percent, and 10.9 percent, respectively).

The high proportion of chairs reporting that they target supporters is certainly consistent with the results of the in-depth interviews, where it was emphasized that the party focused on securing the party base. Substantially fewer chairs reported that they targeted Independents, which is consistent with the argument made in the elite interviews that party organizations emphasize turning out their supporters, while candidates emphasize working on swing voters. That Hispanics are the most targeted minority group is consistent with elite claims as to the importance of the Hispanic vote but also with the fact that Hispanics are the largest, most geographically dispersed minority group in the state. The much smaller proportion of chairs reporting that they target African-Americans and Asian-Americans likely reflects the relative size and geographical distribution of these groups in the state.

Relatively speaking, then, the overall levels of targeting for the various groups are not particularly consistent with hypothesis 2, that *parties will target swing voters*, and hypothesis 3, that *parties will target likely voters*; I might have expected the rich to be targeted more than the poor, for example. At the same time the levels are not inconsistent with these expectations in that the targeting of any single group could be explained by virtue of different hypotheses. Individuals over fifty-five, for example, are targeted at a relatively high rate, perhaps due to their high levels of voter turnout.

A better assessment of hypotheses 2 and hypothesis 3 can be gained from examining the partisan differences in targeting by the party chairs. As shown in the second and third columns of table 5.4, the reports of whom party chairs target are strikingly different. Consistent with hypotheses 1

Table 5.4
Targeting by Party Chairs during 1996 Presidential Campaign

	All chairs	Republicans	Democrats	Chi² (p)
Supporters	85.3%	85.5%	85%	.89
	(442)	(228)	(214)	
Independents	44.9%	48.4%	41.1%	.13
	(434)	(225)	(209)	
Rich	20.9%	25.6%	16%	.01
	(436)	(223)	(213)	
Poor	43.5%	29.6%	58%	.00
	(435)	(223)	(212)	
Christian Right	21.6%	40%	1.9%	.00
	(436)	(225)	(211)	
Women	54%	37.5%	71.4%	.00
	(437)	(224)	(213)	
African-Americans	39.7%	26.8%	53.3%	.00
	(436)	(224)	(212)	
Asian-Americans	10.9%	10.9%	11%	.99
	(430)	(220)	(210)	
Hispanics	60%	47.3%	73.2%	.00
	(437)	(224)	(213)	
Individuals over fifty-five	60.6%	46.4%	75.6%	.00
	(437)	(224)	(213)	
Individuals under thirty	50.2%	40.2%	60.9%	.00
	(436)	(224)	(212)	

Source: 1996 Survey of Texas County Party Chairs.

Note: Table entries represent the percentage of chairs in the entire sample, the percentage of Republican chairs, and the percentage of Democratic chairs, respectively, that report targeting each group. The Chi² p value indicates the probability that the difference in the percentage of Republicans and Democrats targeting each group is significant.

and 2, there is no significant difference between Republicans and Democrats in their likelihood of targeting supporters and Independents.

Hypothesis 3 gains support from examining whether the theory that party leaders target individuals who have a high probability of voting (or being registered to vote) can be tested by comparing the level of targeting across social groups with established patterns of electoral participation. Studies of voter registration and voter turnout, for example, provide abundant empirical evidence that older individuals are more likely to vote than younger individuals, and that high socioeconomic status individuals are more likely to vote than low socioeconomic status individuals. Hence, if party leaders target individuals who are registered, then older individuals and wealthier individuals should be targeted more than younger individuals and the poor, respectively.

It is curious, then, that both parties report targeting the poor more than the rich: 29.6 percent of Republicans and 58 percent of Democrats target the poor, while 25.6 percent of Republicans and 16 percent of Democrats target the rich. This finding might well reflect two things. First, party chairs might not report targeting the rich because they know that they have a high probability of turnout regardless of party efforts. That is, leaders may not respond to a question regarding which groups they targeted to turn out by thinking of the rich—who are likely to vote anyway—even though they are likely to use voter registration lists routinely in their efforts to increase turnout.

Second, and of greater substantive import, party leaders are likely to report targeting members of their support coalitions, regardless of voter turnout. This might well explain the large difference between the proportion of Democrats targeting the poor as opposed to the rich, but it does not explain why Republicans are almost equally likely to report targeting the rich and the poor.

Party chair reports of which social groups they target also provide indirect support for hypothesis 1. The expectation is that Republicans will be more likely to target the rich and the Christian Right than will the Democrats and that Democrats will be more likely to target the poor, women, African-Americans, and Hispanics.[5] These expectations are clearly met, with significant differences (in the expected direction) between Republican and Democratic chairs in the extent to which they report targeting these various groups.

In addition, the Democratic Party chairs are more likely to report targeting younger individuals and older individuals. Although there is no obvious explanation for this, one interpretation might be that the Democratic chairs are simply more likely to be engaged in mobilizing activities (as demonstrated in chapter 3) and hence likely to target more groups overall. As figure 5.6 shows, this is indeed the case. The parties are relatively "equal" in their likelihood of targeting more than five groups (about 25 percent of both Republican and Democratic Party chairs report doing so), but Democratic chairs are far more likely to report targeting four or five groups than are Republican chairs (approximately 47 percent versus 18 percent). Conversely, just over 30 percent of Republican chairs report targeting only one or two groups, compared to only 13 percent of Democratic chairs.

Finally, table 5.4 indicates that there are no partisan differences in targeting Asian-Americans: Asian-Americans are the least likely group to be

[5] Expectations regarding partisan differences in targeting Asian-Americans, individuals under the age of thirty, and individuals over the age of fifty-five are not clear but are included for purposes of comparison.

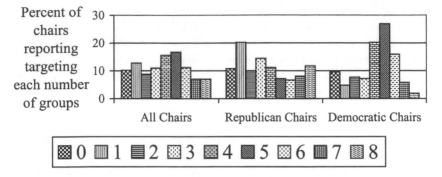

Figure 5.6. Number of Groups Targeted by Party Chairs
Source: 1996 Survey of Texas County Party Chairs

targeted, and the percent of chairs reporting that they target Asian-Americans is essentially the same for Republicans and Democrats. This undoubtedly reflects the relatively small proportion of Asian-Americans and their geographic concentration in the state: smaller numbers result in fewer counties where Asian-Americans are even available to target. But it might also reflect the lower levels of involvement of Asian-Americans in some aspects of partisan or electoral politics—which county chairs may interpret as Asian-Americans as being "apolitical" and therefore result in few efforts to incorporate the group. (On the lack of electoral involvement of Asian-Americans, see table 4.1).

MINORITY TARGETING: THE ROLE OF CONTEXT AND IDEOLOGY

Both the academic literature and the in-depth interviews introduced in chapters 1 and 2 point toward the critical role of ideology in structuring elite mobilization. Party leaders with limited resources must use them wisely. To engage in activities that stimulate one's opponents to vote is simply counterproductive, the democratic ideal of full participation of the citizenry notwithstanding. It is clear that when party leaders or candidates seek to increase turnout, they intend to maximize turnout of their supporters. Thus, parties target strategically where the party is strong early in campaigns and then, as the election approaches, where swing voting is high (i.e., where the race is likely to be competitive). This suggests that, ceteris paribus, Republicans will target Republicans, Democrats will target Democrats, and both will target Independents.

As noted above, scholars studying patterns of party contacting have sought to document this targeting strategy, but they have produced mixed results.

Wielhouwer (1999), for example, disputes Rosenstone and Hansen's conclusion that parties contact supporters. A possible explanation for this is that the individual partisans who are selected into the nationwide probability sample might well represent a mix of partisan neighborhoods, precincts, or counties. Hence, findings based on combining all conservatives nationwide might well be inaccurate due to the diversity of social and political contexts that are being sampled but not incorporated into the model.

Put another way, one of the limitations of studying party contacting using data collected as part of national probability samples (i.e., the American National Election Studies) is that individual survey respondents are chosen "randomly" by household, with the intention of eliminating the effects of context by ignoring it. Thus, little to no information is gathered regarding the individual's political context—although it might well structure the political behavior of interest (such as elites' targeting decisions).

The advantage of using elite reports of targeting strategies is that we can represent a diversity of political contexts as structuring the targeting behavior. More specifically, we can compare the reported targeting decisions of party leaders with either objective data on the political context or their subjective perceptions of the political context. Of particular interest here are two contextual characteristics: the size of the minority group and the extent to which the county is competitive in partisan elections.

The particular contexts I consider here are quite distinct. The first, minority group size, is motivated by the theoretical importance of group size to minority participation. According to Uhlaner's "relational goods" model, minorities residing in areas of large minority group size will be more likely to participate. One of the mechanisms by which this might occur is that minority group leaders may be more likely to recruit group members to participate when they reside in areas of large minority group size. Hence, the analysis that follows tests this aspect of the relational goods model.

The second contextual characteristic that I consider in the analyses below is that of electoral competitiveness. As noted in chapter 4, the closeness of elections is argued to have a substantial effect on both elite mobilization (i.e., campaign spending) and mass participation (i.e., voter turnout). The former finding suggests that elite calculations of the electoral payoffs of engaging in mobilizing activities, or targeting particular groups, is contingent on the competitiveness of the race: if marginal changes in the composition of the electorate or the vote choices of the electorate determine who wins, then efforts devoted toward influencing either of these are worth the effort. Hence, the analyses that follow all consider the role of electoral competitiveness.

Figure 5.7, for example, shows the extent to which targeting African-Americans and Hispanics is affected by minority group size and electoral competitiveness. Group size appears to be particularly important: party

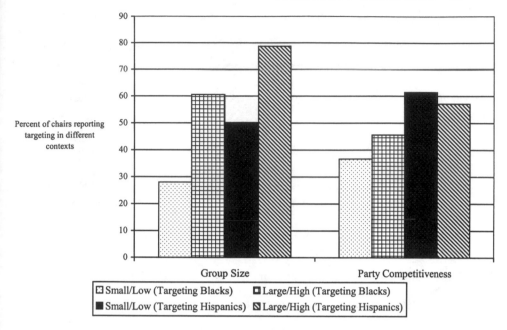

Figure 5.7. Targeting African-Americans and Hispanics in Different Social and Political Contexts

Source: 1996 Texas County Party Chairs Survey

chairs in counties with large Black populations are significantly more likely to target Blacks than are party chairs residing in counties with small Black populations (60.5 percent versus 28 percent, respectively). Similarly, party chairs residing in counties of large Hispanic populations are significantly more likely to target Hispanics than are party chairs residing in counties with small Hispanic populations (78.7 percent versus 50.2 percent).

At the same time, electoral competitiveness seems to be less important as a contextual characteristic associated with minority targeting. While party chairs in competitive counties report targeting Blacks more than party chairs in noncompetitive counties (45.6 percent and 36.7 percent, respectively), the difference is not statistically significant (at conventional probability levels of $p < .05$). The same is true of Hispanic targeting: 57.1 percent of chairs in competitive counties report targeting Hispanics, compared to 61.4 percent of chairs in noncompetitive counties. Again, this difference is not statistically significant.

To test whether this null finding regarding competitiveness is a function of the distinct coalitions of the Republican and Democratic Parties, I also tested whether partisanship affected these findings, and indeed it affirms our earlier findings regarding the critical difference between the parties in

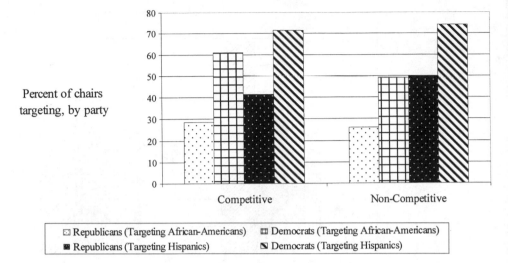

Figure 5.8. Targeting African-Americans and Hispanics by Party, in Competitive and Noncompetitive Counties
Source: 1996 Texas County Party Chairs Survey

mobilizing racial and ethnic minorities. Figure 5.8 shows that Democrats are significantly more likely to target African-Americans and Hispanics in both competitive and noncompetitive counties. This affirms the findings of figure 5.7: it is not competitiveness but party that structures whether minorities are targeted.[6]

Next, I consider whether party leaders are more likely to target individuals who are closer to them ideologically (hypothesis 1) or who are political Independents (hypothesis 2). This analysis provides evidence regarding the general proposition that ideology structures party mobilization, but it also is relevant to the complaint of various Black leaders that Blacks have been marginalized by the Democratic Party due to their high level of voter loyalty. One version of that marginalization is that party leaders devote fewer resources to Blacks because they have essentially been "captured" by the Democrats, in that liberal Blacks do not view the Republican Party as a viable electoral option. So, testing the general premise that parties target groups ideologically close to them also allows us to determine, for example, whether *minority* groups perceived to be more moderate are likewise more likely to be targeted by Republicans.

More specifically, my expectation is that party chairs will target Independents perceived to be moderate (and therefore likely to be true swing

---

[6] Likewise confirming the earlier results, there is no significant difference across competitive and noncompetitive counties in the likelihood that the Republican and Democratic Parties target supporters and Independents: both do, regardless of competitiveness.

voters) and those perceived to be more ideologically close to the party (for Republicans, more conservative, and for Democrats, more liberal). Yet figure 5.9 shows that in only one case is party contacting structured by ideology. In most cases, Republicans and Democrats target African-Americans and Hispanics at the same level, regardless of ideology. The statistical exception to this generalization is for Democrats targeting African-Americans, where Democrats perceiving that African-Americans are liberal in the county are significantly more likely to report targeting African-Americans than those who report that African-Americans are either ideologically conservative or moderate.

Although these reports might be especially sensitive to socially acceptable answers or rationalization on the part of chairs, it is interesting to note that Republicans report targeting Hispanics and African-Americans less when they perceive them to be more conservative than when they perceive them to be moderates or liberals. This is particularly interesting at a time when the Republican leadership has emphasized the particular importance of Hispanics to the party's electoral fortunes in the coming decades.[7]

A MULTIVARIATE ANALYSIS

Because of the possibility that socioeconomic status, group size, and political empowerment are strongly intercorrelated, the most useful analytical evidence is that which tests the independent influence of each of these factors on minority targeting. Table 5.5 presents the results of a probit analysis, where targeting Hispanics and targeting African-Americans are the dependent variables (each a dummy variable where 1 represents targeting, and 0 not targeting), and indicators of socioeconomic status (percentage of the minority group having a high school degree), ideology (on a three-point scale ranging from conservative to liberal, as reported by the county chair), group size (percentage of the county population that is African-American or Hispanic), political empowerment (based on county chair reports as to whether their party had had African-American or Hispanic candidates run for office in the previous two elections), and party (a dummy variable representing the party affiliation of the county chair, where 1 = Democrat) are included as independent variables. In addition, I have included a measure of the size of the voting-age citizen population

---

[7] Similar analyses were run for Republicans' and Democrats' targeting supporters and targeting Independents, by the perceived ideology of supporters and Independents. In both cases (targeting supporters and Independents), there is a significant relationship between ideology and Democratic targeting: supporters who are more liberal are significantly more likely to be targeted by Democratic chairs, as are Independents who are perceived to be more moderate.

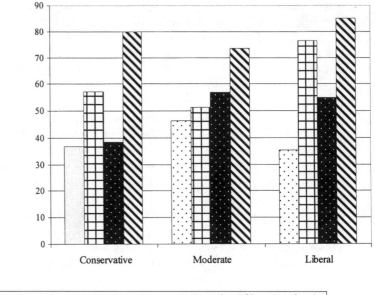

Percent of chairs targeting, by ideology

☐ Republicans (Targeting African-Americans)   ⊞ Democrats (Targeting African-Americans)
■ Republicans (Targeting Hispanics)   ◨ Democrats (Targeting Hispanics)

Figure 5.9. Targeting African-Americans and Hispanics, by Ideology, Controlling for Party
Source: 1996 Texas County Party Chairs Survey

as a control for those counties with relatively large numbers of noncitizen Latinos.[8]

The results for targeting African-Americans and Hispanics are nearly identical substantively and striking. First, as expected based on the party-supporters hypothesis, Democratic chairs are significantly more likely to report targeting both African-Americans and Hispanics. Second, the larger the size of the minority population, the more likely that chairs are to report targeting the particular minority group. Third, none of the other vari-

---

[8] Each of the models was also estimated with the inclusion of the number of mobilizing activities the chair reports engaging in as an additional independent variable, and with party competitiveness and urbanization included as additional independent variables. This variable, which can be interpreted as an indicator of party organizational strength or activity level, is significant as a predictor of targeting any group (minorities, women, party supporters, Independents, etc.). But its inclusion does not affect the substantive findings of any of the models. For reasons of parsimony, I chose to report the models that were made up of variables that had a strong theoretical motivation. Results of the other models are, of course, available upon request.

TABLE 5.5
Multivariate Models of Minority Targeting

	African-Americans	Hispanics
Education	−1.84	−1.98
	(1.91)	(2.01)
Ideology	.11	.21
	(.13)	(.11)
Empowerment	.11	.15
(candidates)	(.22)	(.19)
Group size	2.30°	1.47°°
	(1.21)	(.51)
Competitiveness	.004	.01
	(.18)	(.16)
Party	.81°°	.82°°
	(.19)	(.16)
Percentage voting-age citizens		.29
		(1.27)
Constant	−.23	−.46
	(.65)	(1.13)
N	246	329

Source: 1996 Survey of Texas County Party Chairs.

Note: Table entries are the MLE probit coefficient estimates, followed by the associated standard error in parentheses. The dependent variables are the party chair reports as to whether or not they targeted African-Americans or Hispanics. Education (percentage of African-Americans or Hispanics) and group size (African-American or Hispanic) are county-level measures indicating the percentage of each group with a high school diploma and the population size of the group in the county. Ideology is the county chair's report on whether each group is liberal (1), moderate (2), or conservative (3). Empowerment is based on the chair's report about whether any minorities had been elected in the county during the previous five years; positive responses were coded as "empowered counties" (1) and negative responses were coded as "not empowered" (0). The sample used for estimating the "targeting African-Americans" equation is restricted to those counties where the percentage of Blacks is greater than 1 percent.

°p < .05, two-tailed test of significance. °°p < .01, two-tailed test of significance.

ables is associated with minority targeting. Controlling for party and group size, neither socioeconomic status, group ideology, nor being a high empowerment county is associated with greater targeting of African-Americans or Hispanics.

The latter finding is particularly notable given the prominence of these factors in case studies of electoral politics and journalistic accounts of Black politics. The limitation of those accounts, of course, is that they fail to systematically identify the independent effects of any factors being considered as the reasons why African-Americans or Hispanics are being mobilized.[9]

Finally, I consider whether these general patterns reflect differences in the targeting decisions of Republicans and Democrats. It might be, for example, that Republican chairs are influenced by factors different from those of Democrats when considering whether or not to target African-Americans and Hispanics. Thus I estimated the model in table 5.5 separately for Republican and Democratic chairs. These results are presented in table 5–6.

Although the results are not entirely identical to those presented in table 5.5, they are consistent with regard to socioeconomic status, estimated to be insignificant for each group and party. The only exception for ideology is that Democrats are significantly more likely to target African-Americans who are liberal. The only slightly "positive" difference in these findings is that empowerment is significant for Democratic targeting of Hispanics: where Hispanics are running for office, they are also more likely to be targeted by Democratic chairs. Finally, the size of the minority populations is significant in one case, Republican targeting of Hispanics. Thus, the general finding from table 5.5—where population size is significant and ideology is not—is modestly supported here, with only slight differences in the targeting strategies of Republican and Democratic chairs.

SUMMARY AND CONCLUSION

This chapter began with a simple analysis of party contacting, using individuals' self-reports of being contacted by a political party. These analyses demonstrate that, controlling for class, African-Americans are less likely to be contacted by the Republican Party than are Anglos but are no more likely than Anglos to be contacted by the Democratic Party. This confirms the conventional wisdom that parties target supporters—but that African-Americans are marginalized by the Democratic Party.

Unfortunately, these NES data, though available over a nearly thirty-year period, are restricted to individual—rather than contextual—characteristics. Hence, to confirm these findings regarding class and race at the elite level, as well as to investigate the relative importance of contextual

---

[9] In contrast to these findings, the results for a similar model of targeting women—where socioeconomic status (of whites), ideology of people in the county, women running as candidates, competitiveness, urbanization, and party are included as independent variables—party and ideology are positively associated with targeting women (Democrats and liberal county ideology more likely to report targeting) at $p < 0.05$; socioeconomic status is negatively associated with targeting women (the higher the education level, the less likely women are to be targeted) at $p < 0.05$; and empowerment (women running as candidates) is significant at $p < 0.06$.

Table 5.6
Multivariate Model of Minority Targeting, Controlling for Party

	African-Americans		Hispanics	
	Republicans	Democrats	Republicans	Democrats
Education	−1.63	−2.83	−.37	−4.66
	(2.95)	(2.77)	(2.60)	(3.37)
Ideology	−.10	.40°	.23	.23
	(.18)	(.18)	(.15)	(.19)
Empowerment	−.57	.30	−.18	.62°
(candidates)	(.54)	(.27)	(.26)	(.32)
Group size	1.84	2.98	1.81°°	.49
	(1.67)	(1.86)	(.62)	(.96)
Competitiveness	−.10	.09	−.04	.06
	(.25)	(.26)	(.22)	(.25)
Percentage voting-age			.46	−.08
citizens			(1.7)	(2.03)
Constant	.38	−.03	−1.10	1.35
	(.92)	(.98)	(1.51)	(1.83)
N	116	130	171	158

Source: 1996 Survey of Texas County Party Chairs.
Note: Table entries are the MLE probit coefficient estimates, followed by the associated standard error in parentheses. The dependent variables are the party chair reports as to whether or not they targeted African-Americans or Hispanics. Education (percentage of African-Americans or Hispanics) and group size (African-American or Hispanic) are county-level measures indicating the percentage of each group with a high school diploma and the population size of the group in the county. Ideology is the county chair's report on whether each group is liberal (1), moderate (2), or conservative (3). Empowerment is based on the chair's report about whether any minorities had been elected in the county during the previous five years; positive responses were coded as "empowered counties" (1) and negative responses were coded as "not empowered" (0). The sample used for estimating the "targeting African-Americans" equation is restricted to those counties where the percentage of Blacks is greater than 1 percent.
°$p < .05$, two-tailed test of significance. °°$p < .01$, two-tailed test of significance.

characteristics, additional analyses relied on a survey of party elites during the 1996 presidential election.

The overwhelming substantive conclusion drawn from the party-chair survey is, again, that parties target supporters. That is what party chairs report directly and what indirect evidence based on the relative targeting rates of various social groups suggests. Of particular interest, of course, are the group-related patterns associated with race and ethnicity. Consistent with the party-supporter argument, Democratic chairs are significantly more likely to report targeting African-Americans and Hispanics than are Republicans.

The most consistent "positive" finding about minority targeting is that it is driven by group size: the larger the minority population, the more likely chairs are to report targeting the group. Although this in some senses is a logical constraint—chairs with 0 percent minority populations can hardly report targeting the nonexistent groups—it nonetheless has significant theoretical import, especially at the individual level. What this suggests is that minority individuals living in low-minority areas are less likely to be targeted regardless of their other individual characteristics. It thus emphasizes the importance of the social structure and political context in structuring elite targeting decisions—*not* individual-level characteristics typically considered in studies of party contacting.

Neither socioeconomic status, ideology, nor political empowerment generally has an independent effect on targeting decisions. As null findings go, these are powerful. Although there is considerable dispute regarding the tension between race and class as structuring principles in American politics, the findings here strongly suggest that race and ethnicity structure party politics more than class or ideology. Were socioeconomic status equally effective in influencing targeting patterns, one might believe that increasing economic success of African-Americans and Hispanics would bring with it greater political incorporation. But clearly that is not at work here.

Nor is ideology a counterweight to race and ethnicity. When African-Americans and Hispanics are considered to be more moderate, they are not targeted at higher rates by Republicans and in fact are sometimes targeted *less* by Democrats. Thus, particular groups are ignored "at the extremes" and not necessarily compensated when "in the middle" ideologically.

The one notable exception to these broad conclusions is that of political empowerment, which is associated with greater targeting of Hispanics by Democratic chairs. That political empowerment is not associated with African-American targeting for Democrats suggests that the party is responsive to its minority officeholders, but only in the context of a larger Hispanic population. This finding might be considered a positive one for Hispanics hoping to increase their political clout and be more fully incorporated into electoral politics. But it is likewise discouraging in thinking about future developments in African-American political power.

Each of these findings, of course, must be interpreted within the context of the research design, Texas politics. Although Texas has relatively large and diverse minority communities, the Republican Party now dominates statewide election contests, and the Democrats are in a rebuilding period. At the mass level, the Latino (largely Mexican-American) community has a relatively low turnout rate compared to Latino communities in other states (Shaw, de la Garza, and Lee 2000). Hence, these results may or may not reasonably be generalized to other diverse (yet more competitive) states such as New York and California.

An additional cautionary note is that the evidence is based on the counties and the party county organization as the relevant mobilizing institutions. Electoral mobilization is undoubtedly undertaken by a variety of political elites within sometimes distinct and sometimes overlapping electoral districts and contests. Additional elite-level evidence regarding these other mobilization techniques is necessary to draw broader conclusions regarding the nature of elite mobilization.

Having established the importance of partisanship, group size, and empowerment in the targeting decisions of party chairs, I now consider the individual-level evidence regarding the importance of these factors in structuring the mobilization patterns of racial and ethnic minorities. That is, if these findings based on studies of party elites in Texas are reflected in individuals' self-reports of being mobilized to participate in campaign work—as identified by the CPS—then this enhances the confidence we have in the elite-level evidence presented in this chapter. Furthermore, the CPS allows us to consider mobilization by nonparty institutions, which likewise enhances the findings of this chapter. Hence, the goals of chapter 6 are to consider the extent to which the findings on elite behavior presented in this chapter are reflected in individual self-reports and how mobilization differs across types of participation.

Chapter Six

MINORITY POLITICAL MOBILIZATION

THE literature on Latino and African-American political participation highlights the importance of candidate and group mobilization. This chapter seeks to add to that evidence with an assessment of the relative importance of race/ethnicity versus class, and individual versus contextual factors in structuring who is mobilized to participate.

Unfortunately, data on elite or institutional efforts to mobilize individuals, regardless of race and ethnicity, are not available. Although the CPS has the most comprehensive array of data on minorities, mobilization, and participation, Verba, Schlozman, and Brady's focus is on *institutional*, or *civic, mobilization*, that is, how *nonpolitical* institutions mobilize participation both through direct requests to participate and through developing individuals' skills that can be transferred to political activity (Verba, Schlozman, and Brady 1995: 145–49 and chapter 13).

Given Verba, Schlozman, and Brady's extensive treatment of civic mobilization, I pay little attention to it here. Instead I focus on *particularized mobilization*, which refers to specific requests of individuals to participate in particular types of activities such as campaigning, contacting government officials, or getting involved in local politics. Particularized mobilization, the more traditional conceptualization of political mobilization used in previous empirical studies, is operationalized as individuals' self-reports of being contacted (and asked to vote) by a political party or organization.

Consistent with earlier studies of particularized mobilization, the work of Verba, Schlozman, and Brady finds that high-status individuals are more likely to be mobilized than low-status individuals. They also add to earlier studies, noting that most requests for participation come from personal acquaintances; that not all participation is mobilized (many individuals act "spontaneously" without benefit of being asked to participate); and that not all requests to participate generate a positive response.

Verba, Schlozman, and Brady also find that (particularized) mobilization is structured by race/ethnicity. While 40.1 percent of Anglos report being mobilized to contact a government official, only 19 percent of African-Americans and 9.3 percent of Latinos report being similarly mobilized. Similar gaps are evidenced for local activity and campaign mobilization (see figure 6.1).

In contrast, 24.9 percent of Anglos, 25.5 percent of African Americans,

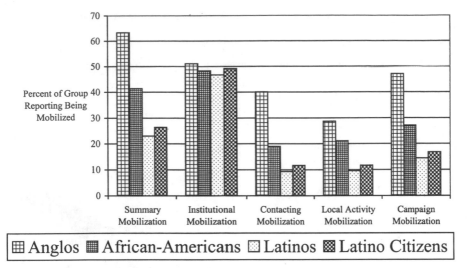

Figure 6.1. Mobilization to Particular Activities, by Race/Ethnicity
Source: CPS. Data are unweighted.

and 23.7 percent of Latinos report being mobilized at church; 16.6 percent of Anglos, 13.2 percent of African-Americans, and 10.7 percent of Latinos report being mobilized on the job; and 26.9 percent of Anglos, 25.9 percent of African-Americans, and 27.1 percent of Latinos report being mobilized in voluntary organizations.[1] Combining the self-reports of respondents across these three measures yields an overall institutional mobilization level that is similar across groups. As shown in figure 6.1, 51.1 percent of Anglos, 48.3 percent of African-Americans, 46.7 percent of Latinos, and 49.2 percent of Latino citizens report being mobilized in one of these institutional contexts.

This contrast between the two types of mobilization likely reflects differences in the extent to which each type of mobilization is structured by political versus nonpolitical institutions. Institutional mobilization reflects more on the extent to which the workplace, church, and voluntary associations are politicized in the United States, while particularized mobilization reflects the strategic efforts of political institutions such as parties, political

---

[1] This data is presented in chapter 3, figure 3.4 and is not repeated here in their entirety. The percentages reported in table 2.4 on institutional mobilization and discussed here differ from Verba, Schlozman, and Brady's (1995) reported data in some cases because I report the percentage of all individuals in the survey reporting that they were mobilized, while they report the percentage of individuals affiliated with each institution who report being mobilized. Hence, the differences in our numbers primarily reflect differences in each racial/ethnic group's level of institutional affiliation.

candidates, and groups to expand conflict in their favor by mobilizing their supporters.

Because involvement in civic institutions is not necessarily structured by race, neither would the level of mobilization within these institutions be distinctive across racial/ethnic groups. This interpretation is broadly consistent with Verba, Schlozman, and Brady's (1995) discussion of the critical importance of civic institutions to the development of political skills—in one sense suggesting that there are political *effects*, rather than *sources*, of institutional mobilization.

Particularized mobilization, however, is presumed to reflect the strategic decisions of political elites regarding who their likely supporters are, as well as who likely participants are (see, e.g., Rosenstone and Hansen 1993). For that reason, this chapter tests the extent to which class, ideology (or partisanship), group size, and minority empowerment—the four components introduced in chapter 1—structure particularized contacting of individuals.

Class and ideology are presumed to reflect the decisions of political institutions to mobilize those individuals likely to participate and party supporters, as suggested in chapter 4. Racial/ethnic group size is a contextual feature that reflects the extent to which race structures elite decision making as well as individuals' calculations of the costs and benefits of both mobilizing others and deciding to engage in political activity. Finally, political empowerment is an indicator of the extent to which minority communities have been successful in gaining access to public authority and, I assume, the potential of minority elites to target members of their own racial/ethnic groups.

Two central questions are addressed: To what extent do these factors account for different mobilization levels across racial/ethnic groups? Is each of these factors equally as important in explaining minority mobilization as well as Anglo mobilization? My assumption is that the extent to which elites seek to mobilize higher-status individuals, supporters, and racial/ethnic minorities will be reflected in individuals' self-reports of whether they have been recruited to political activities. The analyses below thus offer particularly demanding (i.e., conservative) tests of this theoretical model.

THEORETICAL FRAMEWORKS: GROUP SIZE AND POLITICAL EMPOWERMENT

Since no empirical studies to date have examined the relationship between group size and mobilization, and political empowerment and mobilization, I would like to briefly discuss the literatures relevant to group size and emplowerment, clarifying how they might be extrapolated to patterns of political mobilization. Aside from the anecdotal claims described in chapters 1 and 2, group size has been studied primarily as an explanation for whites' voting behavior in the South, while political empowerment has been studied almost exclusively as a predictor of political participation of African-Americans.

Group Size

Group size has been used most extensively by Micheal Giles and various coauthors to study racial politics in the South (see, e.g., Giles and Evans 1985, 1986). Giles extends power conflict theory to the case of white political behavior in the South, arguing that as the threat from Blacks increases, whites will act to protect their interests. Threat is measured by the size of the Black population in the relevant electoral district. Consistent with power conflict theory, the work of Giles and Hertz (1994) finds that high Black population concentrations in Louisana parishes are associated with greater Republican Party identification, while Giles and Buckner (1993) find high Black population concentrations associated with greater support for the senatorial candidacy of conservative segregationist David Duke (but also see Voss 1996a, 1996b, Giles and Buckner 1996).

While individual-level evidence regarding group threat is scarce, various scholars have presented evidence fairly consistent with the notion that racial context is relevant to political attitudes. Oliver and Mendelberg (1998), for example, find that neighborhood and metropolitan racial contexts are occasionally associated with whites' opinions on racial policy preferences. Other scholars have incorporated minority group size in models of turnout using aggregate-level data (see, e.g., Fort 1995; Hill and Leighley 1999; Affigne 1994; Affigne and Tate 1993), typically observing a negative association between minority group size and turnout.

In determining whether group size is associated with higher levels of mobilization (and, in chapter 7, participation) of Latinos as well as Blacks, an additional consideration is the extent to which large concentrations of Latinos is also associated with a high incidence of noncitizenship. De la Garza and DeSipio (1997: 99–111) argue that "high rates of noncitizenship depress community-wide electoral impact and create large constituencies with few votes." As a result, elites devote only limited resources to mobilizing the Latino community and more generally focus on likely participants. Since "likely participants" are typically individuals with high levels of education and income, this, too, disadvantages the Latino community as Latinos—with a relatively large proportion of immigrants and youth—tend to have lower levels of education and income. De la Garza and DeSipio argue further that with the strategic disadvantage of high levels of noncitizenship

compounded by the lower levels of socioeconomic status of Latinos, political parties pay little attention to the Latino community. While de la Garza,
Menchaca, and DeSipio (1994) provide some case-study evidence from
Houston, Texas, on this point, no broader, more systematic evidence has
been offered to test this claim.

Thus, although one of the major implications of Uhlaner's (1989b) formal model is that higher concentrations of minorities should lead to more
highly organized social and political networks and hence higher levels of
mobilization and participation, we have no systematic evidence that group
size in fact structures minority groups' political mobilization. The empirical
evidence in this chapter thus offers an important test of group size as a
stimulus of political mobilization of both majority and minority racial/eth-
nic groups.

Political Empowerment

Political empowerment as a model for minority politics was first offered by
Browning, Marshall, and Tabb (1984) in response to the observation that
"protest was not enough" to secure minority representation in local politics
and decision making. Policy representation, they argue, depends on the
extent to which minorities are incorporated into local government decision-making bodies through their successful election to office and, once
elected, the ability to build coalitions with nonminority elected officials.

Bobo and Gilliam (1990) note the limitations of early studies of Black
participation that relied on data from the early 1960s, a time when few
civil rights gains had been made and thus prior to the dramatic increase in
the number of Black elected officials. They argue that minority empowerment in the post-1960s period should influence mass participation because
the macro political environment structures individuals' calculations of the
costs and benefits of political activity. Hence, where Blacks hold more
positions of power, they should see greater value in participating and
therefore "participate at rates equal to, or possibly greater than, whites"
(Bobo and Gilliam 1990: 379). Moreover, these higher levels of participation result from the more positive civic orientations and political attitudes
held by Blacks living in empowered areas.

Bobo and Gilliam use data from the 1987 General Social Survey to test
these propositions, identifying primary sampling units with a major city
having a Black mayor as high-empowerment areas.[2] They find that, controlling for socioeconomic status, Blacks in high-empowerment areas participate more than whites and that this greater participation is stimulated

[2] These cities included Atlanta, Baltimore, Birmingham, Chicago, Dayton, Detroit, Los Angeles, Newark, Philadelphia, Richmond, and Washington.

by higher levels of political knowledge and engagement (high levels of efficacy and trustfulness).

The psychological "linkage" mechanism between Black political empowerment and participation is consistent with the emphasis of mass behavior research on individual attributes as predictors of participation. Bobo and Gilliam mention that these findings could be interpreted to reflect "that black empowerment is the outcome of higher participation brought about by registration and turnout drives when a viable candidate emerges," but dismiss this possibility "on logical and empirical grounds" (387).[3] However, several alternative mechanisms might also account for this linkage.

Specifically, high-empowerment areas may be more politicized along racially relevant lines. The same cities that elect Black mayors are likely to have an established set of political organizations—either oriented exclusively to Blacks or more generally inclusive of Blacks—and informal patterns of social interaction that increase the likelihood that Blacks are *recruited* to participate. Higher levels of mobilization in political organizations, elite activities, and informal political networks should, in turn, enhance minority participation.

This alternative interpretation is derived in part from Rosenstone and Hansen's (1993) argument that participation patterns reflect the mobilizing activities of political elites and informal patterns of social interaction more than do changes in individuals' attributes (education or income levels, for example). Highly educated individuals, for example, are more likely to participate not solely because they have greater cognitive skills, but also because they are more likely to be targeted by elites (parties and candidates) and recruited to participate.

Despite the persuasiveness of Bobo and Gilliam's evidence—and the acknowledgment of the importance of political empowerment in minority politics—no existing studies have documented its importance as a predictor of *mobilization* for African-Americans or its significance for *Latino* mobilization or participation. Yet one could certainly argue that both historical and contemporary organizing efforts on the part of Latino political communities have stressed the importance of political incorporation—largely through high levels of voter registration and the successful election of Latino candidates.

Hero (1992, chapter 7), for example, discusses the importance of the electoral integration of ethnic minorities in urban politics and offers the example of the election of Federico Peña as mayor of Denver in 1987.

---

[3] Their main points are that Blacks are not newcomers to elective office in most of the empowered cities and the dependent variables are patterns of behavior; that the effects are not restricted to voter turnout; and that if empowerment reflected short-term influences like registration drives, it should have strong direct effects on participation, rather than working almost entirely through Blacks' political attitudes and knowledge.

While Hero notes that Peña emphasized high minority turnout in his second (and successful) run for office in 1987, the consequences of that election for the Latino (and African-American) community in Denver are unknown. We simply have no evidence that, generally, the political empowerment of Latinos stimulates Latino participation in politics. Hence, the implied significance of Latino candidates' successful election to office that motivates these case studies is more an assumption than a carefully established pattern in minority politics.

The need to document this assumption is particularly acute in that one of its premises is that the structure of African-American electoral politics is the same as that of Latino politics: if we understand one minority group, we understand them all. This may not be the case based on the unique historical, social, and legal experiences that have defined the political opportunities available to these two distinctive communities. Without more comparable and systematic evidence as to the effects of political empowerment, the validity of this assumption is also unknown.

In terms of the models introduced in chapter 1, I posit that elite mobilization structures relational goods (i.e., recruitment) of both African-Americans and Latinos to the extent to which both groups have been systematically excluded from positions of political power. Thus, this relationship is likely to be weaker for Latinos than for Blacks, due to the greater likelihood of their participation in broader electoral coalitions with Anglos. Further, I expect group size to be important in structuring the mobilization of both African-Americans and Latinos but weaker for African-Americans than for Latinos. The reasoning behind this expectation is that African-Americans are far less likely to be pivotal groups in electoral politics, and the relevance of African-American group size to political behavior will reflect this.

A NOTE ON EMPOWERMENT AND GROUP SIZE AS POLITICAL CONTEXT

Since previous studies have focused almost exclusively on class and ideology as individual-level factors, there is little precedent as to how best to model the effects of group size and political empowerment on individuals' likelihood of being mobilized. In the analyses that follow, I use two different strategies. First, I use group size and political empowerment as predictors of individual behavior, assuming that they have an independent, linear effect on the probability of being mobilized. This is similar to previous research in which the effects of individuals' political or social context are hypothesized to have an independent influence on their behavior.

Leighley and Nagler (1992), for example, examine the effects of party competition on individuals' likelihood of voting by including party competition—a contextual measure indicating how competitive the state in which the individual resides is—as another independent variable in a turnout model made up primarily of individual-level characteristics such as education, income, and age. As another example, Leighley (1990) tests whether individuals residing in high-status neighborhoods are more likely to participate than individuals residing in low-status neighborhoods by including the individuals' neighborhood education level as a predictor of participation, controlling for the individual's own level of education.

A less typical approach to testing for contextual effects is to estimate (participation) models separately for different levels of the contextual characteristic of interest. The advantage of this approach is that it allows the estimated effects of *all* the predictor variables in a model to vary across contexts. In effect, this approach tests whether the model that is being estimated simply works differently in different contexts. It is thus a more encompassing approach to the study of contextual effects. The disadvantage, of course, is that it tends to lack parsimony: suddenly the sample of interest is split into two or three subsamples. While the use of interaction terms can, theoretically, be used to estimate these models simultaneously, in practice this is usually tenuous as the high number of interaction terms introduces a relatively high level of collinearity into the models being estimated. Nonetheless, because evidence regarding the effects of group size and empowerment on mobilization and participation is either limited or nonexistent, I present both types of analyses below.

DATA AND MEASURES

The analysis below relies on Verba, Schlozman, and Brady's (1995) CPS supplemented with data on minority group size and political empowerment. The CPS, a representative national survey, was conducted in 1989–90 and includes oversamples of political activists, Blacks, and Latinos (see Verba, Schlozman, and Brady [1995] and Verba et al. [1993a] for a more detailed description of the sampling and weighting details). These survey data are supplemented with measures of Black and Latino political empowerment drawn from *Black Elected Officials: A National Roster, 1991* (Joint Center for Political and Economic Studies 1992) and from the *1992 National Roster of Hispanic Elected Officials* (National Association of Latino Elected Officials: 1992). Each roster lists elected Black or Latino officials in local, state, and federal offices as of January 1991.[4]

Empowerment is measured by matching the addresses of mayors, and

---

[4] The listings thus include Blacks or Latinos sworn into office during January 1991, which means that cities with Black or Latino mayors sworn in during that month may not have been high-empowerment areas at the time of the CPS survey. I assume that the error introduced by these few cases is relatively small, though I have not attempted to directly estimate it.

the counties they live in, to CPS respondents' zip codes, by county. That is, the county of the zip code listed for Black and Latino elected mayors was linked to every CPS respondent's county, which was also identified by the respondent's self-reported zip code. Thus, individuals living in a county with a listed Black (or Latino) mayor are coded as "empowered" for either Black (or Latino) empowerment.[5] All individuals living in the same county—though in different zip code areas—would be coded the same on either measure of empowerment.[6] This is similar to Bobo and Gilliam's (1990) measure, where all individuals living in a primary sampling unit where the major city had a Black mayor were coded as living in areas of Black empowerment. More specifically, the empowerment measures are dummy variables, with 1 indicating the presen·e of a Black or Latino mayor in the county. All respondents whose zip codes did not map to an elected Black or Latino mayor were coded as living in a low-empowerment area (0).

The measure of group size is the percentage of the respondent's local context (i.e., zip code) made up of Anglos, Blacks, or Latinos. This measure is similar to that employed by Giles and Evans (1986), Giles and Hertz (1994), and Giles and Buckner (1993), who use the Black percentage of the parish population as an indicator of threat for whites. The population data used to measure group size are taken from the Census Bureau's (1990) *Census of Population and Housing*, where survey respondents are assigned the size of their own ethnic group in their zip code region.[7]

Socioeconomic status is operationalized with standard measures of the individual's education level and reported level of family income. Ideology is measured using three separate dummy variables for Republicans, Democrats, and Independents, with the excluded analytical category being those individuals who claim no party identification, another party identification, or do not know their partisan affiliation.

The potentially negative impact of noncitizenship is tested using two different measures in the analyses below, depending on the dependent variable being used. First, and more important, I have estimated each of the models with and without a variable measuring the percentage of noncitizens in the respondent's zip code region. This is perhaps the most direct test of de la Garza and DeSipio's (1997) claim that Latinos are mo-

---

[5] An exception to this being a county-wide measure was in the case of large metropolitan areas that spanned several counties, where all individuals in the metropolitan area (based on city name) were coded the same.

[6] All of the analyses below were run separately using a citywide (rather than county-wide) empowerment measure, with only marginal differences in the substantive implications. Thus, for reasons of space only those analyses with the county-wide measure are reported.

[7] The population data used to measure group size are taken from the Census Bureau's 1990 Census of Population and Housing, where survey respondents are assigned the size of their own ethnic group in their zip code region.

bilized less in part due to higher levels of noncitizenship. However, since this variable is rarely significant in these models, I note this and, for reasons of parsimony, report the models without this contextual characteristic. I also note whether any substantive changes in the model results occur when including it. Second, in some of the models reported below I include a control for whether the respondent is a U.S. citizen. In some cases this means presenting separate analyses of Latino citizens and Latinos, while in others this is a dichotomous independent variable (where 1 = citizen, 0 = noncitizen) that is added to multivariate equations.

In this as well as subsequent chapters I often analyze Latinos and Latino citizens separately, as it is likely that mobilization efforts are directed toward citizens rather than noncitizens (particularly in the case of electoral mobilization). But determining who is a citizen and who is not is undoubtedly an error-filled exercise for political elites. Moreover, for some types of participation, citizenship is not required, and so examining Latinos, regardless of citizenship, as a group is important. The latter approach also provides the advantage of being able to include substantially more respondents in the analysis, and hence allows for more precise statistical analyses.

The primary dependent variables used in this chapter are a series of three dichotomous variables indicating whether the individual reports being asked to participate in one of three particular ways. *Campaign mobilization* refers to whether the individual was asked to engage in campaign activities; *contacting mobilization* refers to whether the individual was asked to contact a government official; and *local activity mobilization* refers to whether the individual was asked to get involved in a local public or political issue. Occasionally I also use a measure of overall mobilization, which is the sum of the three mobilization items.

SOURCES OF MOBILIZATION

With relatively little survey data available on mobilization patterns across racial/ethnic groups, I begin with some additional descriptive information on the nature of individuals' recruitment into political activity. Uhlaner's (1989b) "relational goods" argument suggests that the sources of effective mobilization efforts will likely differ for Anglos and members of minority groups. One of the key aspects of relational goods is that they result from interpersonal identification and interaction. Hence, more "effective" or successful mobilization efforts directed toward minorities are likely to come from group members, especially those who are known by the mobilization target (see also Chong 1991).

So what are the sources of particularized mobilization, and do they differ for Anglos, African-Americans, and Latinos? Figure 6.2 shows the proportion of each group reporting being mobilized by four different sources:

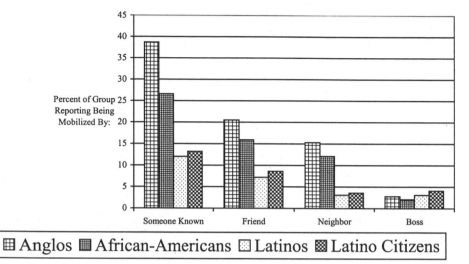

Figure 6.2. Mobilization Sources, by Race/Ethnicity

Note: Each column represents the proportion of each racial/ethnic group recruited by each type of source. The percentages thus reflect different recruitment levels across racial/ethnic groups.

Source: CPS. Data are unweighted.

someone known to them, a friend (or relative), a neighbor, and a boss. These sources are drawn from each type of particularized mobilization used in the analysis below. For each type of mobilization—campaigning, contacting, and local activity—individuals who reported being recruited were then asked whether the individual who asked them was someone they know, a friend, a neighbor, or a boss.

The data reported in figure 6.2 reflect the proportion of the entire racial/ethnic group recruited by each particular source (as opposed to the proportion of those individuals who were recruited, which is reported in figures 6.3a–d). For each mobilization source, then, the relative proportions across groups reflect differential levels of mobilization; Anglos report being mobilized more by each source than do African-Americans, who in turn report being mobilized more than Latinos and Latino citizens.

The point to note in figure 6.2 is that for each group, the proportion of individuals reporting that they were mobilized by a boss is substantially lower than those reporting being mobilized by someone they know, a friend, or a neighbor. Hence, in terms of particularized mobilization, most requests emanate from sources who have a personal acquaintance with the target of their efforts. This suggests a high potential for effective mobilization efforts in general.

Figures 6.3a, b, c, and d show the sources of mobilization as a proportion

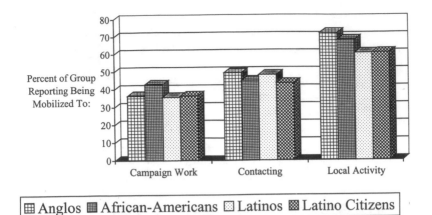

Figure 6.3a. Mobilization by Someone Known, by Race/Ethnicity

Note: Each column represents the proportion of *recruited* individuals within each racial/ethnic group recruited by each particular sources. Individuals not recruited by anyone are coded as missing; individuals who were recruited but not by that particular source are coded as zero, those who were recruited by that particular source are coded as one. The percentages thus reflect the relative incidence of recruitment from each source, controlling for differences in overall levels of recruitment across racial/ethnic groups.

Source: CPS. Data are unweighted.

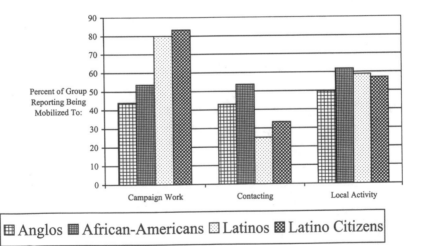

Figure 6.3b. Mobilization by Friend, by Race/Ethnicity

Note: Each column represents the proportion of *recruited* individuals within each racial/ethnic group recruited by each particular sources. Individuals not recruited by anyone are coded as missing; individuals who were recruited but not by that particular source are coded as zero, those who were recruited by that particular source are coded as one. The percentages thus reflect the relative incidence of recruitment from each source, controlling for differences in overall levels of recruitment across racial/ethnic groups.

Source: CPS. Data are unweighted.

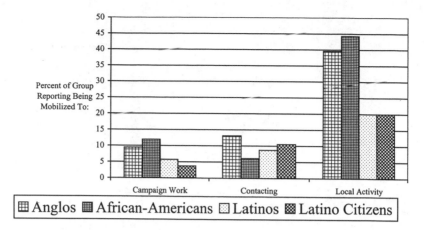

Figure 6.3c. Mobilization by Neighbor, by Race/Ethnicity

Note: Each column represents the proportion of *recruited* individuals within each racial/ethnic group recruited by each particular sources. Individuals not recruited by anyone are coded as missing; individuals who were recruited but not by that particular source are coded as zero, those who were recruited by that particular source are coded as one. The percentages thus reflect the relative incidence of recruitment from each source, controlling for differences in overall levels of recruitment across racial/ethnic groups.

Source: CPS. Data are unweighted.

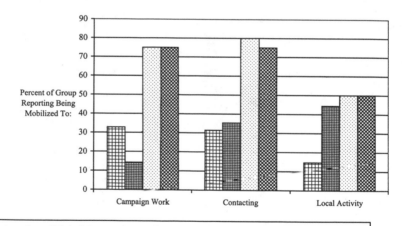

Figure 6.3d. Mobilization by Boss, by Race/Ethnicity

Note: Each column represents the proportion of *recruited* individuals within each racial/ethnic group recruited by each particular sources. Individuals not recruited by anyone are coded as missing; individuals who were recruited but not by that particular source are coded as zero, those who were recruited by that particular source are coded as one. The percentages thus reflect the relative incidence of recruitment from each source, controlling for differences in overall levels of recruitment across racial/ethnic groups.

Source: CPS. Data are unweighted.

of those individuals in each group who report being mobilized. This provides a more accurate basis on which to compare the sources of mobilization across groups. In addition, the mobilization source is presented by each type of political activity to which individuals were recruited. Several points are important to note here.

First, there is little difference across racial/ethnic groups in the proportion of those mobilized who report being mobilized by someone they know, and this is true for each type of mobilization. Approximately 36 percent of Anglos, 43 percent of African-Americans, and 36 percent of Latinos and Latino citizens report being mobilized to do campaign work by someone they know. Higher proportions—and consistently higher for each group—report being mobilized to contact a government official by someone they know, with even higher proportions of individuals recruited to engage in local community activities reporting the same.

Second, the relatively similar levels of mobilization by someone known across racial/ethnic groups evidenced for campaign work mobilization appear to be somewhat different for mobilization by friends (or relatives). African-Americans are more likely than Anglos to report being mobilized by a friend, for campaign work, contacting, and local activity. Neighbors tend to mobilize individuals to local activity, rather than campaign work and contacting, with Anglos and African-Americans much more likely than Latinos to report being mobilized by neighbors. Unfortunately, the relatively small numbers of Latinos and Latino citizens being mobilized by friends and neighbors makes it difficult to confidently assess whether Latinos, too, tend to be mobilized in greater proportion by friends and neighbors.

Third, and related, it is difficult to interpret the numbers of mobilization by bosses, as the numbers even for Anglos are so small. Nonetheless, it appears that Anglos are more likely than African-Americans to be recruited by their boss for campaign work. Overall, then, these data suggest that much of the particularized mobilization that occurs is initiated by individuals known by their targets. This general finding suggests that mobilization of African-Americans and Latinos does not necessarily emanate from "friends and neighbors" (and those with interpersonal relationships) any more so than it does for Anglos. This, combined with the fact that these groups tend to be mobilized less than Anglos, suggests that whether such efforts are more effective in gaining positive responses to requests for participation is especially important.

CLASS, IDEOLOGY, GROUP SIZE, AND EMPOWERMENT

Table 6.1 presents a version of the basic mobilization model estimated separately for each racial/ethnic group; the same model was estimated for

TABLE 6.1

Mobilization Model, Estimated by Race/Ethnicity

	Anglos	African-Americans	Latinos	Latino Citizens
Education	.13°°	.11°°	.04°°	.07°°
	(.01)	(.02)	(.01)	(.02)
Family income	.07°°	.08°°	.04°°	.04°°
	(.01)	(.02)	(.02)	(.02)
Democratic	.22°	.21	.003	.03
	(.12)	(.21)	(.14)	(.21)
Republican	.26°	−.14	.09	.04
	(.13)	(.28)	(.16)	(.23)
Independent	.30°°	.01	−.21	−.24
	(.13)	(.24)	(.17)	(.23)
Group size	−.09	−.19	.20	.13
	(.16)	(.18)	(.22)	(.30)
Minority empowerment	−.06			
	(.06)			
Black empowerment		.09		
		(.11)		
Latino empowerment			−.02	−.04
			(.12)	(.16)
U.S. citizen	.32°	.40°	.09	−.61
	(.14)	(.24)	(.10)	(.74)
Percent noncitizen	.03	−.30	−.63	
	(.58)	(.61)	(.49)	
Constant	−1.65°°	−1.57°°	−.46°	−.65°
	(.27)	(.37)	(.20)	(.33)
Adjusted R2	.23	.23	.12	.12
N	1,232	338	222	152

Source: CPS. Data are unweighted.

Note: Table entries are OLS regression coefficients, with the associated standard error in parentheses. The dependent variable is whether the individual was asked to engage in campaign work, local activity, or contacting government officials, and thus ranges from 0 to 3. Group size refers to the proportion of the population in the individual's neighborhood/zip code region that is the same as the individual's self-identified race/ethnicity. Empowerment refers to Black empowerment for African-Americans, Latino empowerment for Latinos, and minority (either Black or Latino) empowerment for Anglos.
°$p < .05$, one-tailed test of significance. °°$p < .01$, one-tailed test of significance.

the three types of mobilization separately, with few substantive differences, as indicated by statistical significance. Given the centrality of socioeconomic status and ideology in previous analyses of party contacting, it is not surprising to find that education, income, and each of the ideological identifiers is significantly and positively associated with being mobilized for

Anglos. Further, the findings regarding class also hold for African-Americans and Latinos. Thus, high-status individuals—whether Anglo, African-American, or Latino—are more likely to be mobilized than low-status individuals.

The association between ideology and being mobilized varies across groups, but in a pattern that is entirely consistent with anecdotal evidence. While Anglos who claim any ideological position are more likely to report being mobilized than those who do not, neither African-Americans nor Latinos, whether citizens or not, appear to be targeted in mobilization efforts. This likely reflects the central importance of high-status individuals to both parties as well as other political institutions seeking to mobilize political participation.

African-Americans often argue that they are overlooked by the Democratic Party due to their traditional loyalties to the Democratic Party. But even Independent Blacks fail to be mobilized more. Likewise, neither Latino Independents nor partisans are significantly more likely to report being mobilized. This finding might also reflect the lower levels of participation among Latinos in some locales and thus emphasizes how political parties, as well as other institutions, are likely to target those who have higher probabilities of participating (Brady, Schlozman, and Verba 1999).

Finally, although citizenship as an individual- and contextual-level characteristic is included in each model, only individual-level citizenship is significant as a predictor of mobilization: Anglos and African-Americans who are citizens are more likely to report being mobilized. These results might also be interpreted as failing to support de la Garza and DeSipio's (1997) claim that Latinos are less likely to be mobilized due to residing in areas of high noncitizenship. However, their claim that Latinos are targeted less because parties focus on likely participants is indeed supported by the ideology/partisanship results.

Thus, the results on the effects of ideology on mobilization confirm the institutional basis of partisan mobilization: parties contact supporters, and parties contact those who are most likely to participate. One clear consequence of this is that racial and ethnic minorities are typically mobilized less.

To assess the effects of group size and empowerment on mobilization patterns I have included in table 6.1 appropriate group-size and empowerment variables for each group. I assume that African-Americans and Latinos will be affected only by their own groups' characteristics (though I consider a variation on that assumption in chapter 8). Thus, for Blacks, only Black empowerment and Black population size are included as predictors of mobilization, while for Latinos only Latino empowerment and Latino population size are included. For Anglos, I chose to include Anglo population size and an indicator of minority empowerment, that is, the presence of either Black or Latino elected officials in the county.

Political empowerment is insignificant as a predictor of mobilization for Anglos as well as African-Americans and Latinos. Moreover, group size is also not associated with overall levels of mobilization for Anglos, African-Americans, or Latinos. Neither African-Americans nor Latinos are more or less likely to be mobilized when residing in areas of high minority populations, despite Uhlaner's (1989b) claim to the contrary. Also, to the extent that political empowerment reflects formal leadership, it suggests that elected minority leaders do not necessarily target other group members or, indirectly, cannot rely on established social and political institutions to do so.

At the same time, these findings suggest that anecdotal claims about the disadvantages associated with minority group size, or the advantages associated with empowerment, are not sustained when tested simultaneously with class and ideology as predictors of being mobilized.[8] On first blush, then, it appears that the individual-level characteristics of class and ideology structure mobilization far more than any group-related characteristics, regardless of majority or minority group status.

This conclusion must be modified somewhat, however, when one considers the alternative specification of empowerment and group size as contextual characteristics. Table 6.2 presents the results of the basic mobilization model estimated separately for African-Americans and Latinos living in (Black or Latino) nonempowerment areas and those living in empowerment areas. The results are essentially the same as those presented in table 6.1, in that they confirm the central role of class in determining who is mobilized, and find little of importance in terms of empowerment as a contextual characteristic structuring political mobilization of either African-Americans or Latinos.

However, there are two important differences. First, in areas of Black empowerment, African-Americans who identify as Democrats are significantly more likely to report being mobilized. This suggests that one consequence of residing in an area of Black empowerment is that party mobilization directed toward supporters is enhanced—in a way that is not evidenced for African-Americans in areas of Black nonempowerment. This result must be interpreted carefully, of course, in that sharing in formal governance of a community might energize the efforts of the local party in mobilizing individuals to participate—or, alternatively, having energized the party faithful, Blacks might be more likely to hold office.

This problem challenges Bobo and Gilliam's original findings and cannot be resolved here. I would note, however, that this analysis focuses on mo-

---

[8] These models were also estimated including the squared value of minority group size to test for a nonlinear relationship between group size and mobilization. Each of these coefficient estimates was insignificant, and so I chose not to report them. For similar results, see Leighley and Vedlitz (1999).

TABLE 6.2
Overall Mobilization Models, by Empowerment (Blacks and Latinos Estimated Separately)

	African-Americans Overall Mobilization		Latinos Overall Mobilization	
	Black Empowerment	Black Non-empowerment	Latino Empowerment	Latino Non-empowerment
Education	.08°°	.12°°	.03	.05°°
	(.03)	(.03)	(.02)	(.02)
Income	.10°°	.06°°	.05°	.04°
	(.02)	(.02)	(.03)	(.02)
Democratic	1.07°	−.005	.10	−.08
	(.53)	(.23)	(.21)	(.22)
Republican	.46	−.17	.03	.06
	(.60)	(.33)	(.25)	(.24)
Independent	.72	−.09	−.21	−.24
	(.56)	(.28)	(.28)	(.24)
Group size	−.48°	−.04	.04	.32
	(.28)	(.26)	(.32)	(.32)
Citizen	.17	.53°	.07	.13
	(.46)	(.29)	(.18)	(.13)
Percent noncit-	−.89	−.17	.32	−1.11°
izen	(1.01)	(.81)	(.92)	(.64)
Constant	−1.70°	1.69°°	−.45	−.45
	(.83)	(.44)	(.29)	(.34)
Adjusted R2	.25	.21	.08	.12
N	156	182	86	136

Source: CPS. Data are unweighted.

Note: Table entries are OLS regression coefficients, with the associated standard error in parentheses. The dependent variable is whether the individual was asked to engage in campaign work, local activity, or contacting government officials, and thus ranges from 0 to 3. Group size refers to the proportion of the population in the individual's neighborhood/zip code region that is the same as the individual's self-identified race/ethnicity (African-American or Latino).

°$p < .05$, one-tailed test of significance. °°$p < .01$, one-tailed test of significance.

bilization not just to campaign activities, but also to local community activities and contacting government officials. Were this effect limited to mobilization to campaign activities alone—which it is not—then it would be tempting to argue that Black empowerment is a consequence of an invigorated party politics. Since this finding holds for all types of mobilization, I would argue that the alternative interpretation is more appropriate: African-Americans who reside in areas of empowerment are more likely to be targeted by African-American leaders and thus become more active in mobilizing participation of other African-Americans.

Second, it is only in areas of Black empowerment where group size matters for either Blacks or Latinos. In areas of Black empowerment, the larger the size of the Black population, the less likely African-Americans are to be mobilized. Once again, Uhlaner's expectations regarding the positive effect of group size on minorities is challenged. Instead, the negative association between group size and mobilization might reflect on Chong's argument regarding the social incentives of participation, where there would be a greater likelihood of knowing other Blacks—and observing their contributions to collective-action efforts—in smaller Black populations. Alternatively, the extent to which large Black population concentrations are associated with legally mandated electoral districts concentrating Blacks, both elite and citizen responses to large group size may be modified. Taken together, these two contextual findings suggest a challenge for the Black community: the very characteristic that leads to the greater likelihood of being empowered also depresses the mobilizing activities within the Black community.

Similar results are obtained when analyzing group size as a contextual characteristic: class—and not contextual group characteristics—structures mobilization. As shown in table 6.3, education and income are significant predictors of being mobilized, while none of the ideological or partisan affiliation variables is significant. Again, two exceptions emerge. First, in areas of small Black group size, empowerment is a significant predictor of mobilization: African-Americans residing in areas of low Black population are significantly more likely to be mobilized if they reside in an area of Black empowerment. This provides some additional, indirect evidence for the claim I made above, that empowerment increases mobilization within the African-American community.

Second, Latinos who identify as Independents and live in areas of large Latino populations are significantly less likely to be mobilized, while Independent identification has no effect on mobilizing Latinos living in areas of small Latino population size. This might offer some indirect support for de la Garza and DeSipio's claim that Latinos are mobilized less in areas of large Latino population due to citizenship—though the coefficient for the size of the noncitizen population is estimated to be insignificant in both cases.

MOBILIZATION LEVELS ACROSS RACIAL/ETHNIC GROUPS

Up to this point, I have documented that being mobilized, while structured by race, is determined largely by individual characteristics such as education and income, as opposed to contextual characteristics such as group size and empowerment. I began with evidence that African-Americans and Latinos report being mobilized significantly less than Anglos, thus

TABLE 6.3
Overall Mobilization Model, by Group Size (Blacks and Latinos Estimated Separately)

	African-Americans Overall Mobilization		Latinos Overall Mobilization	
	Large Black Group Size	Small Black Group Size	Large Latino Group Size	Small Latino Group Size
Education	.09°°	.14°°	.04°°	.06
	(.02)	(.04)	(.01)	(.05)
Income	.08°°	.06°	.04°	.06°
	(.02)	(.03)	(.02)	(.03)
Democratic	.14	.33	−.003	.17
	(.30)	(.31)	(.15)	(.46)
Republican	−.07	−.82	−.09	.44
	(.35)	(.56)	(.17)	(.46)
Independent	−.18	.36	−.36°	.29
	(.33)	(.38)	(.19)	(.48)
Black/Latino em-	−.02	.48°	.05	.67
powerment	(.11)	(.24)	(.10)	(.74)
Citizen	.07	.60°	.20°	.01
	(.40)	(.32)	(.12)	(.21)
Percent noncitizen	−.24	−.82	.07	−2.09
	(.73)	(1.13)	(.45)	(2.67)
Constant	−1.08°	−2.23°°	−.44°	−.82
	(.53)	(.60)	(.21)	(.56)
Adjusted R2	.22	.29	.12	.09
N	249	88	168	52

Source: CPS. Data are unweighted.
Note: Table entries are OLS regression coefficients, with the associated standard error in parentheses. The dependent variable is whether the individual was asked to engage in campaign work, local activity, or contacting government officials, and thus ranges from 0 to 3. Group size refers to the proportion of the population in the individual's neighborhood/zip code region that is the same as the individual's self-identified race/ethnicity (African-American or Latino). Empowerment refers to Black empowerment for African-Americans and Latino empowerment for Latinos. Individuals residing in areas with their own group-size proportion being greater than the sample mean are coded as "large group size" while those residing in areas with their own group-size proportion being less than the sample mean are coded as "small group size."
°$p < .05$, one-tailed test of significance. °°$p < .01$, one-tailed test of significance.

confirming anecdotal and case-study claims drawn from research on African-American and Latino politics. Of equal importance is whether these differential mobilization levels might be accounted for by the theoretical frameworks discussed above. More specifically, beyond class and ideology, might the racial composition of minority individuals' neighborhoods or political empowerment be associated with the level of mobilization directed toward Blacks and Latinos?

These two factors might account for lower levels of mobilization reported by African-Americans and Latinos because they are contextual cues that structure elite or mass mobilization efforts. That is, if parties and candidates, in general, are less likely to target areas with large minority populations, and Blacks and Latinos are more likely than Anglos to live in those areas, then, ceteris paribus, Blacks and Latinos will be mobilized less than Anglos. Likewise, if Anglos respond positively (i.e., mobilize) to minority populations or empowerment by engaging in more informal recruitment of other Anglos to political action, but Blacks and Latinos do not, then we would also expect to see lower levels of minority mobilization.

To assess whether group size and empowerment are associated with levels of minority mobilization, I estimate a model of overall participation that includes the class, ideology, and citizenship variables included in the analyses above and supplement that with dummy variables for being Black and being Latino. This model is estimated using the entire (weighted) CPS sample, and thus the effects of each independent variable are assumed to be equal across racial/ethnic groups. Given that the sample is made up of predominantly Anglos, these results will largely reflect the nature of the relationships between the independent and dependent variables for Anglos.

However, this strategy allows us to test for differential levels of mobilization across racial/ethnic groups. With Anglos being the excluded category, significant and negative coefficient estimates for the race/ethnicity variables indicate that African-Americans and Latinos are significantly less likely than Anglos to be mobilized, controlling for the other variables in the model. Table 6.4, column 1, presents the OLS regression results for this model, while probit regression results are presented in columns 2, 3, and 4 for each particular type of mobilization.

As expected—given the large proportion of Anglos in the sample—neither group size nor empowerment is a significant predictor of overall mobilization or any particular type of mobilization. Also as expected, socioeconomic status is a consistent predictor of being mobilized across racial/ethnic groups.

Of particular interest is the fact that controlling for whether or not the respondent is a citizen, the contextual measure of citizenship is insignificant as a predictor of mobilization in each case. In contrast, citizens are significantly more likely to report being mobilized to campaign activity and contacting activity, while they are less likely to report being mobilized to local community activity. This suggests that the nature of the desired political activity affects who is mobilized: where electoral politics or contacting government officials is involved, citizens are more likely to be mobilized.

TABLE 6.4
Mobilization Models, Estimated for Entire Sample

	Summary	Campaign Mobilization	Contacting Mobilization	Local Mobilization
Education	.10°°	.16°°	.11°°	.10°°
	(.01)	(.02)	(.02)	(.02)
Family income	.07°°	.07°°	.07°°	.07°°
	(.01)	(.01)	(.01)	(.01)
Democratic	.15	.46°	−.03	.25
	(.10)	(.24)	(.20)	(.24)
Republican	.19°	.47°	.07	.26
	(.10)	(.24)	(.21)	(.24)
Independent	.26°°	.47°	.15	.45°
	(.11)	(.25)	(.21)	(.25)
Group size	.03	−.14	.13	.20
	(.10)	(.18)	(.19)	(.19)
Minority	−.04	.09	−.12	−.10
empowerment	(.05)	(.09)	(.09)	(.10)
Black	−.09	−.21°	−.31°°	.15
	(.07)	(.13)	(.13)	(.13)
Latino	−.26°°	−.50°°	−.54°°	−.44°°
	(.08)	(.16)	(.17)	(.18)
U.S. citizen	.09	.52°°	.49°	−.45°
	(.11)	(.20)	(.24)	(.21)
Percentage noncitizen	.51	.85	.10	.81
	(.39)	(.67)	(.77)	(.71)
Constant	1.22°°	−4.03°°	−3.06°°	−2.79°°
	(.21)	(.47)	(.43)	(.47)
N	1,791	1,790	1,791	1,786
Adjusted R2	.22			
Percent correctly predicted		60.9%	58.6%	58.6%

Source: CPS. Data are weighted.

Note: Table entries for "summary mobilization" are OLS regression coefficients, with the associated standard error in parentheses. Table entries for the other three models are probit coefficients, with the associated standard error in parentheses. "Summary mobilization" is an index of the number of ways in which the individual was asked to engage in campaign work, local activity, or contacting government officials, and thus ranges from 0 to 3. The other three dependent variables are dichotomies, where 1 indicates the individual was asked to engage in the particular activity, and 0 indicates the individual was not asked. Group size refers to the proportion of the population in the individual's neighborhood/zip code region that is the same as the individual's self-identified race/ethnicity. Minority empowerment is a dichotomous variable, with 1 indicating the individual resides in an area with either a Black or Latino elected official; 0 otherwise.

°$p < .05$, one-tailed test of significance. °°$p < .01$, one-tailed test of significance.

On the other hand, where individuals are likely to work together on local activities, some of which require involvement with formal government officials, the disadvantage of noncitizenship is eliminated and, in some senses, becomes a strength, suggesting that noncitizens are more likely to be engaged in community politics by other citizens or political institutions.

Finally, it is important to note that African-Americans and Latinos are significantly less likely to report being mobilized to campaign work and contacting activities. Had I not controlled for citizenship in two ways, as well as the important effects of class, we might have a more "positive" interpretation of this finding. But, as it stands, this evidence suggests that both Blacks and Latinos are marginalized in terms of whom individuals seek to mobilize to political participation. The claim of African-Americans that the Democratic Party fails to be responsive to them as a group certainly seems to be supported. And that African-Americans are no less likely to be mobilized to local activities suggests at the same time that this minority community likely structures participation opportunities independent of the dominant political institutions in our democracy.

The finding that Latinos are significantly less likely to be mobilized likewise suggests that, despite the rhetoric of inclusion and the claims that this growing segment of the population is even now a swing vote, political institutions are not currently targeting these individuals for inclusion. Moreover, the lower levels of mobilization in local activities—independent of electoral considerations and government officials—suggest that Latino organizations have not been able to overcome this disadvantage.

CONCLUSION

Not unlike its central role in explanations of political participation, class is the most consistent predictor of political mobilization. Ideology, while important, reflects the realities of political institutions, with Anglos being more likely to be mobilized and African-Americans and Latinos only occasionally reflecting the result of mobilization by established political institutions.

Alternatively, the role of contextual influences in structuring political mobilization seems to be minimal. The effects of empowerment and group size are typically unimportant though occasionally dependent on one another for African-American mobilization. Neither factor seems to encourage the mobilization of Latinos into any type of political activity. It is important to note that this conclusion holds while controlling for citizenship—and that, contrary to de la Garza and DeSipio's claims, political mobilization of Latinos is not substantially affected by high levels of noncitizenship.

At the same time, this finding, among the others discussed above, is obviously constrained by the extent to which the self-reported measures of political mobilization actually capture the institutional dynamics of party and group contacting. Similar to most studies of party contacting, my work uses individual-level socioeconomic status and ideology characteristics to proxy as indicators of whom party elites mobilize. Yet the findings reported here undoubtedly reflect the strategies and resources of groups other than traditional political parties. Hence, whatever conclusions have been offered regarding a particular type of behavior—or lack of behavior—on the part of political parties should be interpreted gingerly. What we are observing is the result of a social process in which many actors and institutions are engaged.

The evidence we have, however, seems to document more systematically anecdotal claims regarding the relative inattention given to minority groups at the mass level by political elites. Because these groups are disproportionately poor, they are at a mobilization disadvantage in this respect as well. Thus, the first modification required of the models presented in chapter 1 is to eliminate the linkage between racial/ethnic context and mobilization, and to "weaken" that between elite mobilization (i.e., empowerment) and mobilization.

More broadly, the findings presented in this chapter suggest that contextual characteristics only occasionally structure individuals' political mobilization. Much like Anglos, African-Americans and Latinos tend to be mobilized when they enjoy the advantages of high socioeconomic status. Contextual characteristics unique to individuals who happen to be African-American or Latino are, in contrast, relatively unimportant to processes of political mobilization. Whether the same holds true for individuals' decisions to participate is the next question I turn to.

Chapter Seven

MINORITY POLITICAL PARTICIPATION

THIS chapter tests the models of African-American and Latino participation introduced in chapter 1, providing rare systematic evidence regarding how individual and contextual characteristics simultaneously structure minority participation. Of particular importance to this chapter's focus are the relationships among elite mobilization (i.e., political empowerment), racial context, and individuals' decisions to participate. If the rather weak—or at least limited—findings regarding the influence of these factors on mobilization is replicated here regarding political participation, this might indicate serious flaws in either the models' conceptualization or the indicators used to test it. Fortunately that is not the case, and the evidence bears out the models' expectations fairly consistently.

In assessing the validity of these models, this chapter extends previous research in two important ways. First, I test the validity of the political empowerment model—developed and tested regarding Black political participation—for Latino political behavior. Second, I test whether these findings are similar for electoral as well as nonelectoral participation.

THEORETICAL FRAMEWORK

Much of the theoretical motivation for the analysis in the first part of this chapter was discussed in both chapters 1 and 6, and so the discussion here focuses on the particular details of the argument that differ (in substance or magnitude) as I shift to consider political participation rather than mobilization.

Of critical importance as a starting point in this chapter is Bobo and Gilliam's (1990) analysis of Black empowerment. As noted in chapter 6, Bobo and Gilliam argue that Black political participation levels reflect the extent to which Blacks have gained power in the political system. They find that Blacks in high-empowerment areas participate more than whites (controlling for socioeconomic status), and that this greater participation is stimulated by higher levels of political knowledge and engagement. However, it may also be that high-empowerment areas are also likely to be more politicized—in terms of political organizations, elite activities, and informal political networks that produce higher levels of political recruitment. Higher levels of recruitment should, in turn, enhance minority participation.

The importance of political mobilization in structuring participation has been demonstrated more broadly in several ways, in particular with respect to political parties. First, party contacting is a strong predictor of individual voter turnout and campaign activism (see, e.g., Wielhouwer 1995, 1999; Wielhouwer and Lockerbie 1994). Second, party activities—independent of direct contact—are associated with greater turnout (Huckfeldt and Sprague 1992). Third, party ideology and competitiveness are associated with higher turnout (Hill and Leighley 1993, 1994).

Campaign expenditures, often associated with greater turnout, are also considered proxies for the likelihood of contact with, and therefore being recruited by, a candidate. Jackson (1993), for example, finds that senatorial, gubernatorial, and House spending is associated with higher levels of turnout and that the effects of such mobilization are about as influential in predicting turnout as are individual attributes such as education and income (see, e.g., Cox and Munger 1989; Patterson and Caldeira 1983).

It is also possible that the nature of mobilization experience in areas of minority empowerment is simply different—and more effective—than in areas of nonempowerment. That is, areas of political empowerment might well have an underlying social and political structure that provides additional social incentives to participate (see, e.g., Chong 1991). This argument is entirely consistent with Uhlaner's claims regarding relational goods. Specifically, she hypothesizes that turnout should be greater where group members have higher levels of interpersonal interaction and the social networks within the group are denser. Without explicitly incorporating individuals' level of recruitment and the nature of the recruitment process in empirical tests of the Black empowerment thesis, our substantive conclusions regarding the significance of political empowerment for minority individuals may be premature.

Another issue that remains unresolved is whether the empowerment thesis is a unique feature of African-American politics or is valid as well in the context of Latino politics. With historical similarities in the development and efforts of the Chicano and Black civil rights movements, it is tempting to believe that both racial and ethnic groups would react similarly to the symbolic victory of having non-whites elected to office. On the other hand, the positive consequences might not be translated to Latinos so easily.

First, historical differences in the level of segregation (and perhaps discrimination) faced by African-Americans and Latinos reflect that Blacks lived under different systems of law while Latinos could sometimes escape the penalties of race due to the "invisibility" of their color (McClain and Stewart 1999). The resulting higher barriers for African-Americans to full participation in society include higher levels of residential segregation, lower levels of intergenerational mobility, and lower levels of intermarriage (Farley 1996; Hochschild 1995).

Second, there might well be a strategic difference between the two groups, in that Latinos or Hispanics in certain parts of the country have considerably large populations and are more likely to be majority populations. Thus, winning office is, ceteris paribus, easier for Latinos simply due to their larger electoral visibility. Third, the ability of Latino candidates to win Anglo support is likely higher than that of Black candidates, and hence Latino coalitions are likely to include a higher proportion of nonminorities, thus reducing the salience of minority empowerment. Fourth, nationality differences within the Hispanic/Latino population in the United States may diminish the psychological benefits of having "one of our own" elected to office. Thus, the question of whether empowerment enhances the participation of Latinos, both important and theoretically interesting, remains open.

The theoretical import of group size can be viewed in two distinct ways. First, and of lesser importance, group size can be viewed as a simple statistical control to test for the effects of political empowerment. It is in some senses a truism to expect that African-Americans will be more likely to be empowered where their share of the population is large, given the empirical evidence we have of the importance of candidate race to individuals' vote choices (see, e.g., Hero 1992).

Second, however, is Uhlaner's "relational goods" argument, which posits that minority group members will be more likely to participate (i.e., contribute) as their group increases in size. According to this argument, African-Americans and Latinos will be more likely to participate when they reside in a more homogeneous racial environment than when they reside in a less homogeneous environment.

Previous research, however, provides extremely limited empirical evidence as to the effects of the racial group context on individual political participation. Leighley and Vedlitz (1999) find that minorities (i.e., African-Americans, Mexican-Americans, and Asian-Americans) in Texas are no more (or less) likely to participate when residing in more homogeneous group contexts. However, Leighley and Vedlitz's finding may reflect historical, cultural, or institutional factors unique to Texas and must be interpreted cautiously. More specifically, with a relatively weakly organized minority group system and Texas's emergence from a period of one-party-dominant politics, the incentives provided in a more homogenous environment may be insufficient to overcome the costs of participating.

THE RELATIONAL GOODS PARTICIPATION MODEL

The analyses below use much of the same data used in chapter 5 and the CPS, supplemented with contextual data on minority empowerment and group size. However, several new measures of mobilization and participation are introduced.

Three different participation measures are used. *Overall participation* is an additive scale based on individuals' self-reported participation in nine different types of participation (voting in presidential elections, voting in local elections, campaigning, contributing money, attending a local meeting, and contacting officials [local or federal, appointed or elected]. Figure 7.1 shows the distribution of this variable for the full (weighted) sample as well as for each racial/ethnic group.

Consistent with previous research, a substantial group of individuals in the full sample report engaging in no political activities, and relatively few individuals report engaging in more than four activities. Also, Anglos are least likely to report engaging in no activities (about 20 percent) while African-Americans and especially Latinos are more likely to report doing nothing (approximately 30 percent and 50 percent, respectively). Also as expected, Latino citizens are slightly more likely than Latinos as a group to participate.

The other two participation measures indicate how frequently the individual votes in either presidential or local elections: never, rarely, some of the time, most of the time, or all of the time. Table 7.2 shows the distribution of these two variables for the full (weighted) sample, as well as for each racial/ethnic group separately. Approximately 13 percent of the sample reported never voting in presidential elections (compared to 17 percent in local elections); 4 percent reported rarely voting in presidential elections (compared to 7 percent in local elections); 11 percent reported voting in some presidential elections (compared to 18 percent in local elections); 20 percent reported voting in most presidential elections (compared to 33 percent in local elections); and nearly 52 percent reported voting in all presidential elections (compared to 25 percent in local elections). Again, these patterns are similar to those documented in previous research.

Uhlaner's relational goods argument is assessed in the analyses below by including variables indicating whether the individual had been mobilized (recruited); whether the individual knew the person who made the recruitment request; and whether the individual making the recruitment request was of the same race as the respondent. Being mobilized, knowing the recruiter, and having a recruiter of the same racial/ethnic group are factors that either reduce the costs of participation (in the case of being mobilized) or increase the perceived benefits (for the latter two factors).

The particular mobilization variables used differ for overall participation and the frequency of voting variables. For overall participation, mobilization is measured as the number of times the individual reports being asked to engage in one of three activities: campaign work, local activities, or

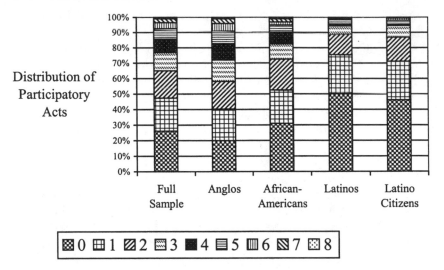

Distribution of Participatory Acts

Figure 7.1. Distribution of Participatory Acts

contacting government officials. This is the same measure of "overall mobilization" used in the last chapter. For the voting frequency models, I use the indicator for campaign mobilization—whether the individual had been asked to engage in campaign work. This is not a direct solicitation to turn out to vote on election day, but it does indicate the extent to which the individual has been targeted for electoral politics.[1]

The other two mobilization characteristics included in the models resulted from follow-up questions to the campaign work, local activity, and contacting recruitment questions described above. For each of these three types of recruitment, individuals were asked if they knew who made the request and if the person was of the same racial/ethnic group. If the individual responded positively to knowing the recruiter, then that person is coded as "knowing the mobilizer" (1 = yes, 0 = no). If the person reported that the individual was of the same racial/ethnic group, then he was coded the same (1 = yes, 0 = no). Individuals who were not asked to participate in any of these three ways—and thus did not "know" a mobilizer and were not mobilized by someone of the same race—were coded as 0 in both cases.

Again, I must note how these mobilization characteristics are not particularly precise measures of encounters with recruiters, in that they are not directly tied to the specific activities undertaken by the individual or to a

[1] The CPS does not include a more precise measure of electoral mobilization (such as party contacting) during a particular campaign.

TABLE 7.1
Frequency of Voting in Presidential and Local Elections

	Full Sample (%)	Anglos (%)	African-Americans (%)	Latinos (%)	Latino Citizens (%)
Presidential elections					
Never	13.2	9.5	13.9	33.1	31.4
Rarely	4.1	3.4	6.0	5.8	7.0
Some of the time	10.8	8.7	16.1	14.5	15.7
Most of the time	20.0	20.3	21.4	14.1	16.8
All of the time	51.9	58.1	42.7	32.6	29.2
N	2,382	1,618	454	242	185
Local elections					
Never	16.7	12.3	19.3	36.8	35.7
Rarely	7.2	6.9	6.8	9.5	10.8
Some of the time	17.9	18.0	18.6	17.4	18.9
Most of the time	32.7	36.1	29.4	17.8	20.0
All of the time	25.5	26.7	25.9	18.6	14.6
N	2,385	1,620	456	242	185

Source: CPS. Data are unweighted, except for estimates for full sample.
Note: Table entries represent the percentage of each group in each category.

particular election in which recruitment took place (or did not). Although a set of questions more similar to this is available in the CPS, they yield so few cases suitable for analysis that it is virtually impossible to use them to assess differences and similarities across the racial and ethnic groups. Instead, I use these basic mobilization characteristics as indicators of the extent to which the individual is "connected" to other individuals or institutions that seek to engage individuals in politics (see Zuckerman and West's 1985 use of a similar measurement strategy).

A fourth measure of relational goods is also included in the models as an indicator of group identity. As Uhlaner argues, experiences of racial discrimination are likely to increase the (minority) individual's willingness to identify as a racial group member (see Uhlaner 1991). Thus, those individuals who report having experienced racial/ethnic discrimination are hypothesized to be more likely to participate as the higher level of group identity they experience acts as a "relational good" and thus increases the benefits of participation. The particular variable used is based on individuals' responses as to whether they had ever been discriminated against because of their race or ethnicity (1 = yes, 0 = no).

Finally, two citizenship variables are included in the models, one indicating whether the respondent is a U.S. citizen and the other indicating the proportion of U.S. citizens residing in the individual's zip code region.

OVERALL PARTICIPATION AND VOTER TURNOUT

Contextual analyses of participation model indiduals' political activity as a function of both individual and social characteristics. In one of the first individual-level studies of this type, Huckfeldt (1979) finds that individual and contextual measures of social class had independent effects on individuals' participation. Moreover, Huckfeldt demonstrates that these contextual effects are likely to differ in magnitude (and even direction) as a function of individual social status as well as the type of participation.

On the latter point, Huckfeldt develops and tests indices for individually based and socially based political participation, based on the level of social interaction required of particular types of participation. Voting in elections, sending messages to leaders, making views known to public officials, and writing letters to editors of newspapers are all considered individually based participation, while campaign activity, joining community groups, talking to others about politics, and supporting a political party are socially based types of participation. The thrust of Huckfeldt's argument—that one should expect contextual effects on participation only if the activity requires social interaction—is indeed intuitive and generally supported in his analysis of a survey of Buffalo, New York.

To ensure that the substantive conclusions drawn in this chapter do not reflect the peculiar nature of any one type of participation, I test the relational goods model on the two (presidential and local) voting frequency measures and the overall participation index. Thus, instead of imposing an analytical distinction of individual (versus social) on particular types of activities, I make instead an institutional discrimination, asking whether the same patterns hold for voter turnout as for overall participation, and for presidential as well as local elections. This seems like an important distinction in an effort to identify any potential influences of a local social and political context.

More specifically, my expectation is that contextual characteristics should be more important in the case of local turnout than in presidential turnout, but that the same patterns of differences between African-Americans and Latinos identified in the participation models introduced in chapter 1 will emerge: empowerment will be more important for African-Americans, while group size will be more important for Latinos.

Table 7.2 presents the statistical estimates for the relational goods participation model of voter turnout frequency and overall participation for

TABLE 7.2
Relational Goods Model of Frequency of Voting in Presidential and Local Elections and
Overall Participation (African-Americans Only)

	Presidential Election Voting Frequency	Local Election Voting Frequency	Overall Participation
Education	.06°	.07°	.13°°
	(.03)	(.03)	(.04)
Income	.004	−.01	.04
	(.02)	(.02)	(.03)
Democratic	1.44°°	1.36°°	.87°°
	(.36)	(.34)	(.35)
Republican	.92°	.74°	.32
	(.45)	(.43)	(.46)
Independent	1.21°°	.96°°	.77°°
	(.40)	(.38)	(.40)
Black empowerment	.37°	.38°°	.14
	(.16)	(.16)	(.18)
Black group size	−.20	.25	.21
	(.28)	(.27)	(.30)
Mobilized	.42°	.24	.55°°
	(.21)	(.21)	(.14)
Knew mobilizer	.21	.30	.70°°
	(.22)	(.22)	(.27)
Black mobilizer	.42°	.63°°	.29
	(.24)	(.23)	(.27)
Experienced racial discrimination	−.24	−.18	.19
	(.18)	(.17)	(.19)
U.S. citizen	.42	−.05	−.40
	(.47)	(.48)	(.41)
Percent noncitizens	−.28	.96	−1.15
	(.96)	(.95)	(1.02)
Constant	.93	.89	−1.31°
	(.69)	(.68)	(.63)
Adjusted R2	.18	.23	.43
N	319	320	336

Source: CPS. Data are unweighted.

Note: Table entries are OLS regression coefficients, with the associated standard error following in parentheses. The dependent variables are individuals' self-reports on the frequency with which they vote in presidential or local elections (ranging from values of 1 ("never") to 5 ("all of the time"); and an index of the number of political activities the individual reports engaging in (ranging from 0 to 8). Minority empowerment is a dummy variable, where 1 indicates that either Blacks or Latinos have been elected to office; 0 otherwise. The mobilization variable used in the model of overall participation is a dummy variable, where 1 indicates that the individual was asked to do campaign work, contact government officials, or engage in local activities. The mobilization variable used in the two voting equations is a dummy variable indicating whether the individual reports having been contacted to do campaign work (1 = yes, 0 = no).
°$p < .05$, one-tailed test of significance. °°$p < .01$, one-tailed test of significance.

African-Americans, and table 7.3 presents the same for Latinos.[2] The striking feature in table 7.2 is the prominence of the empowerment and relational goods variables. In stark contrast to the null findings in chapter 6 for the effects of empowerment on recruitment, here we see that African-Americans are significantly more likely to vote more when they reside in areas of Black empowerment, and this is true for both presidential and local elections. These findings confirm Bobo and Gilliam's previous conclusions regarding the importance of Black empowerment, as well as Uhlaner's hypotheses regarding relational goods and voter turnout. However, it is important to note that empowerment, group size, and having a mobilizer of the same race are not associated with higher levels of overall participation. Thus, these contextual and relational goods characteristics seem to be effective for electoral participation in a way that they are not for nonelectoral participation.

Finally, and as expected, table 7.2 demonstrates the importance of education and ideology as determinants of political participation. In every case, African-Americans with higher levels of education are significantly more likely to vote and participate more, and the ideological identification variables are, with one exception, positively associated with turnout and overall participation.

In contrast, table 7.3 shows that for Latinos, the effects of education on turnout and overall participation are essentially null, while those of income are significant and positive. This suggests that class structures political participation differently for African-Americans and Latinos. The results for ideology are more consistent with those previously reported for African-Americans, in that both Republican and Democratic identifiers report being more likely to vote than nonidentifiers. With the analysis restricted to Latino citizens, the only significant ideology coefficient is that of Republican identifiers, possibly reflecting the larger proportion of Cuban-Americans in the smaller Latino citizen pool. Of particular note is the fact that Latino empowerment fails to stimulate voter turnout, while Latino population size is a strong and significant predictor of turnout in both presidential and local elections as well as overall participation. Thus, as anticipated in the models introduced in chapter 1, I find that political empowerment is critical to understanding African-American political participation, while group size is critical to understanding Latino participation.

To test whether these contextual effects might interact with one another—that group size might matter for African-Americans when empowered, or that empowerment might matter for Latinos when residing in

[2] I have chosen to test these models using Latinos but not restrict the subsample to citizens because the number of cases in the latter case is prohibitively small. My assumption is that including the two citizenship variables in the model—individual-level and contextual-level citizenship—minimizes the bias introduced by including noncitizens in the model.

TABLE 7.3

Relational Goods Model of Frequency of Voting in Presidential and Local Elections and Overall Participation (Latinos and Latino Citizens Only)

	Latinos			Latino Citizens	
	Presidential Elections	Local Elections	Overall Participation	Presidential Elections	Local Elections
Education	.03	.02	.02	− .05	− .02
	(.04)	(.04)	(.04)	(.05)	(.05)
Income	.07°	.03°	.06°	.12°°	.06
	(.04)	(.04)	(.03)	(.04)	(.04)
Democratic	.95°°	.81°	.64°°	.67	.54
	(.38)	(.37)	(.25)	(.41)	(.41)
Republican	1.43°°	1.51°°	.57°	.85°	1.07°
	(.43)	(.42)	(.28)	(.47)	(.47)
Independent	.66	.57	.48	.48	.40
	(.45)	(.43)	(.30)	(.48)	(.47)
Latino empowerment	− .13	.03	− .14	− .48	− .20
	(.29)	(.28)	(.20)	(.33)	(.33)
Latino group size	1.90°°	1.67°°	1.43°°	2.33°°	2.08°°
	(.58)	(.56)	(.39)	(.62)	(.62)
Mobilized	.20	.001	.62°°	− .08	.12
	(.35)	(.35)	(.16)	(.36)	(.38)
Knew mobilizer	1.09°°	.79°	.84°°	1.37°°	.92°
	(.41)	(.40)	(.33)	(.46)	(.46)
Latino mobilizer	− .32	.10	− .17	− .10	.09
	(.55)	(.53)	(.38)	(.59)	(.53)
Experienced racial discrimination	.54°	.38	.32	.43	.23
	(.33)	(.31)	(.22)	(.35)	(.35)
U.S. citizen	− .41	− .40	− .14		
	(.27)	(.26)	(.18)		
Percent noncitizens	− 2.22°°	− 2.26°	− 2.28°°	− 5.06°°	− 3.83°°
	(1.31)	(1.27)	(.89)	(1.52)	(1.51)
Constant	1.21°	1.31°	− .56	1.98°°	1.60°°
	(.54)	(.52)	(.36)	(.67)	(.66)
Adjusted R2	.16	.12	.32	.17	.12
N	186	187	217	141	141

Source: CPS. Data are unweighted.

Note: Table entries are OLS regression coefficients, with the associated standard error following in parentheses. The dependent variables are individuals' self-reports on the frequency with which they vote in presidential or local elections (ranging from values of 1 ("never") to 5 ("all of the time")); and an index of the number of political activities the individual reports engaging in (ranging from 0 to 8). Minority empowerment is a dummy variable, where 1 indicates that either Blacks or Latinos have been elected to office; 0 otherwise. The mobilization variable used in the model of overall participation is a dummy variable, where 1 indicates that the individual was asked to do campaign work, contact government officials, or engage in local activities. The mobilization variable used in the two voting equations is a dummy variable indicating whether the individual reports having been contacted to do campaign work (1 = yes, 0 = no).

°$p < .05$, one-tailed test of significance. °°$p < .01$, one-tailed test of significance.

areas of large Latino group size, for example—I next estimated these same models of overall participation and voting frequency separately by empowerment. I can thus compare the estimates for African-Americans residing in areas of empowerment to estimates for African-Americans residing in nonempowerment areas and do the same for Latinos. These results are presented in table 7.4.

These analyses essentially confirm the findings of tables 7.1 and 7.2. Whether in an area of Black empowerment or not, Black group size has no effect on African-Americans' decisions to participate; whether in an empowerment area or not, Latino group size has a positive and significant effect on Latinos' participation decisions. The effects of many of the other variables in the model fail to achieve statistical significance, again underscoring the importance of empowerment for African-Americans in particular.

Tables 7.5 and 7.6 offer similar analyses of African-American and Latino voting frequency, again estimated separately for empowerment and nonempowerment areas. Perhaps the most striking feature of table 7.5 is that when empowerment is controlled, none of the relational goods indicators, save one, is significantly associated with turnout. This is a substantial deviation from the earlier findings that confirmed so consistently the importance of relational goods to individuals' decisions to participate. Hence, the empirical evidence again points toward the critical role of empowerment in stimulating electoral turnout: the importance of relational goods as incentives for group members to participate is diminished when Blacks are elected to office. The one exception to this point is for Blacks residing in an area of nonempowerment, where being mobilized by a Black continues to increase the likelihood of participating.

Quite a different picture emerges from table 7.6, which presents the Latino relational goods models of voter turnout estimated separately by Latino empowerment. While group size was a significant predictor of overall participation and voter turnout in the basic model, here the effects of group size are restricted, for both presidential and local elections, to areas of nonempowerment. Thus, it appears that group size acts as an incentive (i.e., relational good) to participate only when the Latino resides in an area of nonempowerment. Alternatively, group size has no independent effect on turnout in areas of Latino empowerment. This undoubtedly reflects the point I made earlier: Latinos have far greater potential for empowerment due to their much larger—and hence more pivotal—role in electoral politics, and Latinos residing in an empowerment area fail to react to the incentives associated with group size.

Similar contextual analyses on the effects of group size are offered in tables 7.6 and 7.8. Table 7.7 shows that the effects of most relational goods are consistent across group size contexts. In particular, being mobilized

TABLE 7.4
Relational Goods Model of Overall Participation by Empowerment (Estimated Separately for African-Americans and Latinos)

	African-Americans		Latinos	
	Black Empowerment	Black Nonempowerment	Latino empowerment	Latino Nonempowerment
Education	.13°	.14°°	.04	−.01
	(.05)	(.05)	(.04)	(.04)
Income	.09°°	−.003	.10°	.06
	(.04)	(.04)	(.05)	(.03)
Democratic	1.78°	.78°	.78°	.24
	(.83)	(.41)	(.38)	(.38)
Republican	1.18	.24	.80°	.14
	(.93)	(.59)	(.47)	(.41)
Independent	1.64°	.67	.37	.21
	(.86)	(.49)	(.48)	(.42)
Black/Latino population	.10	.19	1.02°	1.69°°
	(.45)	(.47)	(.55)	(.56)
Mobilized	.54°°	.54°°	.49	.62°°
	(.19)	(.23)	(.31)	(.19)
Knew mobilizer	.53	.76°	.77	.90°
	(.41)	(.39)	(.72)	(.39)
Black/Latino mobilizer	.01	.60	.91	−.96°
	(.38)	(.40)	(.66)	(.50)
Experienced racial discrimination	.16	.19	−.38	.51°
	(.27)	(.28)	(.46)	(.25)
Citizen	−.34	−.46	−.37	−.07
	(.71)	(.52)	(.31)	(.23)
Percent noncitizens	−1.86	−.84	−2.78°	−3.07°°
	(1.56)	(1.49)	(1.65)	(1.15)
Constant	−2.13°	−1.10	−.68	.04
	(1.30)	(.82)	(.50)	(.59)
Adjusted R2	.44	.39	.38	.30
N	155	181	82	135

Source: CPS. Data are unweighted.
Note: Table entries are OLS regression coefficients, with the associated standard error in parentheses. The dependent variable in each model is an index of the number of political activities the individual reports engaging in (ranging from 0 to 8). The mobilization variable is a dummy variable, where 1 indicates that the individual was asked to either do campaign work, contact government officials, or engage in local activities. Black empowerment equations are estimated using Blacks only, and using Black group size and Black mobilizer; Latino empowerment equations are estimated using Latinos only, and using Latino group size and Latino mobilizer.
°$p < .05$, one-tailed test of significance. °°$p < .01$, one-tailed test of significance.

TABLE 7.5

Relational Goods Model of Voting Frequency in Presidential and Local Elections by Empowerment (African-Americans Only)

	Frequency of Voting in Presidential Elections		Frequency of Voting in Local Elections	
	Black Empowerment	Black Nonempowerment	Black Empowerment	Black Nonempowerment
Education	.01	.09°	.03	.09°
	(.05)	(.05)	(.05)	(.05)
Income	.01	−.004	−.01	−.02
	(.03)	(.04)	(.03)	(.04)
Democratic	.82	1.66°°	1.50°	1.46°°
	(.88)	(.41)	(.69)	(.39)
Republican	.31	1.25°	1.21	.67
	(.97)	(.57)	(.79)	(.55)
Independent	1.02	1.05°	1.53°	.70
	(.91)	(.49)	(.73)	(.47)
Black group size	.37	−.69	.97°°	−.14
	(.40)	(.44)	(.38)	(.43)
Mobilized	.17	.30	.22	.20
	(.17)	(.21)	(.16)	(.21)
Knew mobilizer	.43	−.07	.40	.08
	(.36)	(.36)	(.34)	(.35)
Black mobilizer	.23	.53	.20	.90°°
	(.34)	(.37)	(.32)	(.36)
Experienced racial discrimination	−.30	−.21	−.26	−.17
	(.25)	(.27)	(.23)	(.26)
Citizen	.33	.49	.28	−.13
	(.88)	(.58)	(.84)	(.62)
Percent noncitizens	1.49	1.57	3.57°°	−1.18
	(1.38)	(1.42)	(1.31)	(1.41)
Constant	2.20	1.48°	.70	.79
	(1.41)	(.86)	(1.26)	(.86)
Adjusted R2	.08	.20	.12	.24
N	149	170	150	170

Source: CPS. Data are unweighted.

Note: Table entries are OLS regression coefficients, with the associated standard error in parentheses. The dependent variables are individuals' self-reports on the frequency with which they vote in presidential or local elections ranging from values of 1 ("never") to 5 ("all of the time"). "Mobilized" is a dummy variable indicating whether the individual reports having been contacted to do campaign work (1 = yes, 0 = no). °$p < .05$, one-tailed test of significance. °°$p < .01$, one-tailed test of significance.

TABLE 7.6

Relational Goods Model of Voting Frequency in Presidential and Local Elections by Empowerment (Latinos Only)

	Frequency of Voting in Presidential Elections		Frequency of Voting in Local Elections	
	Latino Empowerment	Latino Nonempowerment	Latino Empowerment	Latino Nonempowerment
Education	.09°	− .05	.06	− .03
	(.06)	(.06)	(.06)	(.05)
Income	.08	.10°	.08	.04
	(.07)	(.05)	(.07)	(.05)
Democratic	1.31°°	.55	1.14°	.33
	(.55)	(.56)	(.57)	(.54)
Republican	1.41°	1.08°	1.85°°	.98°
	(.65)	(.62)	(.67)	(.60)
Independent	.35	.60	.20	.48
	(.68)	(.62)	(.68)	(.59)
Latino group size	.92	2.64°°	.93	2.21°°
	(.83)	(.83)	(.86)	(.79)
Mobilized	− .59	.17	− .54	.002
	(.42)	(.26)	(.45)	(.25)
Knew mobilizer	1.32	1.37°°	.65	1.18°
	(.98)	(.55)	(1.02)	(.53)
Latino mobilizer	.16	− .53	.87	− .29
	(.98)	(.72)	(1.01)	(.70)
Experienced racial discrimination	.33	.67°	− .09	.57
	(.65)	(.39)	(.67)	(.37)
Citizen	− .83°	.08	− .54	− .18
	(.48)	(.35)	(.49)	(.34)
Percent noncitizens	.84	− 4.58°°	− .93	− 3.80°°
	(2.36)	(1.67)	(2.42)	(1.61)
Constant	.70	1.81°	.96	1.90°
	(.73)	(.80)	(.76)	(.79)
Adjusted R2	.20	.19	.11	.10
N	72	114	72	115

Source: CPS. Data are unweighted.

Note: Table entries are OLS regression coefficients, with the associated standard error in parentheses. The dependent variables are individuals' self-reports on the frequency with which they vote in presidential or local elections ranging from values of 1 ("never") to 5 ("all of the time"). "Mobilized" is a dummy variable indicating whether the individual reports having been contacted to do campaign work (1 = yes, 0 = no). °$p < .05$, one-tailed test of significance. °°$p < .01$, one-tailed test of significance.

TABLE 7.7
Relational Goods Model of Overall Participation by Group Size
(African-Americans and Latinos Estimated Separately)

	African-Americans		Latinos	
	Large Black Group Size	Small Black Group Size	Large Latino Group Size	Small Latino Group Size
Education	.13°°	.09	.02	−.04
	(.04)	(.06)	(.03)	(.07)
Income	.05°	.06	.05	.06
	(.03)	(.05)	(.03)	(.06)
Democratic	1.07°°	−.17	.73°°	.37
	(.51)	(.47)	(.28)	(.68)
Republican	.76	.78	.73°°	.09
	(.60)	(.86)	(.32)	(.70)
Independent	1.65°°	−.29	.53	.14
	(.56)	(.57)	(.35)	(.72)
Empowerment	.03	−.22	.16	−.58
	(.19)	(.38)	(.19)	(1.18)
Mobilized	.59°°	.64°°	.71°°	.49°
	(.18)	(.23)	(.21)	(.28)
Knew mobilizer	.56°	.89°	.83°°	1.17°°
	(.32)	(.49)	(.45)	(.53)
Black/Latino mobilizer	.24	.34	.10	−1.91°
	(.33)	(.47)	(.44)	(.85)
Experienced racial discrimination	.10	.52	.40	.40
	(.23)	(.38)	(.28)	(.41)
Citizen	−1.15°	−.32	−.02	−.46
	(.68)	(.50)	(.22)	(.35)
Percent Noncitizens	−1.83	−.01	−1.34	−8.84°
	(1.26)	(1.74)	(.87)	(4.06)
Constant	−1.12	−.47	−.16	.92
	(.90)	(.98)	(.39)	(.86)
Adj. R2	.42	.48	.32	.35
N	247	88	163	52

Source: CPS. Data are unweighted.
Note: Table entries are OLS regression coefficients, with the associated standard error in parentheses. The dependent variable in each model is an index of the number of political activities the individual reports engaging in (ranging from 0 to 8). The mobilization variable is a dummy variable, where 1 indicates that the individual was asked to do campaign work, contact government officials, or engage in local activities. Black group-size equations are estimated using Blacks only, and using Black empowerment and Black mobilizer; Latino group-size equations are estimated using Latinos only, and using Latino empowerment and Latino mobilizer.
°$p < .05$, one-tailed test of significance. °°$p < .01$, one-tailed test of significance.

TABLE 7.8
Relational Goods Model of Voting Frequency, Estimated Separately by Black Group Size (African-Americans Only)

	Frequency of Voting in Presidential Elections		Frequency of Voting in Local Elections	
	Large Black Group Size	Small Black Group Size	Large Black Group Size	Small Black Group Size
Education	.05	.04	.08°°	−.01
	(.04)	(.07)	(.04)	(.06)
Income	−.01	.06	−.03	.05
	(.03)	(.05)	(.03)	(.05)
Democratic	2.05°°	.92°	1.51°°	1.06°
	(.54)	(.51)	(.50)	(.46)
Republican	1.81°°	−.68	1.00°	.12
	(.61)	(.87)	(.58)	(.79)
Independent	1.96°°	.27	1.18°	.41
	(.58)	(.60)	(.54)	(.54)
Black empowerment	.40°	.04	.48°°	.08
	(.17)	(.39)	(.17)	(.35)
Mobilized	.25	.17	.18	.30
	(.16)	(.23)	(.17)	(.21)
Knew mobilizer	.01	.36	−.02	.45
	(.29)	(.48)	(.29)	(.44)
Black mobilizer	.53°	.10	.72°°	.34
	(.29)	(.47)	(.29)	(.42)
Experienced racial discrimination	−.40°	.42	−.27	.23
	(.21)	(.38)	(.21)	(.35)
Citizen	1.39°	−.18	.15	−.17
	(.76)	(.64)	(.91)	(.58)
Percent noncitizens	.48	.08	1.42	.73
	(1.18)	(1.71)	(1.19)	(1.56)
Constant	−.66	1.86°	.51	1.72°
	(1.00)	(1.09)	(1.11)	(.99)
Adjusted R2	.18	.18	.20	.28
N	234	84	235	84

Source: CPS. Data are unweighted.

Note: Table entries are OLS regression coefficients, with the associated standard error in parentheses. The dependent variables are individuals' self-reports on the frequency with which they vote in presidential or local elections ranging from values of 1 ("never") to 5 ("all of the time"). "Mobilized" is a dummy variable indicating whether the individual reports having been contacted to do campaign work (1 = yes, 0 = no). Individuals residing in areas with less than the sample mean for Black group size are coded as residing in "small Black group size" areas; those residing in areas with greater than or equal to the sample mean are coded as residing in "large Black group size" areas.

°$p < .05$, one-tailed test of significance. °°$p < .01$, one-tailed test of significance.

and knowing the mobilizer are significant and positive in each case. At the same time, having a mobilizer of the same race is significant in only one of the four cases—for Latinos in areas of smaller Latino populations—but contrary to theory, the estimated relationship is negative. Experience with racial discrimination, being a citizen, and residing in areas with higher levels of noncitizens are in most cases insignificant as predictors of overall participation. Hence, the overall conclusion to be drawn from table 7.7 is simply that the effects of most relational goods remain significant regardless of group size.

Slightly more interesting results obtain from the estimates for frequency of voting in presidential and local elections for African-Americans, as shown in table 7.8. Here, it is clear that ideology is particularly important in areas of large Black group size. For both presidential and local elections, African-Americans identifying as Democrats, Republicans, or Independents are significantly more likely to vote. In contrast, such identification is related to voter turnout in areas of small Black group size only for Democrats. Finally, another important point is that being mobilized by another Black is significant (and positive) only for those African-Americans residing in areas of large Black group size. This, again, is consistent with Uhlaner's relational goods argument: individuals mobilized by (minority) group members should be more likely to participate (i.e., contribute) than those individuals mobilized by nonmembers.

Table 7.9 presents similar models for Latinos, but unfortunately the sample size is reduced sufficiently such that the reliability of these estimates is doubtful. For voting frequency in both presidential and local elections, the sample size is reduced to fewer than fifty cases. It is not surprising that across the four equations few coefficients achieve statistical significance—not even the standard workhorses of education and income. Thus, I include the table for review, but make no further substantive comments.

CONCLUSION

This chapter in some senses offers the most direct evidence regarding my argument, first posed in chapter 1, about the fundamental importance of mobilization to individuals' decisions to participate and of the political and social context to *minorities'* decisions to participate. As such, the empirical evidence both replicates and extends previous research on political participation and offers several interesting insights along the way.

First, it is clear that individuals' decisions to participate are determined in large part by whether they have been recruited to do so. Both the magnitude of this effect and its consistency across racial/ethnic groups

TABLE 7.9

Relational Goods Model of Voting Frequency, Estimated Separately by Latino Group Size (Latinos Only)

	Frequency of Voting in Presidential Elections		Frequency of Voting in Local Elections	
	Large Latino Group Size	Small Latino Group Size	Large Latino Group Size	Small Latino Group Size
Education	.05	−.09	.03	−.04
	(.04)	(.12)	(.04)	(.12)
Income	.05	.03	.04	−.05
	(.05)	(.11)	(.05)	(.11)
Democratic	1.05°°	.87	.85°	.86
	(.42)	(.97)	(.41)	(.96)
Republican	1.68°°	.44	1.71°°	.73
	(.49)	(1.03)	(.48)	(1.01)
Independent	.76	.02	.42	.60
	(.52)	(1.08)	(.50)	(1.05)
Latino	.15	−1.57	.23	.82
empowerment	(.26)	(1.81)	(.26)	(1.78)
Mobilized	−.10	.83°	−.15	.36
	(.29)	(.42)	(.29)	(.41)
Knew mobilizer	1.16	1.11	.86	.92
	(.61)	(.83)	(.60)	(.82)
Latino mobilizer	.33	−3.35°	.62	−2.63°
	(.62)	(1.58)	(.61)	(1.57)
Experienced racial	.46	.96	.23	.91
discrimination	(.41)	(.71)	(.40)	(.69)
Citizen	−.54	−.14	−.34	−.67
	(.33)	(.57)	(.32)	(.55)
Percent noncit-	−1.62	1.18	−1.42	.92
izens	(1.23)	(7.08)	(1.20)	(7.01)
Constant	1.91°°	2.37°	1.76°°	2.36°
	(.62)	(1.23)	(.61)	(1.22)
Adjusted R2	.23	.13	.09	.03
N	43	141	142	43

Source: CPS. Data are unweighted.

Note: Table entries are OLS regression coefficients, with the associated standard error in parentheses. The dependent variables are individuals' self-reports on the frequency with which they vote in presidential or local elections ranging from values of 1 ("never") to 5 ("all of the time"). "Mobilized" is a dummy variable indicating whether the individual reports having been contacted to do campaign work (1 = yes, 0 = no). Individuals residing in areas with less than the sample mean for Latino group size are coded as residing in "small Latino group size" areas; those residing in areas with greater than or equal to the sample mean are coded as residing in "large Latino group size" areas.

°$p < .05$, one-tailed test of significance. °°$p < .01$, one-tailed test of significance.

clearly establish its preeminence in terms of the causal factors structuring individuals' decisions to participate. Moreover, it is not simply being asked to participate that matters, but also knowing the individual who asks. Each of these robust empirical findings confirms Uhlaner's relational goods argument in a striking fashion, and these findings hold across racial/ethnic groups and whether one considers individuals' overall levels of political activity or, more specifically, voter turnout. Evidence regarding other aspects of the relational goods model is not quite as straightforward. Experiencing racial discrimination is only occasionally associated with minority participation, while the race of the mobilizer—an indirect measure of group identity or interaction—is associated with participation only for African-Americans with respect to voter turnout, and not overall participation.

Second, a stunningly consistent finding is the insignificance of political empowerment for Latinos. Thus, while Bobo and Gilliam's conclusions regarding political empowerment are confirmed for African-Americans and electoral turnout, they are clearly not replicated for Latinos. The risk of generalizing across racial and ethnic groups—whether of minority status or not—is indeed highlighted by these two findings.

Third, the analyses suggest that the effects of group size are robust across types of participation, but only for Latinos. For African-Americans, the only significant effects of group size are in the context of voting in local elections, where numbers apparently matter in African-Americans' strategic decisions to participate. This finding thus conflicts with earlier research suggesting that the creation of minority-majority districts for African-Americans is a disincentive to participation. Given the potential importance of this finding for practical matters of public policy, this conclusion should not be taken lightly. The racial context, political empowerment, and relational goods incentives indeed structure minority participation as well as the form that such participation takes (i.e., local versus presidential elections).

Taken as a whole, these distinct findings provide substantial support for the participation models introduced in chapter 1. They especially highlight the broader point that theories developed in the context of one group's politics cannot be easily applied to other groups. Instead, such theories need to be carefully evaluated with systematic evidence. To illustrate this point more broadly, the next chapter considers the effects of racial context on Anglo participation.

Chapter Eight

ANGLO POLITICAL PARTICIPATION IN CONTEXT

I HAVE thus far oriented the analyses toward two major goals: first, improving our understanding of elite strategies of minority mobilization and African-Americans' and Latinos' responsiveness to such efforts, and second, testing whether the factors identified in minority studies literatures—relying largely on anecdotal and case-study evidence—are confirmed when subjecting them to more systematic analysis. These analyses point toward the importance of (minority) group size in structuring the behavior of political elites as well as Latinos; the importance of empowerment in structuring the behavior of African-Americans in electoral politics; and the critical role of mobilization in stimulating Latinos' and African-Americans' political participation.

To put these findings into a broader perspective, in this last analytical chapter I address three questions. First, to what extent do these findings hold true for Anglos? Second, how does the nature of the racial composition of Anglos' neighborhoods affect their political participation? Third, how do these findings reflect on traditional approaches to the study of race and political participation?

The first two questions are particularly important, as Uhlaner's (1989b) formal model poses individuals' decisions to participate as a reflection of group ties, yet she suggests that these group ties may be less important as explanations of political participation for some groups than others. Her examples suggest that these relational goods are more important for minority groups, compared to racial/ethnic "majority" groups. However, to conclude from this that relational goods and the racial context (i.e., minority empowerment or group size) are not relevant to Anglo behavior may be premature. In fact, that very issue is central to understanding how the mass public responds to more diverse political and social environments.

THEORETICAL EXPECTATIONS

My strongest expectation in the analyses below is that the consistent findings regarding the association between socioeconomic status and participation will be confirmed without doubt. One of the motivations for this research program was the observation that most of what we know about political behavior is based on "representative" national surveys of Anglos.

Hence, I fully expect that this generalization will hold when including only Anglos in our sample.

Similarly, I expect to confirm earlier findings regarding ideological patterns in participation: individuals who are most likely to identify with political parties are most likely to be mobilized by them and to perceive advantages to participating; further, there are no costs associated with either party for mobilizing Anglos. Hence, Democrats, Republicans, and Independents alike should be more likely than nonidentifiers to participate.

Thus far I have discussed the effects of group size primarily as an "objective" measure of costs and benefits of participation, where individuals use group size in a strategic decision regarding the likely benefits of engaging in political activity. With respect to minority groups in particular, the larger the size of the group, the more likely minorities will believe that their participation could yield some particularized benefits for group members. This is broadly consistent with Uhlaner's discussion of relational goods, as well as her prediction that the greater the concentration of group members, the higher the level of turnout.

Previous empirical research suggests two alternative hypotheses regarding the relationship between minority group size and Anglo behavior. First, increasing minority group size may have a negative effect on Anglo turnout. Hill and Leighley (1999) draw on historical analyses of Key (1949), Burnham (1982), and Piven and Cloward (1989), all of whom claim that racial politics has defined numerous electoral systems; more recently, the twentieth century (i.e., the "fourth" party system) has been marked by "a host of demobilizing forces nationwide, and destroyed the positive linkages of ethnic groups to the political parties that existed in the third party system" (Hill and Leighley 1999: 277).

Moreover, Burnham argues that the "size of race is most evident at the state and local levels, because the political system is more likely to reflect the geographic concentration of minority groups there" (Hill and Leighley 1999: 278). Hill and Leighley's (1999) aggregate-level evidence shows that states with more ethnically diverse populations have significantly lower levels of voter turnout. To the extent that Anglos make up the majority of state electorates, this suggests that the greater the presence of minorities, the lower the level of Anglo turnout.

Similarly, Leighley and Vedlitz (1999) find that the more heterogeneous the residential context of Anglos (i.e., the greater the presence of minorities in the immediate environment), the less likely Anglos are to participate. This expectation is also consistent with Oliver's (1996) argument that the greater the homogeneity in a community, the higher the level of participation, as heterogeneity breeds conflict. Since conflict is costly, in terms of individuals' rational decisions to vote or not, it acts as a disincentive to participation. However, at odds with this evidence is an alternative expectation, drawing on the research of Giles and various coauthors on racial politics in the South, that the greater the minority group size, the *more* likely Anglos are to participate. Giles and Evans (1985, 1986) argue that as the threat to the dominant group from the minority group increases, individuals belonging to the dominant group will act to protect their interests.

In terms of political behavior, Key wrote about this group-based political phenomenon in *Southern Politics*: as the size of the Black population increased, so did fear within the white community, which resulted in greater negative, controlling behaviors by whites. Similarly, Matthews and Prothro (1966) found that as the proportion of Blacks in Southern counties increased, white support of Blacks' right to vote decreased. The group threat argument—based almost entirely on aggregate-level data—can reasonably be interpreted as a political mobilization argument as well, where Anglos who feel threatened are *more* likely to engage in political activity as they act to protect their interests. Thus, for Anglos, the larger the size of the minority group present, the larger the threat, and therefore the greater the level of political activity.

This, in fact, was how Leighley and Vedlitz (1999) had framed their expectations: Anglos would respond to minority group threat by engaging in political activity to protect their advantaged position. Their evidence, based on a statewide survey of Texans that included oversamples of African-Americans, Latinos, and Asian-Americans, suggested just the opposite: Anglos participated significantly *less* when threatened by the presence of minorities, while individuals of racial/ethnic minority status were not affected (either negatively or positively) by the racial context. It is unclear whether these findings would be sustained outside of the particular historical, cultural, and institutional contexts of Texas politics.

Thus, the analyses below provide critical empirical evidence regarding how Anglos' racial context influences their political behavior. Particularly notable is the fact that this is only the second empirical test of the group-conflict model and its implications for political participation—as opposed to vote choice or candidate preference. Also notable is the fact that I am using individual-level rather than aggregate-level data to test these hypotheses about individual behavior (unlike Hill and Leighley's [1999] evidence).

Bobo and Gilliam (1990) offer the only existing empirical evidence regarding political empowerment, emphasizing its critical importance for Black participation and concluding that whites' political participation is not associated with Black empowerment. Instead, education, occupation, and age are significant predictors of political engagement, as are various psychological orientations toward politics. However, these findings might be restricted to the time period they were investigating (1987), and one might argue that the politics of the 1990s has become more racially charged and divisive. To the extent that that is true, we might expect to see minority empowerment negatively associated with Anglo participation. This interpretation would be consistent with the positive argument for the symbolic value that Blacks associate with empowerment—which might be perceived as equally important by Anglos, but yielding the opposite effects.

RACIAL CONTEXT AND ANGLO PARTICIPATION

To test these competing hypotheses regarding the effects of racial context and minority empowerment on Anglos, I have estimated the "relational goods" model used in the last chapter but restricted the sample to Anglos. I use the same set of dependent variables used in the last chapter as well: individuals' overall level of political participation and individuals' self-reports of the frequency with which they vote in presidential and local elections.

I also use three different measures of racial group context. The first measure is the equivalent of that used for African-Americans and Latinos in chapter 7, and is the percentage of (non-Hispanic) Anglos in the individual's neighborhood (i.e., zip code region). This allows for a direct comparison on the importance of group size for Anglos to the findings reported in the last chapter.

The second measure of racial context is an indicator of racial/ethnic diversity that combines the relative proportions of Anglos, Blacks, and Latinos in a neighborhood. This measure indicates how heterogeneous the population is with respect to non-Hispanic whites, Hispanics, and Blacks.[1] To compute the measure, U.S. census data on the relative size of these three populations in the CPS respondent's zip code region are merged by zip code for each respondent. The measure varies from 0 to 1, with larger values indicating greater ethnic diversity.[2] Since it is the same measure used by Hill and Leighley (1999), it allows for a direct comparison of these analyses to their aggregate-level findings on state politics.

The third measure of racial context, perceived racial homogeneity, is the survey respondent's description of the neighborhood in which she resides as being composed entirely of the individual's racial/ethnic group, composed mostly of the individual's racial/ethnic group, "mixed," or composed of a few of the individual's racial/ethnic group, where higher values indicate greater homogeneity consistent with the survey respondent's race/ethnicity. This, of course, introduces some measurement error as the racial composition of individuals' neighborhoods may not correlate highly with

[1] The formula for this measure is: $1 - ([\text{percent of the white population}^2] + [\text{percent of the black Population}^2] + [\text{percent of the Hispanic population}^2])$. See Hill and Leighley (1999) for a discussion of this measure.

[2] This measure is correlated with "percentage white" at $-.77$.

the relative size of the group in the local community and therefore its presence or importance in local politics. It does, however, allow the individual to cue on a potentially meaningful social context ("the neighborhood") rather than focus on the zip code region.

Table 8.1 presents the initial results for the relational goods models of overall participation and turnout estimated for Anglos. The results for socioeconomic status and ideology are quite consistent, as are the results for minority empowerment and group size. As is the case for African-Americans and Latinos, Anglos of higher socioeconomic status are more likely to participate than Anglos of lower socioeconomic status; this holds true for overall participation, voting in presidential elections and voting in local elections.

With one exception, ideological identifiers are significantly more likely to participate, suggesting that for Anglos, party identifiers are more likely to be mobilized and therefore participate. On the other hand, neither Anglo group size nor minority empowerment is associated with Anglos' overall participation or voting frequency. These findings together suggest that, at least initially, the racial context has little effect on Anglos' participation decisions and that the political parties as political institutions are more critical to structuring Anglo participation.

Except for the measure of racial discrimination—originally included as an indirect measure of individuals' identity with their racial/ethnic (minority) group—each of the "relational goods" indicators is consistently related to Anglo participation. Being mobilized and knowing the person doing the recruiting increases the overall level of participation as well as the frequency of voting in both presidential and local elections.

Somewhat unexpectedly, experience with racial discrimination is associated with Anglos' overall levels of participation, indicating that Anglos (more so than Latinos and African-Americans) are more likely to participate in response to racial discrimination. This is a particularly interesting finding, especially in light of Hochschild's (1995) claim that Anglos are less likely to perceive racial discrimination toward African-Americans. It is possible that such responses have emerged at the same time that the issue of affirmative action has elicited particularly strong opposition from the mass public (see, e.g., Carmines and Sniderman 1999; Kinder and Sanders 1996).

Table 8.2 shows that virtually identical results are produced when the population diversity measure is substituted for Anglo group size: socioeconomic status and ideology are strong and consistent predictors of overall participation and voting frequency, while neither minority empowerment nor population diversity is associated with either type of participation. Further, the relational goods indicators of being mobilized and knowing the mobilizer also have significant, positive effects on Anglo participation.

TABLE 8.1
Relational Goods Models of Overall Participation and Voting Frequency
(Anglos Only)

	Overall Participation	Presidential Election Voting Frequency	Local Election Voting Frequency
Education	.08°°	.07°°	.02
	(.02)	(.02)	(.02)
Income	.05°°	.04°°	.04°°
	(.01)	(.01)	(.01)
Democratic	.52°°	1.20°°	1.13°°
	(.20)	(.15)	(.15)
Republican	.26	1.27°°	1.05°°
	(.20)	(.15)	(.15)
Independent	.35°	.93°°	.84°°
	(.21)	(.15)	(.16)
Anglo group size	−.01	−.09	.26
	(.25)	(.18)	(.19)
Minority	.08	−.12	−.03
empowerment	(.10)	(.07)	(.07)
Mobilized	.92°°	.53°°	.49°°
	(.06)	(.08)	(.08)
Knew mobilizer	.53°°	.17°	.31°°
	(.12)	(.07)	(.08)
Experienced racial	.56°°	−.17	−.15
discrimination	(.18)	(.14)	(.14)
U.S. citizen	−.20	.51°°	.18
	(.23)	(.18)	(.18)
Percent noncitizen	−.69	.0002	.23
	(.92)	(.68)	(.71)
Constant	−.48	1.09°°	1.30°°
	(.43)	(.32)	(.34)
N	1,220	1,192	1,190
Adj. R2	.45	.24	.17

Source: CPS. Data are unweighted.

Note: Table entries are OLS regression coefficients, with the associated standard error following in parentheses. The dependent variables are individuals' self-reports on the frequency with which they vote in presidential or local elections ranging from values of 1 ("never") to 5 ("all of the time") and an index of the number of political activities the individual reports engaging in (ranging from 0 to 8). These same variables were used in chapter 7. Minority empowerment is a dummy variable, where 1 indicates that either Blacks or Latinos have been elected to office; 0 otherwise. The mobilization variable used in the model of overall participation is a dummy variable, where 1 indicates that the individual was asked to do campaign work, contact government officials, or engage in local activities. The mobilization variable used in the two voting equations is a dummy variable indicating whether the individual reports having been contacted to do campaign work (1 = yes, 0 = no).

°$p < .05$, one-tailed test of statistical significance. °°$p < .10$, one-tailed test of statistical significance.

TABLE 8.2
Relational Goods Models, Using Racial/Ethnic Diversity Measure (Anglos Only)

	Overall Participation	Presidential Election Voting Frequency	Local Election Voting Frequency
Education	.08°°	.07°°	.02
	(.02)	(.02)	(.02)
Income	.05°°	.04°°	.04°°
	(.01)	(.01)	(.01)
Democratic	.52°°	1.21°°	1.13°°
	(.20)	(.15)	(.15)
Republican	.26	1.27°°	1.05°°
	(.20)	(.15)	(.15)
Independent	.36°	.93°°	.84°°
	(.21)	(.15)	(.16)
Minority empowerment	.08	−.12°	−.03
	(.09)	(.07)	(.07)
Racial/ethnic diversity	−.14	.11	.17
	(.25)	(.18)	(.18)
Mobilized	.92°°	.53°°	.48°°
	(.06)	(.08)	(.08)
Knew mobilizer	.53°°	.17°	.30°°
	(.12)	(.07)	(.08)
Experienced racial discrimination	.56°°	−.17	−.15
	(.18)	(.14)	(.14)
U.S. citizen	−.19	.51°°	.17
	(.23)	(.18)	(.18)
Percent noncitizen	−.41	−.04	.26
	(.91)	(.68)	(.71)
Constant	−.48	1.00°°	1.57°°
	(.36)	(.27)	(.29)
Adjusted R2	.45	.24	.17
N	1,220	1,192	1,190

Source: CPS. Data are unweighted.

Note: Table entries are OLS regression coefficients, with the associated standard error following in parentheses. The dependent variables are individuals' self-reports on the frequency with which they vote in presidential or local elections ranging from values of 1 ("never") to 5 ("all of the time") and an index of the number of political activities the individual reports engaging in (ranging from 0 to 8). These same variables were used in chapter 7. Minority empowerment is a dummy variable, where 1 indicates that either Blacks or Latinos have been elected to office; 0 otherwise. The mobilization variable used in the model of overall participation is a dummy variable, where 1 indicates that the individual was asked to do campaign work, contact government officials, or engage in local activities. The mobilization variable used in the two voting equations is a dummy variable indicating whether the individual reports having been contacted to do campaign work (1 = yes, 0 = no).
°$p < .05$, one-tailed test of statistical significance. °°$p < .10$, one-tailed test of statistical significance.

To investigate further Anglos' responsiveness to the racial context, I next estimated the relational goods model using Anglos' perceptions of neighborhood racial context (where higher values indicate more homogeneous racial contexts). As shown in table 8.3, perceived neighborhood racial composition is significantly associated with Anglos' frequency of voting in presidential and local elections. Anglos residing in neighborhoods that they perceive to be more homogeneous vote are significantly *more* likely to vote than are Anglos residing in neighborhoods perceived to be less homogeneous (more racially diverse), and this effect holds for both presidential and local elections. Thus, in contrast to the initial findings that the "objective" racial context has no effect on Anglo participation, this evidence suggests that Anglos' involvement in electoral politics is indeed affected by their *perceptions* of the racial context.

To put these findings into context, I estimated the last two models—those including the population diversity and perceived neighborhood homogeneity measures—separately for African-Americans and Latinos as well.[3] Table 8.4 presents the results for African-Americans, where population diversity is included in models of overall participation and frequency of voting in presidential and local elections. Table 8.5 presents the results for the same models, but substitutes individuals' perceptions of neighborhood homogeneity for population diversity.

The two sets of model estimates are generally consistent with each other. African-Americans residing in more diverse neighborhoods are significantly less likely to vote frequently in local elections, but are not less likely to participate or vote less frequently in presidential elections. Note that this differs from the findings in chapter 6, where the size of the Black population is not a significant predictor of participation. This might reflect the fact that high Black population neighborhoods are often the result of Voting Rights Act enforced districts decisions and might thereby nullify the incentives provided by more homogeneous group environments. The evidence that the "objective" racial composition of the neighborhood affects African-Americans' electoral participation is mirrored in the findings in table 8.5, where perceived neighborhood homogeneity is negatively associated with frequency of voting in presidential and local elections.

The different signs on these coefficients, however, merely reflect coding conventions, and the substantive conclusion is the same: African-Americans residing in areas of less diversity/more homogeneity are significantly more likely to vote in local elections; the same holds true for presidential elections in the case of perceptions of neighborhood homogeneity. And, similar to Anglos, neither the objective nor the subjective

[3] The initial model presented in table 8.1 is directly comparable to table 7.2 for African-Americans and to table 7.3 for Latinos.

TABLE 8.3
Relational Goods Models, Using Perceived Neighborhood Racial/Ethnic
Homogeneity Measure (Anglos Only)

	Overall Participation	Presidential Election Voting Frequency	Local Election Voting Frequency
Education	.07°°	.07°°	.02
	(.02)	(.01)	(.02)
Income	.06°°	.04°°	.03°°
	(.01)	(.01)	(.01)
Democratic	.51°°	1.23°°	1.14°°
	(.20)	(.15)	(.15)
Republican	.28	1.30°°	1.08°°
	(.20)	(.15)	(.15)
Independent	.39°	.98°°	.88°°
	(.20)	(.15)	(.16)
Minority empowerment	.06	− .08	− .01
	(.09)	(.07)	(.07)
Perceived neighborhood homogeneity	− .14°°	.11°°	.15°°
	(.06)	(.04)	(.04)
Mobilized	.90°°	.51°°	.46°°
	(.05)	(.07)	(.08)
Knew mobilizer	.56°°	.19°°	.34°°
	(.11)	(.07)	(.07)
Experienced racial discrimination	.48°°	− .16	− .12
	(.18)	(.13)	(.14)
U.S. citizen	.03	.54°°	.26
	(.21)	(.17)	(.17)
Percent noncitizen	− .83	.63	.39
	(.80)	(.60)	(.63)
Constant	− .22	.62°	.99°°
	(.40)	(.30)	(.31)
Adjusted R2	.45	.24	.18
N	1,261	1,233	1,231

Source: CPS. Data are unweighted.

Note: Table entries are OLS regression coefficients, with the associated standard error following in parentheses. The dependent variables are individuals' self-reports on the frequency with which they vote in presidential or local elections ranging from values of 1 ("never") to 5 ("all of the time") and an index of the number of political activities the individual reports engaging in (ranging from 0 to 8). These same variables were used in Chapter 7. Minority empowerment is a dummy variable, where 1 indicates that either Blacks or Latinos have been elected to office; 0 otherwise. The mobilization variable used in the model of overall participation is a dummy variable, where 1 indicates that the individual was asked to do campaign work, contact government officials, or engage in local activities. The mobilization variable used in the two voting equations is a dummy variable indicating whether the individual reports having been contacted to do campaign work (1 = yes, 0 = no).

°$p < .05$, one-tailed test of statistical significance. °°$p < .10$, one-tailed test of statistical significance.

TABLE 8.4
Relational Goods Models, Using Racial/Ethnic Diversity Measure
(African-Americans Only)

	Overall Participation	Presidential Election Voting Frequency	Local Election Voting Frequency
Education	.13°°	.06°	.06°
	(.04)	(.03)	(.03)
Income	.04	.004	−.01
	(.03)	(.03)	(.02)
Democratic	.82°°	1.43°°	1.39°°
	(.35)	(.36)	(.34)
Republican	.18	.93°°	.78°
	(.47)	(.46)	(.44)
Independent	.72°	1.24°°	1.02°°
	(.40)	(.40)	(.38)
Black empowerment	.22	.34°°	.49°°
	(.16)	(.15)	(.14)
Racial/ethnic diversity	.58	−.30	−.73°
	(.43)	(.40)	(.39)
Mobilized	.62°°	.58°°	.50°°
	(.13)	(.19)	(.19)
Knew mobilizer	.77°°	.40°	.55°°
	(.26)	(.20)	(.19)
Experienced racial discrimination	.19	−.23	−.17
	(.19)	(.18)	(.17)
U.S. citizen	−.43	.45	.11
	(.41)	(.47)	(.49)
Percent noncitizen	−1.70	.27	1.67°
	(1.09)	(1.03)	(1.01)
Constant	1.37°	1.02	1.12
	(.64)	(.69)	(.69)
Adjusted R2	.43	.17	.22
N	336	319	320

Source: CPS. Data are unweighted.

Note: Table entries are OLS regression coefficients, with the associated standard error following in parentheses. The dependent variables are individuals' self-reports on the frequency with which they vote in presidential or local elections ranging from values of 1 ("never") to 5 ("all of the time") and an index of the number of political activities the individual reports engaging in (ranging from 0 to 8). These same variables were used in Chapter 7. Minority empowerment is a dummy variable, where 1 indicates that either Blacks or Latinos have been elected to office; 0 otherwise. The mobilization variable used in the model of overall participation is a dummy variable, where 1 indicates that the individual was asked to do campaign work, contact government officials, or engage in local activities. The mobilization variable used in the two voting equations is a dummy variable indicating whether the individual reports having been contacted to do campaign work (1 = yes, 0 = no).

°*p* < .05, one-tailed test of statistical significance. °°*p* < .10, one-tailed test of statistical significance.

TABLE 8.5
Relational Goods Models, Using Perceived Neighborhood Racial/Ethnic
Homogeneity Measure (African-Americans Only)

	Overall Participation	Presidential Election Voting Frequency	Local Election Voting Frequency
Education	.13°°	.06°	.07°
	(.04)	(.03)	(.03)
Income	.04	.01	−.001
	(.03)	(.02)	(.02)
Democratic	.86°°	1.45°°	1.39°°
	(.35)	(.36)	(.34)
Republican	.29	.96°	.76°
	(.46)	(.45)	(.43)
Independent	.77°°	1.26°°	1.00°°
	(.40)	(.40)	(.38)
Black empowerment	.22	.29°	.42°°
	(.16)	(.15)	(.14)
Perceived neighborhood homogeneity	.02	.16°	.23°°
	(.09)	(.08)	(.08)
Mobilized	.62°°	.58°°	.49°°
	(.13)	(.19)	(.19)
Knew mobilizer	.76°°	.37°	.51°°
	(.26)	(.20)	(.19)
Experienced racial discrimination	.19	−.22	−.15
	(.19)	(.18)	(.17)
U.S. citizen	−.39	.36	−.06
	(.41)	(.47)	(.48)
Percent noncitizens	−1.12	.17	1.23
	(1.01)	(.94)	(.93)
Constant	1.28°	.46	.29
	(.68)	(.72)	(.72)
Adjusted R2	.42	.18	.23
N	32	320	321

Source: CPS. Data are unweighted.

Note: Table entries are OLS regression coefficients, with the associated standard error following in parentheses. The dependent variables are individuals' self-reports on the frequency with which they vote in presidential or local elections ranging from values of 1 ("never") to 5 ("all of the time") and an index of the number of political activities the individual reports engaging in (ranging from 0 to 8). These same variables were used in chapter 7. Minority empowerment is a dummy variable, where 1 indicates that either Blacks or Latinos have been elected to office; 0 otherwise. The mobilization variable used in the model of overall participation is a dummy variable, where 1 indicates that the individual was asked to do campaign work, contact government officials, or engage in local activities. The mobilization variable used in the two voting equations is a dummy variable indicating whether the individual reports having been contacted to do campaign work (1 = yes, 0 = no).

°$p < .05$, one-tailed test of statistical significance. °°$p < .10$, one-tailed test of statistical significance.

racial context measure is associated with African-Americans' overall level of participation.

Similar models are estimated for Latinos in tables 8.6 and 8.7. As is the case for Anglos, objective neighborhood population diversity is not associated with Latino overall participation or either of the voting frequency measures. However, Latinos' perceptions of neighborhood homogeneity are associated with the frequency of voting in local elections: Latinos perceiving their neighborhoods to be more homogeneous are significantly more likely to vote more frequently in local elections. Thus, perceptions of the racial composition of neighborhoods are important for all three racial/ ethnic groups, with individuals being more likely to vote in elections when they perceive their neighborhoods to be more homogeneous. Yet the only group for which the *objective* racial composition of the neighborhood is important—with the nature of the relationship being the same—is African-Americans.

Nonetheless, since more homogeneous neighborhoods for Blacks and Latinos are essentially more diverse neighborhoods for Anglos, it appears that these findings basically support Hill and Leighley's (1999) aggregate analysis that suggests that voter turnout is lower in more diverse states: turnout is generally lower in more diverse neighborhoods, controlling for individual characteristics such as socioeconomic status and ideology.

TRADITIONAL APPROACHES TO RACE, ETHNICITY, AND PARTICIPATION

I noted in chapter 1 that traditional ("mainstream") analyses of race, ethnicity, and political participation typically assess whether particular minority groups participate more or less than Anglos. I chose to ignore this traditional approach up to this point because there were compelling theoretical reasons to do so: theories of minority politics had been developed but not rigorously tested. The previous chapters have provided preliminary evidence on a variety of these issues. To finish this undertaking, however, it is useful to briefly reconsider the question of differences in participation levels across racial and ethnic groups.

To do so, I first estimate a variation of the "relational goods" model tested in previous chapters, using the entire (nationally "representative") sample, with overall participation and frequency of voting in presidential and local elections as the dependent variables. This model includes the measures of socioeconomic status, ideology, minority empowerment, and group size used in the previous section on Anglo mobilization and participation.

I also include a measure of mobilization that differs depending on which

TABLE 8.6
Relational Goods Models, Using Racial/Ethnic Diversity Measure (Latinos Only)

	Overall Participation	Presidential Election Voting Frequency	Local Election Voting Frequency
Education	.004	.02	.01
	(.03)	(.04)	(.04)
Income	.05	.06	.02
	(.03)	(.04)	(.04)
Democratic	.64°°	1.03°°	.86°
	(.26)	(.39)	(.38)
Republican	.47	1.32°°	1.38°°
	(.29)	(.44)	(.43)
Independent	.43	.66	.57
	(.31)	(.46)	(.44)
Latino empowerment	.34°	.33	.44°
	(.18)	(.26)	(.25)
Racial/ethnic diversity	.44	− .46	− .30
	(.42)	(.62)	(.59)
Mobilized	.63°°	.18	.03
	(.16)	(.36)	(.35)
Knew mobilizer	.88°°	1.10°°	.92°°
	(.33)	(.39)	(.38)
Experienced racial discrimination	.27	.53	.38
	(.22)	(.34)	(.32)
U.S. citizen	− .01	− .15	− .19
	(.18)	(.27)	(.26)
Percent noncitizens	− .63	.36	.07
	(.76)	(1.12)	(1.08)
Constant	− .36	1.70°°	1.69°°
	(.38)	(.61)	(.59)
Adjusted R2	.29	.12	.08
N	217	186	187

Source: CPS. Data are unweighted.

Note: Table entries are OLS regression coefficients, with the associated standard error following in parentheses. The dependent variables are individuals' self-reports on the frequency with which they vote in presidential or local elections ranging from values of 1 ("never") to 5 ("all of the time") and an index of the number of political activities the individual reports engaging in (ranging from 0 to 8). These same variables were used in chapter 7. Minority empowerment is a dummy variable, where 1 indicates that either Blacks or Latinos have been elected to office; 0 otherwise. The mobilization variable used in the model of overall participation is a dummy variable, where 1 indicates that the individual was asked to do campaign work, contact government officials, or engage in local activities. The mobilization variable used in the two voting equations is a dummy variable indicating whether the individual reports having been contacted to do campaign work (1 = yes, 0 = no).

°$p < .05$, one-tailed test of statistical significance. °°$p < .10$, one-tailed test of statistical significance.

TABLE 8.7

Relational Goods Models, Using Perceived Neighborhood Racial/Ethnic Homogeneity
Measure (Latinos Only)

	Overall Participation	Presidential Election Voting Frequency	Local Election Voting Frequency
Education	.004	.02	.01
	(.03)	(.04)	(.04)
Income	.05°	.07°	.03
	(.03)	(.04)	(.04)
Democratic	.67°°	1.09°°	1.82°
	(.26)	(.39)	(.38)
Republican	.49°	1.37°°	1.38°°
	(.28)	(.44)	(.42)
Independent	.46	.77°	.61
	(.31)	(.46)	(.44)
Latino empowerment	.25	.31	.43°
	(.18)	(.26)	(.25)
Perceived neighborhood	.03	.12	.43°
homogeneity	(.10)	(.26)	(.25)
Mobilized	.66°°	.23	.11
	(.17)	(.36)	(.36)
Knew mobilizer	.81°°	1.01°°	.85°
	(.34)	(.39)	(.39)
Experienced racial	.27	.54	.38
discrimination	(.23)	(.34)	(.32)
U.S. citizen	−.003	−.28	−.29
	(.18)	(.28)	(.27)
Percent noncitizen	−.56	−.06	−.47
	(.79)	(1.18)	(1.13)
Constant	−.29	1.24°°	1.46°°
	(.41)	(.61)	(.58)
Adjusted R2	.28	.11	.08
N	216	185	185

Source: CPS. Data are unweighted.

Note: Table entries are OLS regression coefficients, with the associated standard error following in parentheses. The dependent variables are individuals' self-reports on the frequency with which they vote in presidential or local elections ranging from values of 1 ("never") to 5 ("all of the time") and an index of the number of political activities the individual reports engaging in (ranging from 0 to 8). These same variables were used in chapter 7. Minority empowerment is a dummy variable, where 1 indicates that either Blacks or Latinos have been elected to office; 0 otherwise. The mobilization variable used in the model of overall participation is a dummy variable, where 1 indicates that the individual was asked to either do campaign work, contact government officials, or engage in local activities. The mobilization variable used in the two voting equations is a dummy variable indicating whether the individual reports having been contacted to do campaign work (1 = yes, 0 = no).

°$p < .05$, one-tailed test of statistical significance. °°$p < .10$, one-tailed test of statistical significance.

dependent variable is being estimated. For overall participation, the mobilization indicator represents how many times the individual reports being asked to engage in campaign work, to contact government officials, and to engage in local community activity. It thus ranges from 0 to 3. For the voting frequency models, the mobilization measure is a dichotomous variable that indicates whether the individual was recruited to engage in campaign work (1 = recruited, and 0 = not recruited).

In each of the three models, a dummy variable indicating whether the individual knew the recruiter (in any one of the three possible recruitment requests described above) and a dummy variable indicating whether the individual had experienced racial discrimination are included as measures of relational goods. Controls for individual-level and contextual-level citizenship are also included, as are two dummy variables for being "Black" or "Latino."

The advantage of this model specification is that it provides the opportunity to assess whether the components of the relational goods model eliminate differences in the level of participation across racial/ethnic groups. Of particular interest in these "traditional" models is whether the dummy variables for "Latino" and "Black" are significant and if so, whether the estimated coefficients are positive or negative.

Table 8.8 shows that, as expected, socioeconomic status, ideological identification, being mobilized, and knowing the mobilizer are significant predictors of both overall participation and frequency of voting in presidential and local elections (with the exception of "knowing the mobilizer" in the presidential election voting frequency model). Again generally consistent with the earlier models, neither minority empowerment nor experience with racial discrimination is associated with overall participation or with voting in presidential or local elections. Group size, on the other hand, is significantly associated with individuals' frequency of voting in local elections: the greater the size of the individual's racial/ethnic group in the immediate neighborhood, the more likely the individual is to vote in local elections. Finally, the dummy variable for Blacks is insignificant for overall participation and for voting in presidential elections, suggesting that Blacks are no more and no less likely to vote in presidential elections or engage in a wide range of political activities than are Anglos. Blacks are, however, significantly more likely to report voting frequently in local elections. In contrast, Latinos are significantly less likely than Anglos to vote frequently in presidential and local elections, and they participate significantly less than Anglos in a wider range of political activities. Consistent with the group-specific analyses presented in the last chapter, neither the contextual characteristics of empowerment and group size nor the relational goods indicators seemingly overcome the lower levels of participation reported by Latinos.

TABLE 8.8
Relational Goods Models of Overall Participation and Voting Frequency (Full Sample)

	Overall Participation	Presidential Election Voting Frequency	Local Election Voting Frequency
Education	.05°°	.06°°	.02
	(.02)	(.02)	(.02)
Income	.04°°	.04°°	.02
	(.01)	(.01)	(.01)
Democratic	.62°°	1.29°°	1.21°°
	(.13)	(.19)	(.18)
Republican	.41°°	1.33°°	1.09°°
	(.14)	(.20)	(.10)
Independent	.47°°	.93°°	.87°°
	(.15)	(.21)	(.19)
Group size	−.01	.04	.43°°
	(.17)	(.16)	(.16)
Minority empowerment	.08	−.06	.04
	(.08)	(.07)	(.08)
Mobilized	.74°°	.57°°	.48°°
	(.07)	(.08)	(.09)
Knew mobilizer	.46°°	.09	.25°°
	(.15)	(.08)	(.09)
Experienced racial discrimination	.23	−.20	−.19
	(.16)	(.14)	(.16)
Black	−.02	−.09	.20°
	(.12)	(.12)	(.12)
Latino	−.24°	−.46°°	−.33°
	(.14)	(.17)	(.16)
U.S. citizen	−.15	.35	.002
	(.23)	(.22)	(.21)
Percent noncitizen	−.81	−.38	−.31
	(.63)	(.70)	(.64)
Constant	−.14	1.24°°	1.45°°
	(.32)	(.35)	(.35)
N	1,772	1,696	1,696
Adjusted R2	.36	.21	.14

Source: CPS. Data are weighted.

Note: Table entries are OLS regression coefficients, with the associated standard error following in parentheses. The dependent variables are individuals' self-reports on the frequency with which they vote in presidential or local elections ranging from values of 1 ("never") to 5 ("all of the time") and an index of the number of political activities the individual reports engaging in (ranging from 0 to 8). These same variables were used in chapter 7. Minority empowerment is a dummy variable, where 1 indicates that either Blacks or Latinos have been elected to office; 0 otherwise. The mobilization variable used in the model of overall participation is a dummy variable, where 1 indicates that the individual was asked to do campaign work, contact government officials, or engage in local activities. The mobilization variable used in the two voting equations is a dummy variable indicating whether the individual reports having been contacted to do campaign work (1 = yes, 0 = no).

°$p < .05$, one-tailed test of statistical significance. °°$p < .10$, one-tailed test of statistical significance.

Finally, I consider one alternative conceptualization to race/ethnicity-related differences in political participation. One of the most challenging problems in studying political mobilization and participation is that, theoretically and practically, the very factors that predict one predict the other. And these factors are essentially enduring demographic characteristics. Moreover, we typically use cross-sectional survey data to test a process that occurs over time: mobilization leads to participation, which leads to a greater probability of being mobilized, etc. Hence, it is virtually impossible to estimate the effect of mobilization on participation while giving sufficient consideration to the extent to which they are interrelated. Individuals and institutions are likely to mobilize those who are likely to participate, and mobilization always predicts participation successfully. Although this problem is often noted in the political behavior literature, there has been little, if any, success in solving it.

Further compounding this problem is that our survey measures of mobilization and participation are recall measures, and we have little empirical evidence as to the validity and reliability of these self-reports. Perhaps the strong effect of being mobilized on participation is partly spurious, a function of the fact that individuals who have participated simply are more likely to recall being mobilized. Again, we have no evidence on this point, and I have clearly not tried to solve this problem that plagues research on political participation more broadly.

However, I would like to offer one last analysis that might be considered fuel to add to the debate regarding the relative importance of mobilization to participation. Verba, Schlozman and Brady (1995) noted that not all acts of participation are mobilized; indeed a substantial amount of political activity is "spontaneous." I would like to ask the question from the opposite direction: if an individual is mobilized, do the standard predictors of participation still matter?

Obviously the "if" portion of the previous sentence yields a potential firestorm of criticism in that it flagrantly ignores the endogeneity issue directly. To begin with an "if mobilization" statement—when we know that the traditional factors are all highly correlated with mobilization—and then ask whether these same factors matter in predicting individuals' responses to mobilization efforts is indeed a risky venture—and should be undertaken and interpreted with care.

However, given the centrality of mobilization to this assessment of class, race, and political participation, I think it is worth at least a brief consideration. It is possible to examine this question because of the availability of a unique set of mobilization and participation questions in the CPS. In most surveys, individuals are usually asked questions about mobilization and participation that are not directly linked, that is, they are asked whether the parties contacted them, and whether they voted in the last election. The CPS, on the other hand, includes a series of questions that begins by asking individuals whether they were recruited to engage in a particular political activity, some details about the recruiter, and whether they responded positively to such a request. This provides a unique opportunity to assess the effects of mobilization as "responses to a mobilization request."

To do so, I use measures derived from this series of questions to estimate the "relational goods" model used in earlier chapters for the entire sample. The alternative measures are each dichotomous dependent variables, where 1 indicates that the individual reports being mobilized to participate in a particular activity and said yes, and 0 indicates that the individual reports being mobilized to participate and said no.[4] More specifically, three specific types of mobilization requests are used as dependent variables: requests for campaign work, contacting government officials, and engaging in local campaign activities. (These are the same measures used in the analysis of political mobilization presented in chapter 6).

Table 8.9 shows the results for these three model estimates, calculated for the full sample. Two findings here are particularly striking. First, socioeconomic status is clearly unrelated to saying yes to mobilization requests: once one is mobilized, class matters little in predicting whether individuals will engage in political activity. Instead, what seems to matter most as a predictor of subsequent activity is whether the individual knows the mobilizer.

Second, when considering individuals' responses to mobilization, neither African-Americans nor Latinos are significantly less likely to respond positively to such a request. This is especially notable given the finding in table 8.8 that Latinos are consistently less likely than Anglos to participate overall or to vote in presidential and local elections. Here, once mobilization is "accounted for," Latinos are no less likely to participate than are Anglos.

To summarize, traditional approaches to modeling the effects of race, or racial context, on individuals' political participation have typically focused on the question of whether minorities participate more or less than Anglos. As an example of this approach, I have estimated the "relational goods" model for the entire sample and concluded that Latinos are significantly less likely than Anglos to participate. Solving the bigger issue of endogeneity in estimates of the effects of mobilization on participation (and

---

[4] These models will necessarily suffer from selection bias: individuals who were not mobilized did not have the opportunity to say yes or no and hence are excluded from this analysis. Thus, conclusions regarding the effect of individuals' characteristics on saying yes or no to a question for mobilization will not be based on a representative sample. In this case, for example, we know that individuals with higher levels of education and income are more likely to be mobilized. Because of this the estimates for the effects of education and income on "saying yes" do not reflect the true population parameters (Greene 1999).

TABLE 8.9
Relational Goods Models of "Saying Yes" (Full Sample)

	Campaign Mobilization	Contact Mobilization	Local Activity Mobilization
Education	−.01	−.01	.04
	(.04)	(.04)	(.04)
Income	.02	−.02	.08°°
	(.02)	(.02)	(.03)
Democratic	.17	−.01	.72°
	(.51)	(.45)	(.41)
Republican	.12	.08	1.00°°
	(.51)	(.45)	(.42)
Independent	.02	−.13	.57
	(.52)	(.46)	(.42)
Group size	−.16	−.20	.58
	(.30)	(.35)	(.38)
Minority empowerment	−.13	.10	.14
	(.14)	(.17)	(.18)
Knew mobilizer	.45°°	.70°°	.57°°
	(.14)	(.16)	(.21)
Experienced racial discrimination	.11	.16	.30
	(.24)	(.26)	(.27)
Black	.20	−.09	.11
	(.23)	(.28)	(.29)
Latino	.35	−.06	.08
	(.30)	(.35)	(.36)
U.S. citizen	.42	−.32	−.03
	(.30)	(.44)	(.42)
Percent noncitizen	.21	1.23	−1.11
	(1.30)	(1.48)	(1.50)
Constant	−1.04	.51	−2.72°°
	(.77)	(.85)	(.86)
N	680	563	456
Percent correctly predicted	20.1	21.3	15.5
Mean participation	45.8%	66.9%	59.8%

Source: CPS. Data are weighted.

Note: Table entries are probit regression coefficients, with the associated standard error following in parentheses for all models. The dependent variable is a dichotomous variable indicating whether the individual responded positively to a specific request for campaign activity, contacting a government official, or engaging in local community activity. Minority empowerment is a dummy variable, where 1 indicates that either Blacks or Latinos have been elected to office; 0 otherwise.

°$p < .05$, one-tailed test of statistical significance. °°$p < .10$, one-tailed test of statistical significance.

vice versa) is particularly important given the tentative findings I report on requests for mobilization: if we consider only individuals who are mobilized, neither Latinos nor African-Americans are less likely than Anglos to participate. Were this conclusion sustained with a more appropriate empirical analysis, it would indeed underscore the importance of mobilization to understanding who participates.

CONCLUSION

The main intellectual contribution of this chapter is its consideration of how the racial context structures Anglos' political participation. The strongest theoretical framework motivating this analysis was group-conflict theory, which suggests that Anglos respond to threats from other groups by mobilizing to protect their interests. However, almost all of the empirical evidence on this point focused not on participation, but instead on attitudinal and electoral behaviors (i.e., vote choice). In addition, this evidence relied on aggregate-level data; operationalized racial group threat with respect to Blacks only; and assumed group threat to be experienced by Anglos only.

Contradicting this theoretical framework was some limited evidence that diversity depresses political participation. But, in one case, this evidence was based only on data analyzed at the aggregate level; in the other case, it relied on survey data only from Texas. Hence, how the racial context structures Anglos' political participation was unresolved.

The evidence offered in this chapter provides a set of convincing answers to that question and illuminates this process in greater detail. I find that the racial context consistently structures Anglos' participation, in that Anglos are less likely to vote in more diverse environments—and this finding is similar to that for both Latinos and African-Americans. Individuals residing in areas that are "more like them" are simply more likely to vote.

However, it is important to note that for Anglos, this finding is restricted to perceptual measures of neighborhood homogeneity, in that "objective" measures of diversity are not associated with Anglos' decisions to vote or participate. Although I had no theoretical reason to expect conflicting findings when using the alternative measures, the finding that the perception of diversity is more "important" than objective realities is curious. One interpretation of this finding is that individuals' attitudes toward racial and ethnic minorities may be critical to understanding individuals' participation in more diverse contexts. Alternatively, this might suggest that a more diverse community has more politically relevant issues in the public arena and that the incentives for individuals to participate are therefore enhanced.

Finally, I concluded with a brief presentation of the relational goods model, estimated in the traditional manner, where the main question focuses on whether minorities participate less than Anglos. The evidence here suggests that Latinos are less likely to participate than Anglos. But this finding must be interpreted in light of findings in earlier chapters that suggested that in certain racial/political contexts, this might not be the case. Rather than concluding that there is something innate to Latino individuals or cultures that would depress participation, the alternative explanation points to the importance of the racial and political contexts in structuring those patterns. That Latinos participate less than Anglos reflects in part the reality that Latinos are mobilized less in civic institutions such as the workplace or voluntary associations (Verba, Schlozman, and Brady 1995). But it might also reflect the need for greater, more positive socialization into participatory democracy (see Cho 1999).

This finding, as well as the evidence from this part of the analysis that racial context has no effect on individuals' participation decisions, of course reflects very specific theoretical assumptions (of traditional approaches) and research design issues. In those respects the presentation of these results emphasizes further the observation that motivated my research here: mainstream studies of political participation have ignored theories and evidence regarding the participation of racial and ethnic minorities, while at the same time the latter have been developed less systematically than is needed.

And so we return to our original questions: Do individuals engage or disengage in response to diversity? Under what conditions do they do so? Generally, individuals are more likely to participate when they reside in more racially/ethnically homogeneous contexts; the more the surrounding environment is "like them," the more likely they are to participate.

Although these findings seem to point us toward a conclusion that highlights different patterns of participation across racial and ethnic groups, it is also clear that the other incredibly consistent set of findings is that regarding relational goods. Not just being mobilized but knowing who initiated the mobilization request increases the likelihood of participation for Latinos, African-Americans, and Anglos alike. It thus appears that the similarities regarding why individuals participate might be as great as the differences. And those "relational goods" might well be the incentives that build stronger communities in a more diverse democratic society.

Chapter Nine

SUMMARY AND CONCLUSION

M OST discussions of race and class in American politics are awash in rhetoric and anecdote—each undoubtedly serving its unique purpose—yet the extent to which these issues are central to the most fundamental political questions in our nation demands that we treat them more seriously in our scholarship. That is what I have tried to do here, in an effort to think more systematically about and understand more generally citizens' responses to racial and ethnic diversity.

I began with a broad criticism of "traditional" or "mainstream" models of political participation, which have focused for decades now almost exclusively on individual characteristics as determinants of individuals' decisions to engage in political activity. Considerations of the significance of race or ethnicity were often limited to the question of whether Blacks or Latinos participated more or less than Anglos. Much of this research assumed that the effects of individual characteristics such as socioeconomic status and ideology are similar across racial and ethnic groups. Although the evidence for these basic theories was abundant, it nonetheless was generated by a research tradition dominated by the use of "representative" national surveys made up almost entirely of Anglos.

Perhaps the most serious consequence of this dominant approach is, first, that we learned very little about the very factors that scholars of African-American and Latino politics emphasized in their arguments regarding political participation. In contrast to the emphasis in mainstream studies on individual characteristics, these scholars noted the critical importance of mobilization for minority communities. In this research tradition, however, most evidence was drawn from anecdotal accounts and a handful of case studies of minority politics. Second, little effort had been devoted to assessing whether theories developed in the context of one group's politics were valid for others.

My goal, then, was to explicitly test for systematic differences in the level, nature and effects of mobilization on political participation, and to do so in a way that provided insight as to differences (or similarities) across racial/ethnic groups. At one level the analytical approach was quite simple. Based on the traditional and minority studies literatures I identified five factors—socioeconomic status, ideology/partisanship, group size, political empowerment, and relational goods—that were argued to structure individual participation and, except for the latter, mobilization. I systematically tested how these factors were associated with elite decisions to mobilize and individuals' decisions to participate—as well as whether these patterns varied across groups.

The simplicity of this approach nonetheless yielded original empirical evidence on numerous points. First, I provided systematic evidence regarding elite decisions to mobilize and target various groups. Although this evidence is restricted to party elites in Texas, it is unique as evidence that tests what elites do (or say they do) to mobilize the mass public and does not rely on survey data. Second, I extended this research by examining not just the level of mobilization oriented toward minorities, but also the nature of these mobilization activities. This elite data on mobilization strategies and techniques suggested that the relative size of minority groups determines the likelihood that they will be targeted, and that socioeconomic status and ideological considerations are of little importance to party elites.

Third, I tested whether the political empowerment thesis extended to Latino political participation. An implicit assumption of some scholars is that what "works" or is important to one minority community does as well in other minority communities. Students of African-American and Latino politics would be quick to dispute this. The evidence regarding the empowerment thesis is especially valuable as it provides a simultaneous test of the thesis across these two groups. Substantively, this evidence sustained earlier findings on the importance of empowerment for Black political participation, but did not do so for Latino political participation.

Fourth, I have systematically considered the effects of group size on individuals' political participation, assessing these effects separately across racial/ethnic groups and across types of participation. These analyses are valuable contributions to group-conflict theory, for which most previous evidence was restricted to Anglos and to political behaviors other than participation and relied almost exclusively on aggregate-level data. Moreover, this new evidence helped resolve conflicting theoretical expectations regarding whether group threat would act to depress or stimulate Anglo political participation. Of particular interest here is the comparison of the role of racial/ethnic diversity in structuring political participation across racial and ethnic groups—and how that role is especially important in understanding Anglo political behavior.

Although the major empirical findings are summarized at the end of each chapter, I would like to highlight here what I believe are the most important substantive contributions. Each of these, I believe, is sufficiently important to warrant further research.

POLITICAL MOBILIZATION

The empirical findings regarding political mobilization identify socioeconomic status as the most consistent predictor of mobilization across racial/ethnic groups. In contrast, the role of ideology is structured by political institutions and its importance or relevance as a predictor of mobilization thus varies across groups. For example, while Anglo ideological identifiers (Republicans, Democrats, and Independents) are more likely to be mobilized than nonidentifiers, this pattern does not hold for African-Americans or Latinos. The patterns for African-Americans—significant only for African-American Democrats but no Latino groups—seem to reflect the current institutional affiliations of these groups as a whole, rather than individuals' particular political orientations. The patterns are also consistent with the findings on elite mobilization that suggested that only Democratic chairs targeted African-Americans (in Texas).

One of the more interesting issues that emerges from this finding is whether party elites will alter their current strategies as minority populations increase in size (i.e., electoral importance)—a virtual reality in states such as California and Texas—and if minorities are perceived to be more ideologically diverse. Perhaps unfortunately, both African-Americans and Latinos are perceived by the mass public as well as elites as being strongly liberal in their political orientations, which is not entirely accurate (see McClain and Stewart 1999). Assuming the Black and Latino middle classes continue to grow, the possibilities for the Republican Party to make inroads would seem to increase—and there is at least some elite recognition of the need to do so in states where minorities will make up a majority of the population in the not-so-distant future.

The challenge to party leaders in this scenario, of course, will be to reach out to an increasingly diverse electorate without losing the support of its current members. As Carmines and Stimson (1989) and Huckfeldt and Kohfeld (1989) have demonstrated, the party system of the mid- to late-twentieth century has been structured in part by issues of race. And, despite dramatic changes in Anglos' (explicitly) racial attitudes, it would be surprising if parties competing for minority voters did not have this contemporary history in mind when targeting potential supporters and building elite coalitions.

Since parties are most likely to target supporters (as demonstrated here and elsewhere), the question reduces to how this dynamic of support/mobilization might begin. And that is where there is an interesting opportunity to extend this research by documenting who, and how, the parties are mobilizing at the local level—and what factors are associated with these decisions. I would assume, of course, that where minorities are wealthier, they would be more likely to be targeted. But it might also be that minorities in highly competitive districts would be more likely to be targeted. A more systematic approach at the elite level—and beyond the state of Texas—is certainly warranted, given the importance of race to electoral coalitions and the projections of population changes anticipated over the next two decades in several states.

Yet to focus on party elites alone would be shortsighted, as both African-American and Latino activists have developed and sustained a set of mobilization institutions directed toward engaging African-Americans and Latinos into the political realm. To ignore these groups in future research would effectively limit our understanding of the political mobilization of racial/ethnic minorities to political institutions (i.e., party elites and candidates) dominated by Anglos. The possibly distinctive conceptualizations and strategies of minority leaders for mobilizing participation—as well as their interactions with party elites—must be studied more systematically to extend our understanding of political mobilization in U.S. politics and the extent to which racial/ethnic minorities are incorporated into the political system.

A second important substantive finding is that empowerment increases the probability that African-Americans are mobilized, but not in the case of Latino mobilization. Instead, empowerment has no effect on Latino mobilization, and group size has the *opposite* effect of what was anticipated. These findings are important for several reasons. First, they highlight the fact that we cannot generalize empirical findings on one minority group to another—a seemingly obvious point, but one that is probably not as evident in traditional studies of political participation. Second, these findings are important because they are largely consistent with the (brief) argument I made earlier regarding the differences in the two communities' political "infrastructure." The distinctive organizational, residential, historical, and cultural differences between the two groups, I argued, likely result in differential opportunities to participate—consistent with the political opportunity structure emphasis currently in vogue in studies of comparative social movements.

While my argument was sufficiently developed to provide a general sense of differences that we might expect to find between these two groups, it is clear that we could learn much more about the seemingly distinctive mobilization processes within these two communities by pursuing this theoretical framework further. "Borrowing" from comparative studies of social movements might provide some innovative ideas for both theory and research design and allow us to answer more precise questions about the unique dynamics—organizationally, socially, culturally—that structure minority groups' opportunities (i.e., incentives) to either mobilize or participate.

Third, and perhaps related, these findings regarding political empowerment and group size might also reflect the different nature of electoral coalition building, candidate strategies, and individual voting behavior available to African-Americans and Latinos. Throughout these chapters I have been quite clear as to the importance of studying these groups separately, but in various ways I have labeled them together as "racial/ethnic" groups. One might easily take issue with this, arguing that the barriers to full participation in our political system as well as society are far greater for African-Americans than for Latinos. A fair amount of empirical evidence suggests that this is the case, even in terms of various aspects of political behavior. For example, while we have consistent evidence regarding racialized voting (where Anglos are less likely to vote for Black candidates, and Blacks are significantly more likely to vote for Black candidates), there is some evidence that this type of voting is less common for Latinos—that is, the effects of ethnicity on Anglo voting behavior are weaker than those of race—and that Latinos are only slightly more likely, if at all, to vote for Latinos, regardless of other characteristics (Hero 1992).

Some discussions of urban politics suggest that Latinos have been more likely to enter into coalitions with Anglos than have African-Americans. This "color line" in electoral politics is undoubtedly strengthened by the existence of electoral district lines that are drawn either explicitly or implicitly to ensure minority representation (Swain 1995). This suggests the importance of examining the nature of racial and ethnic coalition building—at both the mass and elite level—and how these electoral strategies might well result in differential mobilization opportunities across racial and ethnic groups.

Finally, it is impossible to assess how my conclusions regarding political mobilization, empowerment, group size, and participation might be modified by explicitly considering the effects of racial redistricting. Although the contextual unit of analysis used in earlier chapters is smaller and not contiguous with such district lines, we would surely have a more thorough understanding of the role of elites in mobilizing participation of racial/ethnic minorities were we able to incorporate more explicitly details regarding *political* districts, both theoretically and empirically. The challenges of designing research projects that integrate individual, contextual, and electoral data relevant to political behavior would certainly be worth the effort.

POLITICAL PARTICIPATION

In some senses, the relative importance of my various findings regarding the factors that structure individuals' political participation is not proportional to the amount of evidence, or text, devoted to them in the previous chapters. The more traditional analyses presented pointed toward the critical importance of mobilization in determining who participates. Not just being mobilized but also knowing the individual who engaged in the mobilization effort were strong and consistent predictors of participation. Both of these aspects of mobilization were identified in Uhlaner's (1989b) formal model as "relational goods" that provide individuals the necessary incentives to engage in collective action.

Although previous research has documented the importance of mobilization to participation (e.g., Rosenstone and Hansen 1993), two other types of "relational goods" structure participation, as Uhlaner (1989b) suggests. Individuals experiencing racial discrimination (and therefore more likely to identify with their group), for example, were often more likely to participate than those who had not experienced racial discrimination. And group size—the proportion of Latinos in the individual's local context— was associated with greater participation for Latinos. Hence, the evidence in these chapters is the most systematic and widespread empirical treatment that has been afforded Uhlaner's (1989b) formal model—and the proof is rather positive for the general outlines of her model.

The evidence, however, is not entirely consistent with Uhlaner's predictions, which suggests that a more complex model might be required. For example, it is not African-Americans or Latinos for whom racial discrimination typically increases participation levels—it is Anglos. And Black population size enhances only Blacks' participation in local elections—not other types of participation, as it does for Latinos—while Latino population size also seems to enhance Anglo participation. Hence, it is likely that these relational goods operate within a particular political or social context, which should be specified more fully.

Finally, I have offered a more systematic treatment of group conflict theory, which suggests that, when threatened, individuals will act to protect their group interests. As chapter 7 indicated, previous research on group conflict focused almost exclusively on Anglos, relied heavily on aggregate-level data, and produced somewhat mixed results. My evidence helps resolve these inconsistencies, in finding that the effects of group threat on Anglo political participation differ according to the type of participation.

More specifically, individuals—whether Anglo, African-American, or Latino—are *less* likely to vote in diverse environments. These patterns have potentially enormous social and political implications, for the underlying principle that seems to structure participation—where homogeneity increases electoral involvement—is necessarily a zero-sum game: what advantages Anglos in electoral involvement necessarily disadvantages Blacks and Latinos. A most interesting question to pursue is the extent to which these differential responses of the mass public reflect, in part, the different strategies adopted by political elites in more diverse environments.

ON LEARNING MORE ABOUT POLITICAL PARTICIPATION

My criticisms of the standard socioeconomic status model and mainstream approaches to the study of political participation result in part from rejecting the assumption in these studies that individuals think and act politically independent of their social and political context. This assumption has been sustained, in part, by our choice of research design, with most studies relying on nationally "representative" surveys. These surveys, of course, are designed to randomize contexts across individual respondents. Accordingly, they not only restrict our attention to those individual characteristics easily ascertained through the course of an interview, but implicitly confuse the effects of individual characteristics with those of political and social context.

Incorporating aspects of individuals' political and social contexts more explicitly in our models of participation, and behavior more generally, is important as it enhances the *political* nature of our theories of political participation. As my discussion in this chapter suggests, the patterns of mobilization and participation I observed indicated that indeed both political and social institutions translate demographic characteristics into politically relevant behaviors or attitudes. Until we change our research designs to incorporate those institutions more directly, our explanations of political participation are likely to become irrelevant.

Some of this, of course, has already occurred. The study of voter turnout, for example, has shifted dramatically from Wolfinger and Rosenstone's now classic (1980) study of the demographic correlates of turnout to encompass factors such as political advertising, campaign spending, party competition, and registration laws, to name a few. The challenge in sustaining this exciting intellectual agenda is in being able to conceptualize the nature of mobilization beyond electoral politics. What institutions (elites) are relevant to study? How do we incorporate informal mobilization? How can we document mobilization independent of individuals' self-reports? Each of these questions is infinitely more difficult to address in the case of nonelectoral participation.

Future efforts at trying to synthesize the study of mainstream and minority participation, however, will have to deal precisely with these theoretical issues, as well as their implications for research design. While I am sympathetic to complaints regarding the paucity of data that allow us to study systematically how race and ethnicity structure political behavior, I nonetheless remain convinced that we must address the theoretical developments first. Doing so will benefit students of mass political behavior, as well as minority politics.

STRENGTH IN NUMBERS?

Finally, I return to the basic question: how will citizens respond politically to a more diverse social and political environment? The answer, I believe, is threefold. First, citizens in general will engage—*if mobilized to do so by political elites*. The trick, I might surmise, is whether such mobilization will be conducted in a racially polarizing manner or instead in a racially neutral way by appealing to voters on the basis of substantive issues. Second, citizens will engage if they are mobilized in direct rather than mediated ways by individuals they know. This provides a potentially important limit to political elites' abilities to motivate political behavior using mediated, often negative symbols and rhetoric. Third, racial and ethnic minorities will engage more when they reside among others "like themselves." Hence, there is *strength in numbers* with respect to the representation of minorities as political activists.

The challenge, of course, is that Anglos, too, are more likely to participate when residing in more homogeneous contexts. The future of democratic politics is thus likely to rest on the nature of those political involvements and the extent to which political elites seek to build coalitions across groups, rather than escalate any social and political differences that might exist between them. Thus, while this book has not dealt directly with elites' strategic use of race and ethnicity as political issues or the political consequences of doing so, it certainly points out the critical importance of further research in that direction.

Appendix A

TEXAS A&M / RICE UNIVERSITY 1996 TEXAS COUNTY PARTY CHAIR POST-ELECTION SURVEY

1) How long have you been active in the county party organization?
___ months ___ years

2) And how long have you been county chair? ___ months ___ years

3) This fall, approximately how many hours per week did you spend on party activities? ___

4) This fall, did your organization have [**CIRCLE ONE OF THE FOLLOWING**]:
a paid staff   a volunteer staff   a mix of both   or did you not have any staff?

5) In 1996, did your organization [**circle one answer for each question**]:
- have an office with regular hours?   yes   no
- receive money from the state or national party?   yes   no
- provide registration materials to individuals?   yes   no
- provide voter information or volunteers to candidates?   yes   no
- provide voters transportation to the polls during early voting?   yes   no
- provide voters transportation to the polls on election day?   yes   no
- purchase advertisements or distribute literature?   yes   no
- sponsor fundraising events or provide funds to candidates?   yes   no

6) The following is a list of things that parties do. Please rank them in order of importance to your organization in this past election, with **one being most important** and **four being least important**. (You may record the number in the space following the activity.)
- registering voters   _____
- increasing turnout   _____
- persuading voters to support your party's candidates   _____
- providing resources to candidates   _____

7) How much did your county organization spend on the campaign in 1996? $ ___

8) This fall, were any races in the county targeted by the state or national party organization? yes no

9) Next, could you pleace indicate which of the following types of individuals your organization targeted to turn out for this fall's elections? [**CIRCLE ONE ANSWER FOR EACH QUESTION**]
- individuals likely to support your party   yes   no
- African-Americans   yes   no

• Hispanics	yes	no
• Asian-Americans	yes	no
• Christian Right	yes	no
• Independents or third-party supporters	yes	no
• individuals under 30 years of age	yes	no
• individuals aged 55 and over	yes	no
• high-income individuals	yes	no
• low-income individuals	yes	no
• women	yes	no

10) And did any auxiliaries of your party (like the College Democrats or College Republicans) try to increase voter registration and turnout in your county?

yes   no
[IF NO, SKIP TO QUESTION 12]

11) If so, which groups were these? **[PLEASE LIST GROUP NAMES]**
    1.
    2.
    3.

12) In 1996, were any *non*party organizations active in your county in trying to increase voter registration and turnout?

yes   no
[IF NO, SKIP TO QUESTION 14]

13) If so, which groups were these? **[PLEASE LIST GROUP NAMES]**
    1.
    2.
    3.

14) Did you seriously consider using early voting as part of your campaign strategy, or did you not really think about doing that?

yes (considered it)   no (did not consider it)
[IF NO, SKIP TO QUESTION 20]

15) And did you decide to go through with any activities to increase early voting turnout?   yes   no

[IF NO, SKIP TO QUESTION 20]

16) Approximately how many weeks prior to election day did these activities begin? _____

17) Did you target the same types of individuals for early voting as you did for election-day voting?   yes   no

[IF NO, SKIP TO QUESTION 20]

18) Could you please indicate which of the following types of individuals your organization targeted for early voting?
    [CIRCLE ONE ANSWER FOR EACH QUESTION]
    - registered voters   yes   no
    - individuals likely to support your party   yes   no
    - African-Americans   yes   no
    - Hispanics   yes   no
    - Asian-Americans   yes   no
    - Christian Right   yes   no
    - Independents/third-party supporters   yes   no
    - individuals under 30 years of age   yes   no
    - individuals aged 55 and over   yes   no
    - high-income individuals   yes   no
    - low-income individuals   yes   no
    - women   yes   no

19) And did you emphasize the same issues for early voters as you did for election-day voters?   yes   no

20) In the 1994 gubernatorial and congressional election, did your party target early voters?   yes   no

21) And how about the 1992 presidential election?   yes   no

22) Thinking back to the 1992 and 1994 elections, did any African-Americans run for county or local office as a candidate for your party in your county?
    yes   no

23) Any Asian-Americans?   yes   no

24) Any Hispanics?   yes   no

25) Any Women?   yes   no

26) Now, I'd like to ask you some additional questions about people in your county. On a scale of 1 to 5 with **1 being extremely liberal** and **5 being extremely conservative,** how would you describe the following? **[CIRCLE ONE ANSWER FOR EACH QUESTION]**
    - yourself   1   2   3   4   5
    - people in your county   1   2   3   4   5
    - Democratic Party activists   1   2   3   4   5
    - Republican Party activists   1   2   3   4   5
    - Independents   1   2   3   4   5
    - African-Americans   1   2   3   4   5
    - Hispanics   1   2   3   4   5
    - Asian-Americans   1   2   3   4   5
    - election-day voters   1   2   3   4   5

• early voters	1	2	3	4	5
• absentee voters	1	2	3	4	5

27) In what year were you born? 19_____

28) What is your current occupation? _____

29) We would like to know the general range of your family income, that is, the family living with you for 1996, before taxes. Was your total family income:
[**CIRCLE ONE OF THE FOLLOWING**]

less than $15,000	between $15,000 and $30,000
between $30,000 and $50,000	between $50,000 and $75,000
over $75,000	

30) What is your race or ethnic background? **CIRCLE ONE OF THE FOLLOWING]**

Anglo White	African-American	Hispanic
American Indian or Alaskan native	Asian or Pacific Islander	Other

You may return the completed survey in the enclosed, postage-paid envelope. Thank you again for your assistance!!!

REFERENCES CITED

Acock, Alan C., and Wilbur J. Scott. 1980. "A Model for Predicting Behavior: The Effect of Attitude and Social Class on High and Low Visibility Political Participation." *Social Psychology Quarterly* 43(1):59–72.

Affigne, Anthony. 1994. "Race and Turnout in Memphis: The Persistence of Racial Differentials in Participation." Paper presented at the Annual Meeting of the Midwest Political Science Association, Chicago, April 14–16.

Affigne, Anthony, and Katherine Tate. 1993. "The Limits of Urban Democracy: Voter Turnout, Politics and Race in U.S. Cities." Paper presented at the Annual Meeting of the American Political Science Association, Washington, DC, September 2–5.

Aldrich, John H. 1976. "Some Problems in Testing Two Rational Models of Participation." *American Journal of Political Science* 20 (4 November): 713–33.

———. 1993. "Rational Choice and Turnout." *American Journal of Political Science* 37:246–78.

Almond, Gabriel A., and Sidney Verba. 1963. *The Civic Culture*. Princeton: Princeton University Press.

Ansolabehere, Stephen, Shanto Iyengar, Adam Simon, and Nicholas Valentino. 1994. "Does Attack Advertising Demobilize the Electorate?" *American Political Science Review* 88:829–38.

Arvizu, John R., and F. Chris Garcia. 1996. "Latino Voting Participation: Explaining and Differentiating Latino Voting Turnout." *Hispanic Journal of Behavioral Sciences* 18:104–28.

Barker, Lucius J., and Mack H. Jones. 1994. *African Americans and the American Political System*, 3d ed. Englewood Cliffs, N.J.: Prentice Hall.

Barker, Lucius J., and Ronald W. Walters, eds. 1989. *Jesse Jackson's 1984 Presidential Campaign: Challenge and Change in American Politics*. Urbana: University of Illinois Press.

Barnes, Samuel, and Max Kaase. 1979. *Political Action: Mass Participation in Five Western Democracies*. Beverly Hills, CA: Sage.

Barrera, Mario. 1985. "The Historical Evolution of Chicano Ethnic Goals: A Bibliographic Essay." *Sage Race Relations Abstracts* 10(1):1–48.

Barta, Carolyn. "Parties Roll Out Strategies to Court Hispanic Vote." *The Bryan/College Station Eagle* 20 September 1998.

Beck, Paul A., and M. Kent Jennings. 1979. "Political Periods and Political Participation." *American Political Science Review* 73:737–50.

Berry, Jeffrey M., Kent E. Portney, and Ken Thomson. 1990. "The Political Behavior of Poor People." Paper presented at the Annual Meeting of the American Political Science Association, San Francisco, August 30–September 2.

Bibby, John F. 1999. "State and Local Parties in a Candidate Centered Age." In *American State and Local Politics: Directions for the 21st Century*, ed. Ronald E. Weber and Paul Brace, 194–211. New York: Chatham House.

Bobo, Lawrence, and Franklin D. Gilliam, Jr. 1990. "Race, Sociopolitical Participation, and Black Empowerment." *American Political Science Review* 84:377–93.

Brady, Henry E., Kay Lehman Schlozman, and Sidney Verba. 1999. "Prospecting for Participants: Rational Expectations and the Recruitment of Political Activists." *American Political Science Review* 93:153–68.

Brown, Clifford W., Jr., Roman B. Hedges, and Lynda W. Powell. 1980. "Modes of Elite Political Participation: Contributors to the 1972 Presidential Candidates." *American Journal of Political Science* 24(2):259–90.

Browning, Rufus P., Dale Rogers Marshall, and David H. Tabb. 1984. *Protest Is Not Enough: The Struggle of Blacks and Hispanics for Equality in Urban Politics.* Berkeley: University of California Press.

Bullock, Charles S. 1999. "The Opening Up of State and Local Election Processes." In *American State and Local Politics: Directions for the 21st Century*, ed. Ronald E. Weber and Paul Brace, 212–40. New York: Chatham House.

Burnham, Walter Dean. 1981. "The System of 1896: An Analysis." In *The Evolution of American Electoral Systems*, ed. Paul Kleppner, Walter Dean Burnham, Ronald P. Formisano, Samuel P. Hays, Richard Jensen, and William G. Shade, 147–202. Westport, CT: Greenwood.

———. 1982. *The Current Crisis in American Politics*. Oxford: Oxford University Press.

———. 1987. "The Turnout Problem." In *Elections American Style*, ed. A. James Reichley, 97–133. Washington DC: Brookings Institution.

Button, James W. 1989. *Blacks and Social Change*. Princeton: Princeton University Press.

Calvo, Maria Antonia, and Steven J. Rosenstone. 1989. *Hispanic Political Participation*. San Antonio, TX: Southwest Voter Research Institute, Inc.

Cameron, David R. 1974. "Toward a Theory of Political Mobilization." *Journal of Politics* 36:133–71.

Campbell, Angus, Philip E. Converse, Warren E. Miller, and Donald E. Stokes. 1960. *The American Voter*. New York: Wiley.

Canon, David T. 1999. *Race, Redistricting and Representation: The Unintended Consequences of Black Majority District Changes*. Chicago: University of Chicago Press.

Carmines, Edward G., and Paul M. Sniderman, eds. 1999. *Reaching beyond Race*. Cambridge, MA: Harvard University Press.

Carmines, Edward G., and James A. Stimson. 1989. *Issue Evolution: Race and the Transformation of American Politics*. Princeton: Princeton University Press.

Carmines, Edward G., Robert Huckfeldt, and Carl McCurley. 1995. "Mobilization, Counter-mobilization and the Politics of Race." *Political Geography* 14:601–19.

Carson, Clayborne. 1981. *In Struggle*. Cambridge, MA: Harvard University Press.

Carton, Paul. 1984. *Mobilizing the Black Community: The Effects of Personal Contact Campaigning on Black Voters*. Washington, DC: Joint Center for Political Studies.

Cavanagh, Thomas E. 1985. *Inside Black America*. Washington, DC: Joint Center for Political Studies.

———. 1987. *Strategies for Mobilizing Black Voters: Four Case Studies*. Washington, DC: Joint Center for Political Studies.

Census of Population and Housing. 1990. Summary Tape File 3 on CD-Rom. Washington, DC: Bureau of the Census.

Champagne, Anthony, and Edward J. Harpham, eds. 1998. *Texas Politics: A Reader*, 2d ed. New York: W. W. Norton.

Cho, Wendy K. Tam. 1999. "Naturalization, Socialization, Participation: Immigration and (Non-)Voting." *Journal of Politics* 61:1140–55.

Chong, Dennis. 1991. *Collective Action and the Civil Rights Movement*. Chicago: University of Chicago Press.

Clark, Kenneth B. 1970. "The Civil Rights Movement: Momentum and Organization." In *Roots of Rebellion*, ed. Richard P. Young, 270–97. New York: Harper and Row.

Conway, M. Margaret. 1981. "Political Participation in Midterm Congressional Elections: Attitudinal and Social Characteristics during the 1970s." *American Politics Quarterly* 9:221–44.

———. 1991. *Political Participation in the United States*. Washington, DC: CQ Press.

Cook, Constance Ewing. 1984. "Participation in Public Interest Groups." *American Politics Quarterly* 12(4):409–30.

Cox, Gary W., and Michael C. Munger. 1989. "Closeness, Expenditures, and Turnout in the 1982 U.S. House Elections." *American Political Science Review* 83: 217–31.

Crotty, William. 1991. "Political Participation: Mapping the Terrain." In *Political Participation and American Democracy*, ed. William Crotty, New York: Greenwood Press.

Curtis, James E., Edward G. Grabb, and Douglas E. Baer. 1992. "Voluntary Association Membership in Fifteen Countries: A Comparative Analysis." *American Sociological Review* 57:129–52.

Dalton, Russell J. 1988. *Citizen Politics in Western Democracies*. Chatham, NJ: Chatham House.

Danigelis, Nicholas L. 1982. "Race, Class and Political Involvement in the U.S." *Social Forces* 61:532–50.

Davidson, Chandler. 1990. *Race and Class in Texas Politics*. Princeton, NJ: Princeton University Press.

Dawson, Michael C. 1994. *Behind the Mule: Race and Class in African-American Politics*. Princeton, NJ: Princeton University Press.

Dawson, Michael C., Ronald E. Brown, and Richard L. Allen. 1990. "Racial Belief Systems, Religious Guidance, and African-American Political Participation." *National Political Science Review* 2:22–44.

De la Garza, Rodolfo O., and Louis DeSipio. 1994. "Overview: The Link between Individuals and Electoral Institutions in Five Latino Neighborhoods." In *Barrio Ballots: Latino Politics in the 1990 Elections*, ed. Rodolfo de la Garza, Martha Menchaca, and Louis DeSipio, 8. Boulder, CO: Westview.

———. 1997. "Save the Baby, Change the Bathwater, and Scrub the Tub: Latino Electoral Participation after Twenty Years of Voting Rights Act Coverage." In *Pursuing Power: Latinos and the Political System*, ed. F. Chris Garcia, 72–126. Notre Dame: University of Notre Dame Press.

———. eds. 1992. *From Rhetoric to Reality: Latino Politics in the 1988 Elections*. Boulder, CO: Westview.

————. eds. 1996. *Ethnic Ironies: Latino Politics in the 1992 Elections*. Boulder, CO: Westview.

————. eds. 1999. *Awash in the Mainstream: Latino Politics in the 1996 Elections*. Boulder, CO: Westview.

De la Garza, Rodolfo O., Martha Menchaca, and Louis DeSipio. 1994. *Barrio Ballots: Latino Politics in the 1990 Elections*. Boulder, CO: Westview.

DeSipio, Louis. 1996. *Counting on the Latino Vote: Latinos as a New Electorate*. Charlottesville: University of Virginia Press.

DeSipio, Louis, and Gregory Rocha. 1992. "Latino Influence on National Elections: The Case of 1988." In *From Rhetoric to Reality: Latino Politics in the 1988 Elections*, ed. Rodolfo de la Garza and Louis DeSipio, 3–22. Boulder, CO: Westview.

Diaz, William A. 1996. "Latino Participation in America: Associational and Political Roles." *Hispanic Journal of Behavioral Sciences* 18:154–74.

Downs, Anthony. 1957. *An Economic Theory of Democracy*. New York: Harper and Row.

Dubin, Jeffrey A., and Douglas Rivers. 1989/90. "Selection Bias in Linear Regression, Logit and Probit Models." *Sociological Methods and Research* 18:360–90.

Dyer, James A., Jan E. Leighley, and Arnold Vedlitz. 1998. "Party Identification and Public Opinion in Texas, 1984–1994: Establishing a Two-Party System." In *Texas Politics: A Reader*, 2d ed., Anthony Champagne and Edward J. Harpham, 107–22. New York: W. W. Norton.

Ellison, Christopher G., and David A. Gay. 1989. "Black Political Participation Revisited: A Test of Compensatory, Ethnic Community and Public Arena Models." *Social Science Quarterly* 70:101–19.

Engstrom, Richard L., and Victoria M. Caridas. 1991. "Voting for Judges: Race and Roll-Off in Judicial Elections." In *Political Participation and American Democracy*, ed. William Crotty, 171–92. New York: Greenwood Press.

Falcon, Angelo. 1988. "Black and Latino Politics in New York City: Race and Ethnicity in a Changing Urban Context." In *Latinos and the Political System*, ed. F. Chris Garcia, 171–94. Notre Dame: University of Notre Dame Press.

Farley, Reynolds. 1996. *The New American Reality*. New York: Russell Sage Foundation.

Ferejohn, John A., and Morris P. Fiorina. 1974. "The Paradox of Not Voting: A Decision Theoretic Analysis." *American Political Science Review* 68:525–36.

Fiorina, Morris P. 1976. "The Voting Decision: Instrumental and Expressive Aspects." *Journal of Politics* 38:390–415.

Flores, Henry, and Robert Brischetto. 1992. "Texas Mexicans in the 1988 Election." In *From Rhetoric to Reality: Latino Politics in the 1988 Elections*, ed. Rodolfo de la Garza and Louis DeSipio, 87–97. Boulder, CO: Westview.

Fort, Rodney. 1995. "A Recursive Treatment of the Hurdles of Voting." *Public Choice* 85:45–69.

Frymer, Paul. 1995. "In Pursuit of the Persuadables: African-American Mobilization in Democratic Party Campaigns." Paper presented at the Annual Meeting of the Western Political Science Association, Portland, Oregon, March 15–18.

Garcia, F. Chris. 1988. "Part II: Input to the Political System: Participation." In *Latinos and the Political System*, ed. F. Chris Garcia, 119–24. Notre Dame: University of Notre Dame Press.

———. ed. 1988. *Latinos and the Political System*. Notre Dame: University of Notre Dame Press.

———. ed. 1997. *Pursuing Power: Latinos and the Political System*. Notre Dame: University of Notre Dame Press.

Garcia, John A., and Carlos H. Arce. 1988. "Political Orientations and Behaviors of Chicanos: Trying to Make Sense Out of Attitudes and Participation." In *Latinos and the Political System*, ed. F. Chris Garcia, 125–51. Notre Dame: University of Notre Dame Press.

Gibson, Martha Liebler. 1989. "Motivations of Individual Participation in the Sanctuary Movement." Paper presented at the Annual Meeting of the Midwest Political Science Association, Chicago, April 13–15.

Giles, Micheal W., and Melanie Buckner. 1993. "David Duke and Black Threat: An Old Hypothesis Revisited." *Journal of Politics* 55(3):702–13.

———. 1996. "Comment." *Journal of Politics* 58(4):1171–80.

Giles, Micheal W., and Marilyn K. Dantico. 1982. "Political Participation and Neighborhood Social Context Revisited." *American Journal of Political Science* 26:144–50.

Giles, Micheal W., and Arthur S. Evans. 1985. "External Threat, Perceived Threat and Group Identity." *Social Science Quarterly* 66(1):50–66.

———. 1986. "The Power Approach to Intergroup Hostility." *Journal of Conflict Resolution* 30(3):469–86.

Giles, Micheal W., and Kaenan Hertz. 1994. "Racial Threat and Party Identification." *American Political Science Review* 88(2):317–26.

Gilliam, Frank D. 1996. "Exploring Minority Empowerment: Symbolic Politics, Governing Coalitions and Traces of Political Style in Los Angeles." *American Journal of Political Science* 40:56–81.

Goldenberg, Edie N., and Michael W. Traugott. 1984. *Campaigning for Congress*. Washington, DC: CQ Press.

Grafstein, Robert. 1991. "An Evidential Decision Theory of Turnout." *American Journal of Political Science* 35:989–1010.

Greene, William H. 1999. *Econometric Analysis*. New York: Prentice-Hall.

Gurin, Patricia, Shirley Hatchett, and James S. Jackson. 1989. *Hope and Independence: Blacks' Response to Electoral and Party Politics*. New York: Sage.

Guterbock, Thomas M., and Bruce London. 1983. "Race, Political Orientation, and Participation: An Empirical Test of Four Competing Theories." *American Sociological Review* 48:439–53.

Hardy-Fanta, Carol. 1993. *Latina Politics, Latino Politics: Gender, Culture and Political Participation in Boston*. Philadelphia: Temple University Press.

Harris, Fredrick C. 1994. "Something Within: Religion as a Mobilizer of African-American Political Activism." *Journal of Politics* 56:42–68.

Hero, Rodney E. 1986. "Explaining Citizen-Initiated Contacting of Government Officials: Socioeconomic Status, Perceived Need, Or Something Else?" *Social Science Quarterly* 67:626–35.

———. 1992. *Latinos and the U.S. Political System: Two-Tiered Pluralism*. Philadelphia: Temple University Press.

———. 1998. *Faces of Inequality: Social Diversity in American Politics*. New York: Oxford University Press.

Hero, Rodney E., and Anne G. Campbell. 1996. "Understanding Latino Political

Participation: Exploring the Evidence from the Latino National Political Survey."
Hispanic Journal of Behavioral Sciences 18:129–41.

Herrnson, Paul S. 1988. *Party Campaigning in the 1980s*. Cambridge, MA: Harvard University Press.

Hill, Kevin A., and Dario Moreno. 1996. "Second Generation Cubans." *Hispanic Journal of Behavioral Sciences* 18:175–93.

Hill, Kim Quaile, and Jan E. Leighley. 1992. "The Policy Consequences of Class Bias in State Electorates." *American Journal of Political Science* 36:351–65.

———. 1993. "Party Ideology, Organization and Competitiveness as Mobilizing Forces in Gubernatorial Elections." *American Journal of Political Science* 37: 1158–78.

———. 1994. "Mobilizing Institutions and Class Representation in U.S. State Electorates." *Political Research Quarterly* 47:137–50.

———. 1999. "Racial Diversity and Voter Mobilizing Institutions in the U.S." *American Politics Quarterly* 27:275–95.

Hinich, Melvin J. 1981. "Voting as an Act of Contribution." *Public Choice* 36:135–40.

Hinich, Melvin J., and Michael C. Munger. 1997. *Analytical Politics*. New York: Cambridge University Press.

Hirlinger, Michael W. 1992. "Citizen-Initiated Contacting of Local Government Officials: A Multivariate Explanation." *Journal of Politics* 54:553–64.

Hirschman, Albert O. 1970. *Exit, Voice, and Loyalty: Responses to Decline in Firms, Organizations, and States*. Cambridge, MA: Harvard University Press.

Hochschild, Jennifer. 1995. *Facing Up to the American Dream: Race, Class, and the Soul of the Nation*. Princeton: Princeton University Press.

Huckfeldt, Robert. 1979. "Political Participation and the Neighborhood Social Context." *American Journal of Political Science* 23:579–92.

———. 1986. *Politics in Context: Assimilation and Conflict in Urban Neighborhoods*. New York: Agathon Press.

Huckfeldt, Robert, and Carol Weitzel Kohfeld. 1989. *Race and the Decline of Class in American Politics*. Urbana: University of Illinois Press.

Huckfeldt, Robert, and John D. Sprague. 1992. "Political Parties and Electoral Mobilization: Political Structure, Social Structure and the Party Canvass." *American Political Science Review* 86:70–86.

———. 1995. *Citizens, Politics, and Social Communication: Information Influence in an Election Campaign*. New York: Cambridge University Press.

Jackman, Robert. 1992. "Rationality and Political Participation." *American Journal of Political Science* 37:279–90.

Jackson, Robert A. 1993. "Voter Mobilization in the 1986 Midterm Election." *Journal of Politics* 55:1081–99.

———. 1996. "A Reassessment of Voter Mobilization." *Political Research Quarterly* 49:331–50.

Jacobson, Gary C. 1980. *Money in Congressional Elections*. New Haven: Yale University Press.

———. 1990. "The Effects of Campaign Spending in House Elections: New Evidence for Old Arguments." *American Journal of Political Science* 34:334–62.

———. 1996. *The Politics of Congressional Elections*, 4th ed. New York: Addison-Wesley.

Jones-Correa, Michael, and David L. Leal. 1996. "Becoming 'Hispanic': Secondary Panethnic Identification among Latin American Origin Populations in the United States." *Hispanic Journal of Behavioral Sciences* 18:214–54.

Kelley, Stanley, Jr., Richard E. Ayres, and William G. Bowen. 1967. "Registration and Voting: Putting First Things First." *American Political Science Review* 61:359–79.

Kenny, Christopher B. 1992. "Political Participation and Effects from the Social Environment." *American Journal of Political Science* 36:259–67.

Kenny, Christopher B., and Wayne Parent. 1991. "Explaining Campaign Contribution Behavior." Paper presented at the Annual Meeting of the Midwest Political Science Association, Chicago, April 15–20.

Key, V. O., Jr. 1949. *Southern Politics in State and Nation.* New York: Knopf.

Kinder, Donald R., and Lynn M. Sanders. 1996. *Divided by Color: Racial Politics and Democratic Ideals.* Chicago: University of Chicago Press.

Kleppner, Paul. 1979. *The Third Electoral System, 1853–1892.* Chapel Hill: University of North Carolina Press.

———. 1982. *Who Voted? The Dynamics of Electoral Turnout, 1870–1980.* New York: Praeger.

Knoke, David. 1990a. "Networks of Political Action: Toward Theory Construction." *Social Forces* 68:1041–63.

———. 1990b. *Organizing for Collective Action: The Political Economies of Associations.* New York: Aldine de Gruyter.

Krassa, Michael A. 1988. "Context and the Canvass: The Mechanisms of Interaction." *Political Behavior* 10:233–46.

———. 1989. "Getting Out the Black Vote: The Party Canvass and Black Response." In *New Perspectives in American Politics: National Political Science Review, Volume 1,* ed. Lucius J. Barker, 58–75. New Brunswick, NJ: Transaction Publishers.

Leighley, Jan E. 1990. "Social Interaction and Contextual Influences on Political Participation." *American Politics Quarterly* 18:459–75.

———. 1995. "Attitudes, Opportunities and Incentives: A Field Essay on Political Participation." *Political Research Quarterly* 48:181–209.

———. 1996. "Group Membership and the Mobilization of Political Participation." *Journal of Politics* 58:447–63.

Leighley, Jan E., and Jonathan Nagler. 1992. "Individual and Systemic Influences on Turnout: Who Votes? 1984." *Journal of Politics* 54:718–40.

———. 1992. "Socioeconomic Bias in Turnout 1964–1988: The Voters Remain the Same." *American Political Science Review* 86:725–36.

Leighley, Jan E., and Arnold Vedlitz. 1999. "Race, Ethnicity and Political Participation: Competing Models and Contrasting Explanations." *Journal of Politics* 61:1092–1114.

Lenchner, Paul. 1998. "The Party System in Texas." In *Texas Politics: A Reader,* 2d ed., ed. Anthony Champagne and Edward J. Harpham, 156–76. New York: W. W. Norton.

London, Bruce, and Michael W. Giles. 1987. "Black Participation: Compensation or Ethnic Identification?" *Journal of Black Studies* 18:20–44.

London, Bruce, and John Hearn. 1976. "The Ethnic Community Theory of Black

Social and Political Participation: Additional Support." *Social Science Quarterly* 57:883–91.

MacManus, Susan A., and Carol A. Cassel. 1982. "Mexican-Americans in City Politics: Participation, Representation, and Policy Preferences." *Urban Interest* 4:57–69.

———. 1988. "Mexican-Americans in City Politics: Participation, Representation, and Policy Preference." In *Latinos and the Political System*, ed. F. Chris Garcia, 201–12. Notre Dame: University of Notre Dame Press.

Martinez, Valerie J. 1996. "Unrealized Expectations: Latinos and the 1992 Elections in Texas." In *Ethnic Ironies: Latino Politics in the 1992 Elections*, ed. Rodolfo O. de la Garza and Louis DeSipio, 113–30. Boulder, CO: Westview.

Mason, David. 1984. "Individual Participation in Collective Racial Violence: A Rational Choice Perspective." *American Political Science Review* 78:1040–56.

Massey, Douglas S., and Nancy A. Denton. 1993. *American Apartheid: Segregation and the Making of the Underclass*. Cambridge, MA: Harvard University Press.

Masset, Royal. N.d. "Precinct Walking: Walking Your Way to Victory in November." Austin: Republican Party of Texas.

———. N.d. "Introduction to Campaign Management: How to Win in November." Austin: Republican Party of Texas.

———. N.d. "Campaign Planning: Plan Now for Victory in November." Austin: Republican Party of Texas.

Matthews, Donald R., and James W. Prothro. 1966. *Negroes and the New Southern Politics*. New York: Harcourt Brace.

McAdam, Doug. 1982. *Political Process and the Development of Black Insurgency, 1930–1970*. Chicago: University of Chicago Press.

———. 1988. *Freedom Summer*. New York: Oxford University Press.

McAdam, Doug, John D. McCarthy, and Mayer N. Zald. 1996. *Comparative Perspectives on Social Movements*. New York: Cambridge University Press.

McClain, Paula D., and Joseph Stewart. 1999. *"Can We All Get Along?": Racial and Ethnic Minorities in American Politics*. 2d ed. New York: Westview.

McClerking, Harwood K. 1999. "Love Thy Neighbor?: Racial Context and Membership in Neighborhood Voluntary Associations." Paper presented at the Annual Meeting of the Midwest Political Science Association, Chicago, April 15–17.

McPherson, J. Miller. 1977. "Correlates of Social Participation: A Comparison of the Ethnic Community and Compensatory Theories." *Sociological Quarterly* 18:197–208.

Milbrath, Lester. 1965 *Political Participation*. Chicago: Rand McNally.

Miller, Arthur, Patricia Gurin, Gerald Gurin, and Oksana Malanchuk. 1981. "Group Consciousness and Political Participation." *American Journal of Political Science* 25:494–511.

Montoya, Lisa J. 1999. "Señor Smith Didn't Go to Washington: Latinos and the 1996 Texas Elections." In *Awash in the Mainstream*, ed. Rodolfo O. de la Garza and Louis DeSipio, 139–66. Boulder, CO: Westview.

Mormino, Gary R., and George Pozzetta. 1987. *The Immigrant World of Ybor City: Italians and Their Latin Neighbors in Tampa, 1885–1985*. Urbana: University of Illinois Press.

Morris, Aldon. 1981. "Black Southern Student Sit-In Movement: An Analysis of Internal Organization." *American Sociological Review* 46:744–67.

———. 1984. *Origins of the Civil Rights Movement: Black Communities Organizing for Change*. New York: Free Press.

Morton, Rebecca B. 1991. "Groups in Rational Turnout Models." *American Journal of Political Science* 35:758–76.

National Asian Pacific American Voter Registration Campaign. 1996. *Basic Facts on Voter Registration*. NAPAVRC: Washington, DC.

Nice, David C. 1988. "Abortion Clinic Bombings as Political Violence." *American Journal of Political Science* 32:178–95.

Nie, Norman H., Sidney Verba, Henry Brady, Kay L. Schlozman, and Jane Junn. 1988. "Participation in America: Continuity and Change." Paper presented at the Annual Meeting of the Midwest Political Science Association, Chicago.

Oliver, J. Eric. 1996. "The Effects of Eligibility Restrictions and Party Activity on Absentee Voting and Overall Turnout." *American Journal of Political Science* 40:498–513.

———. 1999. "The Effects of Metropolitan Economic Segregation on Local Civic Participation." *American Journal of Political Science* 43:186–212.

Oliver, J. Eric, and Tali Mendelberg. 1998. "Social Environments and White Racial Attitudes: The Meaning and Measurement of Context." Paper presented at the Annual Meeting of the Midwest Political Science Association, Chicago, April 23–26.

Olsen, Marvin E. 1970. "Social and Political Participation of Blacks." *American Sociological Review* 35:682–97.

Opp, Karl-Dieter. 1989. *The Rationality of Political Protest: A Comparative Analysis of Rational Choice Theory*. Boulder, CO: Westview.

Pachon, Harry, and Louis DiSipio. 1994. *New Americans by Choice: Political Perspectives of Latino Immigrants*. Boulder, CO: Westview.

Palfrey, Thomas R., and Howard Rosenthal. 1985. "Voter Participation and Strategic Uncertainty." *American Political Science Review* 79:62–78.

Patterson, Samuel C., and Gregory A. Caldeira. 1983. "Getting Out the Vote: Participation in Gubernatorial Elections." *American Political Science Review* 77:675–89.

Pinderhughes, Dianne M. 1987. *Race and Ethnicity in Chicago Politics: A Reexamination of Pluralist Theory*. Urbana: University of Illinois Press.

———. 1992. "The Role of African American Political Organizations in the Mobilization of Voters." In *From Exclusion to Inclusion: The Long Struggle for African American Political Power*, ed. Ralph C. Gomes and Linda Faye Williams, 35–52. New York: Greenwood.

Piven, Frances Fox, and Richard A. Cloward. 1989. *Why Americans Don't Vote*. New York: Pantheon.

Portes, Alejandro, and Rafael Mozo. 1988. "The Political Adaptation Process of Cubans and Other Ethnic Minorities in the United States: A Preliminary Analysis." In *Latinos and the Political System*, ed. F. Chris Garcia, 152–70. Notre Dame: University of Notre Dame Press.

Riker, William H., and Peter C. Ordeshook. 1968. "A Theory of the Calculus of Voting." *American Political Science Review* 62:25–43.

———. 1973. *An Introduction to Positive Political Theory*. Englewood Cliffs, NJ: Prentice-Hall.

Rosenstone, Steven J., and John Mark Hansen. 1993. *Mobilization, Participation, and Democracy in America*. New York: Macmillan.

Rosenstone, Steven J., and Raymond E. Wolfinger. 1978. "The Effect of Registration Laws on Voter Turnout." *American Political Science Review* 72:22–45.

Rosenstone, Steven J., John Mark Hansen, Paul Freedman, and Marguerite Grabarek. 1993. "Voter Turnout: Myth and Reality in the 1992 Election." Paper presented at the Annual Meeting of the American Political Science Association, Washington, DC, September 2–5.

Rothenberg, Lawrence S. 1992. *Linking Citizens to Government: Interest Group Politics at Common Cause*. Cambridge: Cambridge University Press.

Saiz, Martin. 1992. "Cohesion Mobilization and Latino Political Influence: Colorado in 1988." In *From Rhetoric to Reality: Latino Politics in the 1988 Elections*, ed. Rodolfo de la Garza and Louis DeSipio, 69–76. Boulder, CO: Westview.

Salisbury, Robert H. 1975. "Research on Political Participation." *American Journal of Political Science* 19:323–41.

———. 1980. *Citizen Participation in the Public Schools*. Lexington, MA: Lexington Books.

Sapiro, Virginia, Steven J. Rosenstone, Warren E. Miller, and the National Election Studies. 1998. American National Election Studies, 1948–1997 (CD-ROM). ICPSR ed. Ann Arbor, MI: Inter-university Consortium for Political and Social Research.

Schlichting, Kurt, Peter Tucker, and Richard Maisel. 1998. "Racial Segregation and Voter Turnout in Urban America." *American Politics Quarterly* 26:218–36.

Sharp, Elaine B. 1982. "Citizen-Initiated Contacting of Government Officials and Socioeconomic Status: Determining the Relationship and Accounting for It." *American Political Science Review* 76:109–15.

———. 1984. "Citizen Demand Making in the Urban Context." *American Journal of Political Science* 28:654–70.

Shaw, Daron, Rodolfo O. de la Garza, and Jongho Lee. 2000. "Examining Latino Turnout in 1996: A Three-State Validated Survey Approach." *American Journal of Political Science* 44:338–46.

Shingles, Richard D. 1981. "Black Consciousness and Political Participation: The Missing Link." *American Political Science Review* 75:76–91.

Sierra, Christine Maria. 1992. "Hispanos and the 1988 General Election in New Mexico." In *From Rhetoric to Reality: Latino Politics in the 1988 Elections*, ed. Rodolfo de la Garza and Louis DeSipio, 43–68. Boulder, CO: Westview.

Silver, Brian E., Barbara A. Anderson, and Paul R. Abramson. 1986. "Who Overreports Voting?" *American Political Science Review* 80:613–24.

Strate, John M., Charles J. Parrish, Charles D. Elder, and Coit Ford III. 1989. "Life Span Civic Development and Voting Participation." *American Political Science Review* 83:443–64.

Subervi-Velez, Federico A. 1992. "Republican and Democratic Mass Communication Strategies: Targeting the Latino Vote." In *From Rhetoric to Reality: Latino Politics in the 1988 Elections*, ed. Rodolfo de la Garza and Louis DeSipio, 22–39. Boulder, CO: Westview.

Subervi-Velez, Federico A., and Stacey L. Connaughton. 1999. "Targeting the Latino Vote: The Democratic Party's 1996 Mass-Communication Strategy." In

Awash in the Mainstream, ed. Rodolfo O. de la Garza and Louis DeSipio, 47–71. Boulder, CO: Westview.

Swain, Carol M. 1995. *Black Faces, Black Interests: The Representation of African Americans in Congress*. Cambridge, MA: Harvard University Press.

Tate, Gayle T. 1993. "Political Consciousness and Resistance among Black Antebellum Women." *Women & Politics* 13:670–89.

Tate, Katherine. 1991. "Black Political Participation in the 1984 and 1988 Presidential Elections." *American Political Science Review* 85:1159–76.

———. 1993. *From Protest to Politics: The New Black Voters in American Elections*. New York: Russell Sage Foundation.

———. 1994. "Playing the Race Card in U.S. Mayoral Elections." Paper presented at the Annual Meeting of the Midwest Political Science Association, Chicago, April 13–16.

Teixeira, Ruy A. 1987. *Why Americans Don't Vote: Turnout Decline in the United States, 1960–1984*. New York, Greenwood Press.

———. 1992. *The Disappearing American Voter*. Washington, DC: Brookings Institution.

Texas Almanac and State Industrial Guide. 1995. Dallas: Dallas Morning News.

Thielemann, Gregory S. 1998. "Leadership, Power and Emerging Partisanship in the Texas Legislature." In *Texas Politics: A Reader*, 2nd ed., ed. Anthony Champagne and Edward J. Harpham, 66–87. New York: W. W. Norton.

Thomas, John C. 1982. "Citizen-Initiated Contacts with Government Agencies: A Test of Three Theories." *American Journal of Political Science* 26:504–22.

Tostado, Ricardo. 1985. "Political Participation." In *Hispanics in the United States: A New Social Agenda*, ed. Pastora San Juan Caffety and William C. McCready, 235–52. New Brunswick, NJ: Transaction Books.

Uhlaner, Carole J. 1986. "Political Participation, Rational Actors, and Rationality: A New Approach." *Political Psychology* 7:551–73.

———. 1989a. "Rational Turnout: The Neglected Role of Groups." *American Journal of Political Science* 33:390–422.

———. 1989b. "'Relational Goods' and Participation: Incorporating Sociability into a Theory of Rational Action." *Public Choice* 62:253–85.

———. 1991. "Political Participation and Discrimination: A Comparative Analysis of Asians, Blacks and Latinos." In *Political Participation and American Democracy*, ed. William Crotty, 139–70. New York: Greenwood Press.

Uhlaner, Carole J., Bruce E. Cain, and D. Roderick Kiewiet. 1989. "Political Participation of Ethnic Minorities in the 1980s." *Political Behavior* 11:195–231.

Vedlitz, Arnold, Roger Durand, and James Dyer. 1980. "Citizen Contacts with Local Governments: A Comparative View." *American Journal of Political Science* 24:50–67.

Verba, Sidney, and Norman H. Nie. 1972. *Participation in America: Political Democracy and Social Equality*. New York: Harper and Row.

Verba, Sidney, Norman H. Nie, and Jae-on Kim. 1978. *Participation and Political Equality*. Cambridge: Cambridge University Press.

Verba, Sidney, Kay Lehman Schlozman, and Henry Brady. 1995. *Voice and Equality: Civic Voluntarism in American Politics*. Cambridge, MA: Harvard University Press.

Verba, Sidney, Kay Lehman Schlozman, Henry Brady, and Norman H. Nie. 1991. "Resources and Political Participation." Paper presented at the Annual Meeting of the American Political Science Association, Washington, DC, August 29–September 1.

———. 1993a. "Who Participates? What Do They Say?" *American Political Science Review* 87:303–18.

———. 1993b. "Race, Ethnicity, and Political Resources: Participation in the United States." *British Journal of Political Science* 23:453–97.

Villareal, Roberto E., Norma G. Hernandez, and Howard D. Neighbor. 1988. *Latino Empowerment: Progress, Problems and Prospects*. New York: Greenwood Press.

Voss, D. Stephen. 1996a. "Beyond Racial Threat: Failure of an Old Hypothesis in the New South." *Journal of Politics* 58:1156–70.

———. 1996b. "Rejoinder." *Journal of Politics* 58:1181–83.

Walton, Hanes, Jr. 1985. *Invisible Politics: Black Political Behavior*. Albany: State University of New York Press.

Welch, Susan, and Philip Secret. 1981. "Sex, Race and Political Participation." *Western Political Quarterly* 34:5–16.

Whitely, Paul F. 1995. "Rational Choice and Political Participation—Evaluating the Debate." *Political Research Quarterly* 48:211–34.

Wielhouwer, Peter W. 1995. "Strategic Canvassing by the Political Parties, 1952–1990." *American Review of Politics* 16:213–38.

———. 1999. "The Mobilization of Campaign Activists by the Party Canvass." *American Politics Quarterly* 27:177–200.

Wielhouwer, Peter W., and Brad Lockerbie. 1994. "Party Contacting and Political Participation, 1952–1990." *American Journal of Political Science* 38:211–29.

Wilcox, Clyde, and Leopoldo Gomez. 1990. "Religion, Group Identification, and Politics among American Blacks." *Sociological Analysis* 51:271–85.

Williams, Linda F. 1987. "Blacks and the 1984 Elections in the South: Racial Polarization and Regional Congruence." In *Blacks in Southern Politics*, ed. Lawrence W. Moreland, Robert P. Steed, and Tod A. Baker, 77–98. New York: Praeger.

Wolfinger, Raymond E., and Steven J. Rosenstone. 1980. *Who Votes?* New Haven: Yale University Press.

Wright, Frederick D. 1987. "The History of Black Political Participation to 1965." In *Blacks in Southern Politics*, ed. Lawrence W. Moreland, Robert P. Steed, and Tod A. Baker, 9–30. New York: Praeger.

Wrinkle, Robert D., Joseph Stewart, Jr., J.L. Polinard, Kenneth J. Meier, and John R. Arvizu. 1996. "Ethnicity and Nonelectoral Political Participation." *Hispanic Journal of Behavior Studies* 18:142–53.

Zipp, John F. 1985. "Perceived Representativeness and Voting: An Assessment of the Impact of 'Choices' vs. 'Echoes'." *American Political Science Review* 79:50–61.

Zipp, John F., Richard Landerman, and Paul Luebke. 1982. "Political Parties and Political Participation: A Reexamination of the Standard Socioeconomic Model." *Social Forces* 60:1140–53.

Zuckerman, Alan S., and Darrell M. West. 1985. "The Political Bases of Citizen Contacting: A Cross-National Analysis." *American Political Science Review* 79:117–31.

INDEX